# Critical
# Reading
# Improvement

# McGraw-Hill Basic Skills System

**Tools for Learning Success**

## Tests

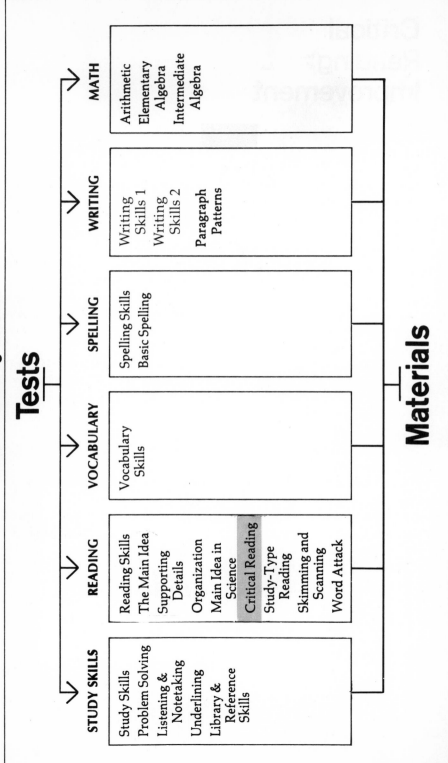

**STUDY SKILLS**

Study Skills
Problem Solving
Listening & Notetaking
Underlining
Library & Reference Skills

**READING**

Reading Skills
The Main Idea
Supporting Details
Organization
Main Idea in Science
Critical Reading
Study-Type Reading
Skimming and Scanning
Word Attack

**VOCABULARY**

Vocabulary Skills

**SPELLING**

Spelling Skills
Basic Spelling

**WRITING**

Writing Skills 1
Writing Skills 2
Paragraph Patterns

**MATH**

Arithmetic
Elementary Algebra
Intermediate Algebra

## Materials

# Editor's Introduction

This book is one of nine parts in a series devoted to instruction in reading skills. This reading series, in turn, is part of a larger system of instructional material—the McGraw-Hill Basic Skills System: Tools for Learning Success. Designed at the University of Minnesota Reading and Study Skills Center, the Basic Skills System is aimed at college-bound high school students, and junior college and college students who need to improve those skills necessary for academic success. The system consists of *tests* to determine instructional needs and *materials* designed to meet those needs, plus instructor's manuals to explain the tests and materials and the relationship between them. The purpose of the *tests* is to find out what instruction a student needs in basic skills, and the purpose of the *materials* is to give him that instruction. Each student gets what he needs without wasting time on unnecessary tasks.

Six basic skill topics—study, reading, vocabulary, spelling, writing, and mathematics—are covered, and two tests (A and B forms) are provided for each topic. Subscales on the tests are matched to accompanying instructional materials: thus a student with a low score on one or more subscales gets instruction in the corresponding skill. The second form of the test may be used to evaluate progress after instruction.

The materials in the Basic Skills System have been field-tested and revised to provide the best possible results. While most of the materials are self-instructional programs, the tests, of course, are designed for supervised administration. These testing instruments have been carefully developed and standardized by California Test Bureau. The latest research techniques and procedures have been utilized to ensure the highest possible validity and reliability.

The instructional materials are designed to be used separately, if desired, and can be purchased as single units. Most of the materials are suitable for adoption as textbooks in such basic skill courses as Freshman English, Communications, How to Study, Vocabulary Development, and Remedial or Developmental Mathematics. Individualized diagnosis and instruction are optional in such settings.

Alton L. Raygor
Consulting Editor
University of Minnesota

# Critical Reading Improvement

**A Program for Self-instruction**

ANITA E. HARNADEK
Lincoln High School
Warren, Michigan

McGRAW-HILL BOOK COMPANY
New York   St. Louis   San Francisco
London   Sydney   Toronto   Mexico   Panama

*Library of Congress Catalog Card Number 69-18713*

07-051383-X

6789011123  HDHD  8107987654

Detroit's two major newspapers, *The Detroit News* and *Detroit Free Press,* have my deep appreciation for their wholehearted cooperation in allowing me to include unusually extensive materials of theirs in this book. Thanks are also due *Reader's Digest* for permission to use some of its materials.

To L. R. Ebbing and E. P. Smith, without whom this book would not have been written.

# To the Student

This book is a combination of a programmed book and a textbook in which all the answers are given. Whereas most programmed books have cut-and-dried answers not subject to question, most of the answers in this book depend upon the individual's interpretation of the material he is reading; consequently, the fact that I may think my interpretation is correct does not necessarily mean that your interpretation is wrong. At best, I can only support my interpretations and try to anticipate and refute others, but this does not mean that I have anticipated and refuted your particular interpretation. Although this book is designed for students who wish to study by themselves, this question of interpretations also makes it appropriate as a textbook for discussion classes.

You will be expected to respond in several ways. Sometimes you will be asked a question. For example,

1. What kind of book are you reading now? Support your answer.

In this case, the answer will be separated from the question by a light rule and from the material following the answer by a darker rule:

Per the first sentence in the first paragraph, this book is a combination of a programmed book and a textbook in which all the answers are given. Per the last sentence in the first paragraph, it is a book designed for self-study, but it may also be used as a textbook for a class. Per the title, it is a book to improve critical reading ability. Count your answer as correct if you answered in any one of these ways.

Since you will not benefit as much from simply reading my answer as you will from thinking of your own answer first, it is suggested that you use the shield provided to block out my answer until you have decided upon your own.

Another type of response will be expected when you are asked to answer a multiple-choice question. (More than one correct answer may be included among the choices.) Here, too, the answer is separated from the question and from the material which follows it. In most cases, the answer(s) I choose will be supported and the answer(s) I reject will be refuted.

2. What do you know so far about this book?
   a. It is supposed to improve critical reading ability.
   b. It is designed to be used as a textbook in discussion classes.
   c. It is written by an expert on critical reading.
   d. It includes answers to the questions asked.

*a, d.* From the answer to question 1 above, we know that answer *a* is correct. From the first sentence of the first paragraph, we know that answer *d* is correct. If you chose *b,* you probably misread the last sentence of the first paragraph: this sentence says that this book is *appropriate* for use as a textbook in a discussion class, but it does not say that this book was *designed* for such use (not *b*). You have been given no information indicating that I am an expert on critical reading (not *c*).

In some cases you will be given certain information and then you will be asked to decide whether each statement following that information is true, is false, or whether you can't tell its truth value from the information given. For example:

Jack and Jill went up the hill to fetch a pail of water. Jack fell down and broke his crown and Jill came tumbling after.

3. Jack and Jill were married.

Can't tell. We are given no information about their relationship. According to the information given, they may or not have been married.

4. There was a well at the top of the hill.

Can't tell. There may or may not have been. Maybe they made arrangements with someone from the other side of the hill to leave a pail of water there for them and they just went to pick it up.

Sometimes sentences containing blank lines or choices of words in parentheses will be written down one side of a page, and the required responses will be written down the other side. In these cases, use your shield to cover the column of answers, uncovering each answer as you respond:

| | |
|---|---|
| It is hoped that this book will help you improve your ability to _____ critically. | read |
| Although this book is designed for self-study, it is also (designed, appropriate) for use as a textbook in a discussion class. | appropriate |
| You will be expected to respond in (only one, several) ways, and it is believed that your ability to read _____ will be improved more if you use your shield as suggested than if you | several critically |

just read the answers given without first thinking of your own answers.

As will be explained in Chapter 1, many facets
of _____ reading will be explored in this     critical
book. As in mathematics, the concepts discussed here (need, do not need) to be thought       need
about if you are to master them.

Therefore, it is suggested that you (try, do not
try) to read this book at two or three sittings;     do not try
instead, read it for a while and then read (it
some more, something else) to see if you can         something else
apply what you have learned so far.

Because newspapers are usually (available, not
available) to almost everyone who will be read-      available
ing this book, much of the material in it has
been taken from newspapers in order that you
can then practice what you have learned by
reading (your own newspapers, more from this
book).                                               your own newspapers

However, the articles selected for this book
from these _____ represent many           newspapers
styles of writing and many kinds of thinking,
and such writing and thinking is likely to be
evident in almost any reading material.

It is hoped, then, that you will recognize and
use your knowledge whenever (you read, you
read newspapers).                                    you read

Anita E. Harnadek

# Contents

# Chapter 1.
# Introduction

If you have not yet read the section "To the Student" preceding this chapter, go back and do so now.

The purpose of this book is to help you improve your ability to read critically. Have you read "To the Student" yet? If so, you're doing fine already. If not, you and I have a long way to go to improve your reading, for already you're ignoring what I say. If you're going to ignore me, then why are you reading this book? Now go back and read that section before reading any further.

In helping you improve your ability to read critically, this book will attempt to teach you many things. The cardinal rule of a critical reader is

**DON'T BELIEVE EVERYTHING YOU READ.**

This cardinal rule sounds cynical, but it isn't: it simply recognizes that everything we read had to be written by someone, that that someone is human, and that humans aren't perfect.

Now "to improve your critical reading ability" sounds like a fine idea, but what, specifically, does a critical reader do which noncritical readers don't do? Among other things, when he reads he

1. doesn't believe everything he reads.
2. questions everything that doesn't make sense to him.
3. questions some things even though they do make sense to him.
4. rereads when he thinks he may have missed something.
5. considers the type of material he is reading before evaluating it.
6. considers the context when he interprets what he reads.
7. considers the audience for whom the writing is intended.
8. tries to determine the author's purpose in writing.
9. decides whether or not he thinks the author has accomplished his purpose.
10. recognizes that the author's attitude will influence what he writes.
11. recognizes that the effect on him of what the author says may be caused more by the author's style of writing than by the facts presented.
12. analyzes arguments.
13. recognizes—in the case of an argument—whether or not the opponent's viewpoint has been refuted.
14. recognizes unsupported opinions and allegations.
15. recognizes conflicting information and inconsistencies.
16. discounts arguments based on fallacious reasoning.
17. recognizes and understands metaphors, figures of speech, idioms, colloquialisms, and slang.

18. recognizes the connotations as well as the denotations of words.
19. distinguishes between what the author really says and what he might seem to say.
20. distinguishes among humor, sarcasm, irony, satire, and straightforward writing.
21. distinguishes between necessary inferences and probable inferences.
22. recognizes and considers intended implications of statements made.
23. recognizes assumptions which are implicit in the author's statements.
24. distinguishes fact from opinion and objective writing from subjective writing.
25. doesn't misinterpret given data.

You should be doing all these things by the time you finish reading this book. Great! But how do you know whether or not you are doing some of these things? For example: Not all statements contain intended implications, so how can you tell when you recognize such implications and when you don't (item 22)? And how do you know that you have distinguished *correctly* between necessary inferences and probable inferences (item 21)? And how can you tell that an author isn't really using irony when you think he's being serious (item 20)?

This book will give you practice in doing all the things above. You will know the answers to the questions above from the answers in this book. So, to the extent of the material in this book, you will be able to tell whether or not you are making progress. But such questions when they apply to the other reading you will be doing are difficult to answer.

To say that you will *know* when you are doing these things is something like telling someone who has never felt pain, "You'll *know* it when you feel pain": his idea of pain is no clearer than it was before. Furthermore, such a statement would not be accurate in many cases, for you and I both know that some people will read this book who will think they're right even when they're dead wrong.

It will be a healthy sign that you're well on your way to reading more critically when two factors are present during your other reading: first, you find yourself automatically asking the kinds of questions asked throughout this book—the questions implied by items 1–25 above; second, you find yourself realizing that you're getting more out of reading than you did before you started reading this book.

Now let's see how you're doing so far.

| Critical reading involves the use of (only a few, many) concepts, (some, all) of which are listed as items 1–25 in this chapter. | many/some |

| | |
|---|---|
| This book will give you practice in using (some, all) of the concepts listed as items 1–25. | all |
| Most of the answers in this book will not only tell you the right answer, but they will (not, also) try to anticipate other answers which might be given. | also |
| Reasons (will usually, will not) be given for rejecting these anticipated answers. | will usually |
| In some cases, however, it is believed that your choice of a wrong answer will be caused by your not considering certain data which would lead you to the right answer; in these cases, only the right answers are given, but the reasoning leading to them is explained. | |
| Roughly speaking, you can be (fairly, very) sure that you are reading critically when you find yourself asking the questions implied in items 1–25 and when you find yourself realizing that you are getting (more, less) out of reading than you did before you started reading this book. | fairly<br><br>more |

If you are now the kind of reader who reads without questioning the author or analyzing his presentation or viewpoint—who pretty much just accepts or rejects what he reads without thinking about why—then you will also be well on the road to critical reading if you find yourself becoming confused about writing which you would have previously simply accepted or rejected. Your confusion will be a sign that you are asking yourself questions about what you read, and asking questions is a characteristic of the critical reader.

As you read the answers given in this book, you are strongly urged to read the reasons for accepting some answers and rejecting others. It is a big temptation simply to read the answer far enough to find out that your answer agrees with mine; but critical reading is not possible without critical thinking, and the answers are designed to show you the thinking which led up to them.

Some concepts are discussed in special sections in order to identify them for you and give you practice in recognizing them. Included in this group are, for example, some of the common fallacies in thinking. Other concepts are not discussed in separate sections but will appear many times throughout this book in the hope that you will learn to look for them automatically when you read. Included in this group are such things as considering the context in interpreting what you read and recognizing conflicting information.

# Chapter 2. Considering the Source

One of the most obvious things to be considered by a reader—and yet one of the things too often not considered at all—is the kind of publication being read.

| | |
|---|---|
| For example, a discussion of the contents of rock formations around Denver, Colorado, is likely to be (less, more) accurate in a novel than in a college geography book, but the beauty of these rocks is likely to be (less, more) easily visualized from the description in a novel than from a college geography book. | less<br><br>more |
| An article on the psychological need for sleep is likely to be (less, more) factual if it appears in *The Psychological Review* than if it appears in *Reader's Digest*. | more |
| An advertisement in *The New Yorker* is likely to be (less, more) sophisticated than an advertisement for the same product in *Life*. | more |

Along with the kind of publication, we must also consider the audience for whom the publication is intended.

| | |
|---|---|
| For example, we can expect the content of the Denver rock formations to be discussed (less, more) thoroughly in a fifth-grade geography book than in a college geography book. | less |
| We can expect a (more, less) objective report of the activities of strikebreakers in a public daily newspaper than we can either in a union newspaper or in a company newspaper. | more |
| We can expect (less, more) sensational handling of the news of a Hollywood divorce in a movie magazine than in a family magazine. | more |
| Reading about a breakthrough in medicine, we can expect (less, more) sensational and (less, | more |

| | |
|---|---|
| more) factual handling in a newspaper than in the American Medical Association's monthly journal. | less |

And, finally, even after considering the kind of publication and the audience for whom it is intended, we must consider both the author and the kind of material he is writing.

| | |
|---|---|
| For example, a newspaper editorial about a proposed revision of abortion laws is likely to be written on (the same, a different) basis than such an article by a Catholic bishop. | a different |
| An article by a commentator will be (less, more) objective than a news release on the same subject by the Associated Press. | less |
| An article on the adoption of a child written by a couple frustrated by adoption laws is likely to be written from (the same, a different) viewpoint (as, than) if written by an adoption agency. | a different than |
| An article by a sympathetic reporter about a couple living on welfare is likely to have (about the same, quite a different) effect on us (as, than) an article by an unsympathetic reporter. | quite a different than |

Several kinds of publications are listed below. For each one, consider its reliability in terms of the grading scale shown here. It is usually helpful to consider the audience toward whom the publication is directed in judging its reliability—for example, is it intended primarily for scholars? for professional people? for conservative people? for the masses? or what? In using this grading scale, you may also use A—, B+, B—, C+, C—, and D+. Count your answer as correct if you are within half a grade of the answer given. (Example: If you have B or C+ and the given answer is B—, count your answer as correct.)

A—HIGHLY RELIABLE: errors and misleading statements are extremely rare; no sensationalism; opinions are clearly distinguished from facts; authors are unusually reliable and qualified.

B—QUITE RELIABLE: few errors or misleading statements; seldom sensational; opinions are usually clearly distinguished from facts; authors are usually reliable and qualified.

C—FAIRLY RELIABLE: some errors or misleading statements, but usually not about the *basic* facts; may be sensational; opinions may not be distinguished from facts; authors may not always be reliable and qualified.

D—SOMEWHAT RELIABLE: careful reading is required to distinguish basic facts from innuendos about them; often sensational; opinions seldom distinguished from facts; authors are almost anyone who has something to say.

X—reliability of the publication will depend primarily on the author, rather than on the type of publication. (Do not include textbooks in this category.)

Here are the publications for you to rate:

1. *Encyclopedia Americana*                              A
2. *Encyclopedia Brittanica*                             A
3. *Journal of Genetic Psychology* (magazine)            A—
4. Movie magazine                                        D
5. Tenth-grade textbook on plane geometry                B+
6. Twelfth-grade textbook on third-year algebra          A
7. *The Scientific American* (magazine)                  B
8. *Better Homes and Gardens* (magazine)                 B—
9. *Reader's Digest* (magazine)                          C
10. Political speech                                      D
11. Reputable daily newspaper                            C
12. *Webster's New Collegiate Dictionary*                A
13. Book: biography by someone who knew the person       X
14. Book: biography by someone who didn't know the person   X
15. *Life* (magazine)                                    C+
16. Historical novel (evaluate on the accuracy of history in the novel)   X
17. This book                                            B—

# Chapter 3. Recognizing What Is Said

When we read, it is natural to call upon our past experiences to help us interpret the words in a way which is meaningful to us.

| | |
|---|---|
| But since we have all had (the same, different) experiences, it follows that we are in danger of interpreting the words in a way which is (the same as, different than) that which the author intended. | different<br><br><br>different than |
| Although this danger cannot be entirely avoided, it can be (eliminated, minimized) by learning not to take too much for granted in our interpretations. | minimized |
| It is one thing to decide what an author means and to know that we might be mistaken; it is (the same, an entirely different) thing—and a stumbling block to critical reading—to take for granted that the author thinks just as we do. | an entirely different |
| One of our problems in reading, then, is to recognize when an author has made certain statements and when he has not made these _____. | statements |

For example, an author might make the statement, "I have to fill the gas tank of my car about three times every week." A truck driver might interpret this to mean, "He drives a lot," whereas a bookkeeper might interpret this as, "His car gets poor gas mileage." We see, however, that the author has said neither that he drives a lot nor that his car gets poor gas mileage, but simply that he must fill the gas tank often. His filling of the gas tank could be for either of the two reasons offered by the truck driver and the bookkeeper, or it could be for a variety of other reasons—for example, maybe someone is continually siphoning gas out of the tank; or maybe he has three teenagers who constantly use the car; or maybe the car's gas tank holds only 5 gallons of gas.

It is necessary, of course, to be able to "read between the lines," to be able to recognize an author's implications. But unless we can definitely distinguish between what the author *says* and what we *infer* from his words, we can never hope to read critically.

As the first step toward shaking up your thinking processes in order to help you recognize the difference between what an author says and what you might *think* he says, most of the rest of this chapter is devoted to material which is so familiar to you that it might even seem rather silly to you to read it. However, this material was chosen precisely *because* it is so familiar to you, for it is when we are on familiar ground that our past conditioning and experience influence us the most in interpreting what we have read, and, consequently, can do the most to mislead us into thinking we have read something which the author did not say at all. The statements following each selection do not pretend to discuss the main idea or even the important aspects of the selection, for their purpose is simply to help you acquire the habit of distinguishing between an author's statements and your inferences about his statements.

Following are some shortened versions of nursery rhymes and fairy tales. Each of these stories is followed by several statements. You are to mark each statement as "true," "false," or "can't tell" on the basis of the story. *In deciding how to mark the statements, you are to accept the story as true and assume good usage of English, but you may not add to the story, and you may not assume any past knowledge of the story.* You may, however, use your knowledge of the world in determining the meanings of common words—such as "house," "girl," and "pie," for example. Again, it is suggested that you keep each answer covered until you have decided on your own answer.

I.   Little Jack Horner sat in the corner
     Eating a Christmas pie.
     He put in his thumb and pulled out a plum
     And said, "What a good boy am I!"

1. Jack Horner was little.

Since the story says "*Little* Jack Horner," an answer of "true" is acceptable; however, an answer of "can't tell" is better, because we don't know whether the author is describing Jack as "little" or whether Jack is 6 feet tall and is being called "Little Jack Horner" to distinguish him from "Big Jack Horner," who is 7 feet tall.

2. Jack was sitting in the corner while he was eating.

True. The story says he "sat in the corner eating." The use of the present participle of the verb "eat" means that he was doing both at the same time.

3. Jack was eating a plum pie.

Can't tell. He pulled a plum out of the pie, but maybe it was an apple pie and the plum fell in by mistake.

4. Jack was sitting on a chair.

Can't tell. The story doesn't say what Jack was sitting on.

5. Jack was a good boy.

Can't tell. Jack *said* he was a good boy, but maybe Jack is a liar.

  II.   There was an old woman who lived in a shoe. She had so many children she didn't know what to do.

1. The woman was old.

True. The story says "old woman."

2. The woman must have been very small in order to be able to live in a shoe.

False. She didn't *have* to be small in order to be able to live in a shoe, because it could have been a big shoe. If the statement had read, "The old woman was small," then we would mark it "can't tell," for we don't know whether she was small or whether the shoe was big.

3. The woman's children lived in the shoe with her.

Can't tell. The story says the old woman had children, but it doesn't tell us where the children lived.

4. The woman didn't really live in a shoe, but her house was so small that she *called* it a shoe.

False. We are told to accept the story as true, and the story says she lived in a shoe.

5. The old woman had a pet cat.

Can't tell. The story doesn't mention a cat, so we can't tell whether or not she had one.

A common error made by readers is to assume that anything not in the story must be false, and many readers will react to statement 5 above, "That's false. The story doesn't say anything about a cat, so if you try to say she could have had one, then you're adding to the story, and you're not allowed to do that." The answer to this line of reasoning is in two parts: first, we do not add to the story by saying that *maybe* the story left something out; second, the person who marks this statement "false" is assuming that the old woman definitely did not have a pet cat, and so this person is adding to the story by making this assumption. Since the story does not mention a pet at all, two possibilities exist: the woman had a pet; the woman didn't have a pet. Since we cannot assume either of these to be true (or false) without adding to the story, we are obliged to mark the statement "can't tell."

When we assume that anything not in the story is false, we are using one form of the reasoning fallacy known as *proof by failure to find a counterexample*. A *counterexample* is a specific example which is used to disprove a generalization. For instance, suppose someone says, "All babies are born with blue eyes." A counterexample would be (choose the correct answer):
*a.* Some babies are not born with blue eyes.
*b.* All babies are born with brown eyes.
*c.* No babies are born with blue eyes.
*d.* Bobby Jackson had brown eyes when he was born.

---

*d.* Statements *a, b,* and *c* are all generalizations, and it was said above that a counterexample is a *specific* example. A *counterexample* names one or more specific *examples* which run *counter* to a generalization.

---

A counterexample to the statement, "All birds can fly," would be:
*a.* An elephant can't fly.
*b.* Not all birds can fly.
*c.* This bird can't fly.
*d.* It is false that all birds can fly.

---

*c.* Statements *b* and *d* are generalizations, and neither names an *example* to refute the given generalization. Although statement *a* names an example of *something* which can't fly, it does not name an example of a *bird* which can't fly, and so it is not a counterexample to the given statement.

---

A counterexample to the statement, "No dog has five legs," would be:
*a.* This dog doesn't have five legs.
*b.* John's dog has five legs.
*c.* Some dogs have five legs.

*d.* This spider has five legs.

---

*b.* Statement *b* names a specific example—John's dog—which runs counter to the given generalization. Statement *a* is a specific example, but it supports the generalization. Statement *c* is a generalization, not a specific example. Statement *d* is a specific example, but it does not refute the statement about *dogs.*

---

Given the statement, "Flying saucers don't exist," which of the following replies is using the fallacy of *proof by failure to find a counterexample?*
*a.* "They can't exist, or someone would have found one by now."
*b.* "If they existed, they'd probably be invisible, anyhow."
*c.* "Earth is the only planet with a civilization capable of having flying saucers, and Earth doesn't have any."
*d.* "I used to think they might exist, but I don't any more."

---

*a.* First we must recognize that the counterexample to the given statement is, "This thing is a flying saucer." The person making statement *a* is assuming that flying saucers don't exist because a flying saucer has never been found. He is assuming that the generalization is true because a counterexample has not been found. He is using proof by failure to find a counterexample. Statement *b* does not accept the truth of the given generalization, and it does not attempt either to prove or disprove the generalization. Statements *c* and *d* support the given generalization, but neither uses the lack of a counterexample as a basis for that support.

---

Given the statement, "All babies are born with blue eyes," which of the following responses indicates the use of the fallacy of proof by failure to find a counterexample?
*a.* "It must be true, because the pigments which cause the other colors aren't active yet at birth."
*b.* "It must be true, because I've delivered thousands of babies and they've all had blue eyes."
*c.* "It must be true, because Bobby Jackson had blue eyes when he was born."
*d.* "It must be true, because it's common knowledge."

---

*b.* Although answers *a* and *d* both assume that no counterexample exists, each of them supports the generalization on a basis other than the non-existence of a counterexample (not *a* or *d*). The person making statement *b* is implying that he surely would have found a counterexample by this time if the given generalization hadn't been true. Although the person making statement *c* is guilty of a fallacy in reasoning (*proof by selected instances*, to be discussed later), he is not using the fallacy of proof by failure to find a counterexample. (Incidentally, the person making statement *b* is also using *proof by selected instances*.)

---

Given the story above about the old woman who lived in a shoe, and given the statement, "She had a pet cat," which of the following responses indicate the use of proof by failure to find a counterexample?

*a.* "She must have had a pet cat, or the story would have told us she didn't."
*b.* "She couldn't have had a pet cat, or the story would have told us she did."
*c.* "If she didn't have a pet cat, then she must have had a pet dog."
*d.* "The story doesn't mention a cat, so we can't tell whether she had one or not."

---

*a, b.* Each of these two statements assumes a generalization to be true because a counterexample wasn't found. Statement *c* may not represent logical reasoning, but any fallacy present does not appear to be based on proof by failure to find a counterexample. Statement *d* tells us that the speaker is unsure of whether or not the woman had a cat, so he is saying neither that she had one nor that she didn't.

---

Now let's try another nursery rhyme. (Remember that each statement following it is to be marked "true," "false," or "can't tell.")

III.   Mary had a little lamb. Its fleece was white as snow,
       And everywhere that Mary went the lamb was sure to go.
       It followed her to school one day; that was against the rule.
       It made the children laugh and play to see a lamb at school.

1. Mary's lamb had white fleece.

---

True. Good English usage demands that the word "its" in the second sentence refer to the antecedent "lamb."

---

2. Mary went to school regularly.

---

Can't tell. The story simply says the lamb followed Mary to school one day; it doesn't tell us whether or not Mary went to school regularly. Maybe she was just taking a lunch to her older sister.

---

3. The lamb followed Mary everywhere she went.

---

Can't tell. We are told only that the lamb *went* everywhere that Mary went, but maybe Mary or someone else sometimes carried the lamb, or maybe he ran ahead of her. (Remember that some authors use words very precisely.)

4. The lamb had a ribbon around its neck.

Can't tell. The story gives us no information at all about a ribbon. Maybe the lamb wore a ribbon and maybe it didn't. (If you answered "false" for this statement, you are probably guilty of using the fallacy of proof by failure to find a counterexample. See page 10.)

5. Mary was a boy.

False. The story says, "It followed *her.*"

6. Mary was a woman.

Can't tell. The story says nothing about Mary's age. Maybe Mary was the teacher.

7. Maybe Mary liked to go to school.

True. Maybe she did. If you answered "can't tell" with the thought, "Maybe she did, and maybe she didn't," your thought is right, but your answer is wrong, for you *are* saying, "Maybe she did," which makes the statement true. (The statement, "Maybe Mary didn't like to go to school," is also true.)

8. Maybe Mary's lamb didn't have white fleece.

False. We are told to accept the story as true, and the story says the lamb had white fleece; therefore, there is no possibility that the lamb did not have white fleece.

Another common error made by readers is to confuse a "maybe" statement with an absolute statement. For example, statement 7 in the above exercise does not say, "Mary liked to go to school," which is an absolute statement. If this had been the statement, then we would have marked it "can't tell." Since the story mentions nothing about Mary's liking or disliking school, two possibilities exist: Mary liked to go to school; Mary did not like to go to school. The use of the word "maybe" is another way of saying, "It is possible," so it follows that both of the following statements would have to be marked "true": "Maybe Mary liked to go to school"; "Maybe Mary didn't like to go to school." However, we see a different situation in statement 8, even though this, too, is a "maybe" statement. Whereas the story gives no information about statement 7, thus leaving open two possibilities for us to consider, the story gives definite information about statement 8, thus leaving open only one possibility—the lamb had white fleece; consequently, to say, "It is possible that the lamb did not have white fleece," is a contradiction of the story, and so the statement is false.

IV.   Little Red Riding Hood's grandmother was ill, and Red decided to take her a basket of goodies to help her get well. The big bad wolf saw Red walking through the woods on the way to the grandmother's house, and he ran ahead to the grandmother's house and ate the grandmother. Although Red didn't recognize the wolf when she first arrived at her grandmother's house, she screamed in time to be rescued by a nearby woodsman.

1. Red's grandmother is alive when the story starts.

True. A person who is dead is not ill, and Red's grandmother was ill; therefore, the grandmother could not be dead and so must have been alive.

2. Red's mother fixed the basket of goodies for Red to take.

Can't tell. The story doesn't mention Red's mother, so we don't know whether or not Red's mother fixed the basket.

3. Red recognized the wolf in time to be rescued.

Can't tell. We know only that she screamed in time to be rescued, not that she recognized the wolf when she screamed. Maybe the wolf fainted and Red thought the wolf was her grandmother having a heart attack and she screamed for help.

4. Red was taking the goodies to her grandmother's house when the wolf saw her in the woods.

Can't tell. The story doesn't say whether or not she took the goodies with her when she went. Maybe she forgot them and left them at home.

5. The wolf was bad.

True. The story says "big *bad* wolf."

6. Maybe Red saw the wolf in the woods at the same time the wolf saw her.

True. Maybe she did. (The statement, "Maybe Red didn't see the wolf in the woods . . .," is also true, for the story doesn't say whether or not Red saw the wolf in the woods. Therefore, both possibilities exist.)

---

7. Red didn't like her grandmother.

---

Can't tell. We aren't told of Red's feelings for her grandmother. The information that Red wanted her grandmother to get well doesn't tell us she liked her grandmother, for maybe the grandmother was rich and had promised Red 6 months ago that Red would inherit her entire fortune if she (the grandmother) lived another full year.

---

8. Red ran all the way from her house to her grandmother's house.

---

False. The story says the wolf "saw Red *walking* . . . to the grandmother's house," so Red could not have run *all* the way.

---

9. Maybe Red had her bicycle with her.

---

True. Maybe she rode her bicycle to the woods, walked it through the woods, and rode it again after she left the woods. (The statement, "Maybe Red didn't have her bicycle with her," is also true, as are the statements, "Maybe Red owned a bicycle," and, "Maybe Red didn't own a bicycle.")

---

10. Maybe Red's grandmother wasn't really ill but was testing Red to see what Red would do.

---

False. We are told to accept the story as true, and the story tells us that the grandmother was ill.

---

11. Red noticed immediately that the wolf was not the grandmother.

---

Can't tell. We are told that Red didn't recognize the wolf at first, but we are not told that Red thought that the wolf was the grandmother. Maybe the grandmother had servants, and Red thought that the wolf was a new servant.

---

12. Red couldn't have been in a big hurry to get to her grandmother's house, or she would have been running, not walking, through the woods.

---

False. Notice that the statement doesn't say, "Red *wasn't* in a big hurry . . .," in which case we would mark it "can't tell," since we don't know whether or not Red was in a hurry. But Red *could* have been in a big hurry, and she could have run until she was exhausted, then walked for a while (during which time the wolf saw her), then started running again.

13. Red was rescued by a passing woodsman.

Can't tell. We don't know whether or not the woodsman was passing, for we are told only that he was nearby. Maybe he lived next door and was in his house when he heard Red scream. Furthermore, we know that she screamed in time to be rescued, but maybe the woodsman just ignored her screams and didn't rescue her at all.

# Chapter 4.
# Recognizing
# Some Common
# Fallacies
# in Thinking

## INTRODUCTION

There has been a lot of talk about ziffers lately, much of which has been behind closed doors, since not everyone is willing to admit his opinions publicly. It seems to me that it's time to discuss the problem publicly and objectively. There is one question to be answered whether or not we have sympathy for ziffers, and that is: Are ziffers undesirable in our society? If the answer is "yes," then we should agree to band together to eliminate them; if the answer is "no," then we should agree to stand together to stop persecuting them; if the answer is not a general one but is to be determined by each man for himself, then we should agree to let each man do as he wishes about ziffers, providing that he doesn't infringe on the rights and privileges of his neighbors.

Now we don't have to know what ziffers are to recognize that the above approach sounds fairly sensible. If we knew what ziffers were, we might or might not agree with this approach, but that doesn't alter the fact that the writer's approach to the problem seems to be a sound one. If we decide that this approach is not a good one, our decision is likely to be based on a difference in value judgments rather than on a fallacy in the writer's reasoning. For example, our agreement with this approach might vary according to whether ziffers are dandelions, rattlesnakes, blue-eyed people, sellers of pornography, or barking dogs.

On the other hand, we don't have to know what mizzigs are to recognize that something is wrong with the following approach:

I wouldn't want to live where everyone had a mizzig, I admit, but I like my mizzig, and I don't intend to give it up. I suppose I wouldn't be too ecstatic about living next door to one, either, and that could be why my next-door neighbors are complaining; nevertheless, I take good care of my mizzig and I don't see why they should complain.

This writer admits, in effect, that he thinks it's all right for him to do what he's doing, but it wouldn't be all right if someone else did it: he isn't willing to extend the same reasoning to other people which he applies to himself. This fallacious line of reasoning will be named and discussed more fully in this chapter.

The purpose of including the above two paragraphs is to show that arguments of writers can be judged on their merits as arguments, rather than on whether or not we agree with the conclusions reached. This is an important point, for if we are to read critically it is not enough to know that we agree or disagree with an author's conclusions; we must also be able to recognize and evaluate the arguments upon which the author bases his conclusions. That the author happens to arrive at a conclusion with which we agree should have no bearing on our evaluation of the merit of his argument; similarly, his arriving at a conclusion with which we disagree should not influence our evaluation of his argument.

This chapter discusses four of the more common informal fallacies in thinking.[1] It should be stressed that true conclusions can be reached through fallacious reasoning, but the fact that the conclusion may be true does not make the argument any stronger than it would be if the conclusion were false. It is the reasoning upon which a conclusion is based that we are concerned with here, not the conclusion itself.

Following are several statements, each of which is to be marked "true" or "false," according to your interpretation of the two paragraphs immediately above this one.

1. If a conclusion is true, then the reasoning upon which it is based is sound.    F
2. In order to read critically, we cannot have any preconceived ideas about the topic being discussed by the author.    F
3. A conclusion reached through fallacious reasoning is a false conclusion.    F
4. A false conclusion is a conclusion reached through fallacious reasoning.    F
5. This chapter will be concerned with the reasoning behind a conclusion rather than with the conclusion itself.    T
6. If we are able to decide whether we agree or disagree with an author's conclusions, then this indicates that we have recognized whether or not his reasoning is sound.    F

[1]For a more thorough treatment of the topic of fallacious thinking, refer to items (1) and (2) in the bibliography at the end of the book. Subsequent numbers in parentheses refer to this list.

7. We should not let the reasoning behind a conclusion influence our decision as to whether or not an argument is a good one.    F

## SPECIAL PLEADING

An argument is called *special pleading* when the arguer is not willing to apply his line of reasoning consistently. It is particularly evident in arguments in which the writer wishes to condone an action of his own while at the same time condemning the same action by others.

Following are several situations. For each one, decide whether or not anyone is using special pleading and, if so, who.

1. Bill: "But Dad, it isn't fair of you to let Mary use the car tonight. I asked you first."

Dad: "I'm sorry, but Mary has convinced me that this is an emergency. You seemed to think it was fair enough last Friday when I let you use the car after Mary had already asked for it."

Bill: "But that was different. Something came up at the last minute and I had to have it."

Bill is guilty of special pleading. Bill thinks it's all right for him to use the car in an emergency after the car was promised to Mary, but it isn't all right for Mary to use the car in an emergency after it was promised to him.

2. Teacher: "Jerry, shut up! I'm sick of your constant interruptions!"

Jerry: "You really get me down. You're always bugging me about something!"

Teacher: "Jerry, that's no way to talk. You should always be courteous to other people."

The teacher is guilty of special pleading. She thinks that Jerry should be courteous to other people, but the way she talked to Jerry tells us that she doesn't think she has to be courteous to other people.

3. Mr. Davis: "I heard you raised the rates on my neighbor's car insurance. It's about time, the way he's always filing claims with you. I didn't think it was right for him to pay the same rates as I pay."

Insurance agent: "Yes, we've been going through our files lately. In fact, that's why I'm here. You've filed quite a few claims on your business policy, and we're going to have to raise your insurance premiums."

Mr. Davis: "Whaddaya mean, raise my rates? When you set the rates, you expect to make money on some people and lose on others. I just happen to be one of the people you lost money on, and now you're crying."

Mr. Davis is guilty of special pleading. He thinks his neighbor's insurance rates should be higher than his own because his neighbor has filed several claims against the company, but he thinks that he himself should be able to file several claims against the company and not pay any more than the policy-holders who don't file claims.

4. Mike: "I don't want to go out with Linda. She's a blonde, and all blondes are dumb."

Mike is not guilty of special pleading.

5. Mike: "I don't want to go out with Linda. She's a blonde, and all blondes are dumb."
Ted: "Then how come you go out with Gail? She's a blonde."
Mike: "She's the exception that proves the rule."

Mike is guilty of special pleading. In his first statement he implies two things: he thinks all blondes are dumb, and he doesn't want to go out with dumb girls. By making an exception for Gail, he is either saying that Gail is not dumb (even though she is a blonde) or that he goes out with Gail even though she is dumb. In either case, he is unwilling to apply his general line of reasoning consistently.

6. Mr. Dalton: "Parents should keep their teen-agers from driving. Teen-aged drivers are a menace on the road."
Mr. Eaton: "But you let your teen-agers drive your car."
Mr. Dalton: "Yes, but I've ridden with them enough to know that they're both careful drivers."

Mr. Dalton is guilty of special pleading. He is not willing to apply his statement to himself.

7. Mr. Fredericks: "People without car insurance shouldn't be allowed to drive."
Mr. Goodrow: "But you drive, and you don't have car insurance."
Mr. Fredericks: "Yes, but I shouldn't be allowed to drive."

No special pleading here. Mr. Fredericks may not follow his convictions, but he is not guilty of special pleading.

8. Dr. Taylor: "The police are certainly taking their time about getting here. I'm going to protest to the Commissioner."

Mrs. Taylor: "Yes, but then you don't always return calls from patients right away, either."

Dr. Taylor: "I gave up on that long ago—99 percent of the time it turns out that if I wait half an hour the illness has cured itself."

Dr. Taylor is guilty of special pleading. He wants immediate service from others, but he—also in a service profession—isn't willing to give immediate service.

9. Jim: "Sure, it's OK for people to steal, as long as they don't steal from me."

Jim is guilty of special pleading. He thinks it's all right if other people have their possessions stolen, but he doesn't think it's all right if his own possessions are stolen.

## AVOIDING THE QUESTION

A person is *avoiding the question* when he talks about something other than the point under discussion. He is also avoiding the question when he talks *around,* but not *at,* the point or question being discussed. Sometimes it is obvious that the speaker is avoiding the question. Other times it is not so obvious, but a little practice on our parts will help us learn to recognize most cases.

Following are several situations. For each one, decide whether or not someone is avoiding the question and, if so, who.

1. Betty: "What's our English assignment for tomorrow?"

Harry: "I think I can get the car tonight. Whaddaya say we forget the homework and go to the dance?"

Harry is avoiding the question.

2. Teacher: "Who was the second President?"

Ken: "George Washington was the first President."

Ken is avoiding the question. If Ken had answered, "George Washington was the second President," he would not have been avoiding the question.

3. Al: "If you had a chance to steal $1 million and know you'd never be caught, would you do it?"

Steve: "How could I be sure I'd never be caught?"

Steve is avoiding the question. He has already been told to suppose that he'd never be caught, and the exact mechanics of making sure of this are irrelevant to the question of whether or not he'd steal the money under those circumstances.

---

4. Student: "How come you always pick on me? The other kids were talking, too."
Teacher: "You always seem to be the one I notice."

The teacher is not avoiding the question, for she has told the student why she always picks on him.

---

5. Teacher: "What did you dislike about previous English courses?"
Student: "I've always tried to look for the good things, rather than the bad things in the courses I've had, and I can honestly say that every course I've ever taken has had many good points."

The student is avoiding the question.

---

6. Jim: "Professor Baker, about how many tests and quizzes will you be giving us in this course?"
Professor Baker: "Oh, I'll be giving a test or quiz any time we've covered enough new material to make me want to be sure that everyone understands it before we go on."

Professor Baker is avoiding the question.

---

7. Doctor: "How do you get along with your children?"
Patient: "Oh, we have the usual ups and downs—some good days, some bad. About the same as other families, I guess."

The patient is not avoiding the question. The doctor has asked a general question, and the patient has given a general answer to that question.

---

8. Student: "What right do you have to tell me what to do?"
Teacher: "The law says while you're in school, your teacher takes the place of your parent."

The teacher takes for granted that the parent has the right to tell the child what to do, so from the teacher's viewpoint he is not avoiding the question. However, if the student believes that his parents have no right to tell him what to do, he may feel that the teacher is avoiding the question.

---

## BEGGING THE QUESTION (CIRCULAR REASONING)

We know that any conclusion we reach is based on underlying assumptions. When someone asks us, "How did you get that idea?" or says to us, "Prove it," we respond by giving information which we believe backs up our idea or conclusion.

We are guilty of *begging the question* when we respond by giving information which is the same as the conclusion—when we assume as true that which we wish to prove.

*Example:* John: "Some birds can't fly."

Mary: "Why do you think so?"

John: "Because not all birds can fly."

Mary has asked John to back up his statement about birds, and John has responded by giving his original statement in different words. If John had answered, "Because newly hatched birds don't have wings strong enough to fly," then he has introduced a new assumption to back up his original statement, and he is not begging the question.

A conclusion which is different from the assumptions does not beg the question, regardless of whether or not the conclusion is justified. An argument which begs the question is, of course, a poor argument. However, an argument which does not beg the question is not necessarily a good argument. For example, John does not beg the question in the following conversation; nevertheless, his argument is a poor one:

John: "Some birds can't fly."

Mary: "Why do you think so?"

John: "Because zebras have black and white stripes."

*Begging the question* is also called *circular reasoning.* It should be understood that begging the question, or circular reasoning, can occur both in conversation and in writing. Begging the question—circular reasoning—occurs whenever a conclusion is the same as an underlying assumption.

Following are several arguments. For each one, tell whether or not someone is begging the question ("BQ" or "Not BQ").

1. Jack: "How come you like chemistry better than the other sciences?" Pat: "I guess because I don't like the other sciences as well as chemistry."

BQ by Pat.

2. Mr. Adams: "You said all of Beethoven's music is good. Why do you think so?"

Mr. Brown: "Because all the music he composed is good."

BQ by Brown.

---

3. Mr. Adams: "You said all of Beethoven's music is good. Why do you think so?"
Mr. Brown: "Because the music critics say that all the music he composed is good."

Not BQ. In problem 2 above, Brown is saying, in effect, "I believe Beethoven's music is good because I believe it is good." In problem 3, Brown is saying, in effect, "Music critics say Beethoven's music is good. I believe what the music critics say. Therefore, I believe that Beethoven's music is good."

---

4. Johnny: "Dogs are the nicest pets."
Debby: "No, cats are the nicest pets."
Johnny: "No, dogs are the nicest, because they're nicer than any other pets."

BQ by Johnny.

---

5. Same conversation as in problem 4 above, but Debby adds, "No, cats are lots nicer than dogs."

Not BQ. If Debby continues her present line of reasoning (eliminating other possibilities one by one), she will have supported her statement without BQ. The fact that we might not agree that cats are nicer than dogs does not mean that Debby is BQ.

---

6. A good teacher knows that in order to encourage his students to think for themselves, he must adopt a questioning attitude of the students and allow his students to question him. Therefore, if a teacher is a good teacher and wishes to help his students enhance their thinking activities, he knows that he must ask them many questions and expect many questions from them.

BQ, for the conclusion says the same thing as the first sentence.

---

7. A good education for all of its citizens is essential to the life of a free society; therefore, if a free society is to continue its existence it must provide a good education for its citizens.

BQ.

---

8. The Himalayan Mountains are the highest in the world because no other mountains are as high as the Himalayas.

_____

BQ.

_____

9. When an acidic solution and a basic solution are chemically combined in proper proportions, water and some salt are formed. This is because the chemical reaction resulting from the proper combining of an acid and a base will be water and a salt.

_____

BQ.

_____

10. That we have so many different kinds of four-legged animals follows from the fact that there is such a wide variety of animals having four legs.

_____

BQ.

_____

11. If we are to maintain our mental equilibrium we must have a sense of humor, for a sense of humor is essential to a balanced outlook on life.

_____

BQ.

_____

12. Mr. Jackson: "Anyone with good taste in art will prefer the old masters—such as Rembrandt and Van Gogh—to the modern op art."
Mr. Kraylor: "How do you determine whether or not a person has good taste in art?"
Mr. Jackson: "That's easy enough. You can tell the ones with good taste by their preference for the old masters over op art."

_____

BQ by Jackson.

_____

## SUBSTITUTION OF CONVERSE OR INVERSE FOR PROPOSITION
Consider the following conversation:
Charlie: "If I marry your daughter, you have to promise not to interfere in our lives."
Mother of girl (later): "How come you broke up with Judy? You said if I promised not to interefere in your lives you'd marry her."
The girl's mother has committed the fallacy of *substituting the converse for the proposition.* Charlie told her that
   if [he marries her daughter] then [she has to promise not to interfere].
The mother has exchanged the "if" and "then" parts of the sentence:
   if [she promises not to interfere] then [he will marry her daughter].

In the following conversation, the wife is guilty of substituting the converse for the proposition:

Husband: "I'll be home later than usual if I pick up the cleaning."

Wife (that evening): "How come you're late and you don't have the cleaning? You said if you were late it would be because you stopped for the cleaning."

We see that the husband has told the wife that

if [he picked up the cleaning] then [he'd be home late].

The wife has exchanged the "if" and "then" parts of his sentence:

if [he'll be home late] then [he has picked up the cleaning].

Following are several statements. State the converse of each one.

1. If we pay low wages, then we'll have to hire incompetent people.

If we have to hire incompetent people, then we are paying low wages.

2. If you use brand X aspirin, then you'll get fast headache relief.

If you get fast headache relief, then you use brand X aspirin.

3. If we don't increase our efficiency, then we won't be able to compete.

If we can't compete, then we didn't increase our efficiency.

4. If we don't at least talk about the problems, then we're not going to be able to solve them.

If we can't solve the problems, then we didn't even talk about them.

5. If a person reads this book thoroughly, then he will improve his critical reading ability.

If a person improves his critical reading ability, then he has read this book thoroughly.

Allied with the fallacy of substituting the converse for the proposition is the fallacy of *substituting the inverse for the proposition*. This latter fallacy occurs when we leave the "if" and "then" parts of the original statement in their original positions but we negate them both. For example:

Statement: If we pay low wages then we will be hiring incompetent people.

Inverse: If we don't pay low wages, then we won't be hiring incompetent people.

State the inverse of each of the following propositions.

1. If I pick up the cleaning on my way home, then I'll be home late.

If I don't pick up the cleaning on my way home, then I won't be home late.

---

2. If you use brand X aspirin, then you'll get fast headache relief.

If you don't use brand X aspirin, then you won't get fast headache relief.

---

3. If we don't increase our efficiency, then we won't be able to compete.

If we increase our efficiency, then we'll be able to compete.

---

4. If we don't at least talk about the problems, then we're not going to be able to solve them.

If we at least talk about the problems, then we'll be able to solve them.

---

5. If a person reads this book thoroughly, then he will improve his critical reading ability.

If a person doesn't read this book thoroughly, then he won't improve his critical reading ability.

---

State both the converse and the inverse of each of the following propositions.

1. If freedom of speech is guaranteed, then men will not hesitate to speak.

Converse: If men won't hesitate to speak, then freedom of speech is guaranteed.
Inverse: If freedom of speech isn't guaranteed, then men will hesitate to speak.

---

2. If we don't act on this problem soon, then it will snowball.

Converse: If the problem snowballs, we didn't act on it soon.
Inverse: If we act on the problem soon, then it will not snowball.

---

3. If a man has good character, then he doesn't steal.

Converse: If a man doesn't steal, then he has good character.
Inverse: If a man doesn't have good character, then he steals.

---

4. You won't win the contest if you don't enter it.

Converse: If you don't win the contest then you didn't enter it.

Inverse: If you enter the contest, then you'll win it.
(Did you have trouble with this one? If so, you probably didn't notice that the "if" part of the given statement is in a different position this time.)

---

Following are several problems. For each one state whether or not one of the two fallacies discussed in this section is committed. If a fallacy has been committed, name it: substitution of converse for proposition, or substitution of inverse for proposition.

1. John: "If I don't get the car tonight, then I won't be over."
Mary (the next day): "You had the car last night and you didn't show up. How come? You said if you got the car you'd be over."

---

Mary has substituted the inverse for the proposition.

---

2. Gary: "If I get the car tonight, then I'll be over."
Janet (that evening): "What are you doing here? Your sister told me you couldn't get the car tonight, and you said that you wouldn't be here if you didn't get the car."

---

Janet has substituted the inverse for the proposition.

---

3. Advertisement: "Parents who buy brand Y toys want their children to be happy."
Reader: "If I don't buy brand Y toys, then I don't want my children to be happy."

---

The reader has substituted the inverse for the proposition.

---

4. Mother: "If you expect to go out tonight, then you'll have to do your homework first."
Son (later that evening): "Well, how come I can't go? You said I could if I did my homework first."

---

The son has substituted the converse for the proposition.

---

5. Advertisement: "This contest is not open to residents of those states whose laws prohibit such contests."
Reader: "My state doesn't prohibit contests, so that means I can enter it."

---

The reader has substituted the inverse for the proposition.

---

6. Book: "All natural redheads have blue eyes."

Reader: "All blue-eyed people have naturally red hair."

The reader has substituted the converse for the proposition.

7. Notice of course requirements: "If you are to get an 'A' in this class, then you must do extra credit work."
Student (at card-marking time): "How come I didn't get an 'A'? I did extra credit work."

The student has substituted the converse for the proposition.

8. Advertisement: "If you don't want to have sparkling clean sheets, then don't use Kleen Detergent for your laundry."
Housewife A: "I'd better buy Kleen Detergent, or I won't have sparkling clean sheets."
Housewife B: "I want sparkling sheets, so I guess I'll buy Kleen Detergent."

Housewife A is substituting the converse for the proposition. She is saying, in effect, "If I don't buy Kleen Detergent, then I won't have sparkling clean sheets." Housewife B is substituting the inverse for the proposition.

## REVIEW
We have discussed five kinds of fallacious reasoning so far:
1) Proof by failure to find a counterexample (page 10)
2) Special pleading (page 19)
3) Avoiding the question (page 21)
4) Begging the question—circular reasoning (page 23)
5) Substitution of converse or inverse for proposition (pages 25, 26)

| | |
|---|---|
| *Proof by failure to find a counterexample* is the assumption that a (specific statement, generalization) is true because one or more (specific examples, generalizations) cannot be found to (agree with, contradict) it. | generalization specific examples contradict |
| *Special pleading* is used when a person is (willing, unwilling) to allow other people to enjoy the same benefits he himself enjoys. | unwilling |
| We are guilty of *special pleading* when we are willing to apply a general line of reasoning (in all cases, in some cases but not in others). | in some cases but not in others |

We are *avoiding the question* when we talk about (the, something other than the) point being discussed or when we talk *around*, instead of *at*, the point being discussed.

something other than the

We are *begging the question*—using *circular reasoning*—when we back up a conclusion with an assumption which is (the same as, different from) the conclusion.

the same as

Given an "if-then" proposition, we are *substituting the* _____ *for the proposition* when we exchange the "if" and "then" parts and assume that the new sentence has the same meaning as the original sentence; when we leave the "if" and "then" parts in their original positions but (accept, negate) both of them, we are *substituting the* _____ *for the proposition.*

*converse*

negate
*inverse*

Name the fallacy (or fallacies) in thinking involved in each of the following problems. Also consider it to be a fallacy if someone has ignored a counterexample.

1. Sam: "I don't believe that flying saucers don't exist."
Tom: "Well, find one, then."
Sam: "I can't."
Tom: "Then they don't exist."

---

Tom is using proof by failure to find a counterexample.

---

2. TV Panel Moderator: "We are here to discuss the effects of foreign trade on our own economy, and this distinguished panel of experts will give us their opinions. Dr. Carter, we'd like to hear from you first, please."
Dr. Carter: "Thank you, sir. I'm pleased that you asked me to be on your panel today. We agreed beforehand that the foreign trade to be discussed was two-way trade, so in giving my opinion I shall ignore those cases where the trading is a one-way proposition, either from our country to another, or from another country to ours."

---

Dr. Carter cannot really be accused of avoiding the question, for he seems to be leading up to it.

---

3. Dr. Carter continues: "First of all, in considering a two-way trade, we must necessarily assume that we have something the other country wants, and that

they have something that we want. A problem is created, however, when one of the countries has more of the commodity than either of us wants, for in that case, the country having the surplus will be obliged to find an additional outlet for its goods. This problem of maintaining just the proper balance of goods, I think, is the most difficult problem we encounter today in foreign trade."

Dr. Carter is guilty of avoiding the question. We see that he is discussing the question of the problems encountered in foreign trade, rather than the question of the effects of foreign trade on our own economy.

4. Professor Simpson: "And so we see that some changes in behavior can be attributed to physiological, or maturational, changes, while others can be attributed to experience or conditioning."
Student: "It takes experience to learn to ride a bicycle, and yet a child can't ride a bicycle until he's developed physiologically to the point where he has enough sense of balance to ride one. To which of these causes would you attribute being able to ride a bicycle?"
Professor Simpson: "I think you have just answered your own question."

Professor Simpson is avoiding the question.

5. Scott: "Boy, you really bug me! I loaned you $5 three weeks ago and you still haven't paid it back! That's the last time I'll loan you any money."
Rich: "You seem to forget that I loaned you money six months ago and you took five weeks to pay it back, and then you turned right around and borrowed it again a week later."
Scott: "We're talking about the money you owe me right now, not money that I've already paid back to you."

Scott is guilty of special pleading: he expects favors of others which he, in turn, is not willing to grant. Rich is avoiding the question.

6. Rod: "All blondes are dumb."
Walt: "Marsha's a blonde, and she isn't dumb."
Rod: "She's just the exception that proves the rule."
(Hint: Two fallacies are present here.)

Rod is guilty on two counts: special pleading; ignoring a counterexample.

7. Mr. Meyers: "Our union contract expires next week and we take a strike vote. You going to be there?"

Mr. Young: "Sure, and I'm going to vote to strike, too. Our working conditions are bad enough, but we're underpaid besides."

Mr. Meyers: "That's the way I feel, too. And speaking of strikes, what do you think of these teachers not starting to work in September because their contracts aren't settled?"

Mr. Young: "I think they've got a lot of nerve keeping our kids from getting an education. We ought to have a law against that kind of thing."

Mr. Young is guilty of special pleading. He thinks it's all right for him not to work if he doesn't have a contract, but he thinks teachers should work whether they have a contract or not.

8. (conversation from problem 7 continued) Mr. Meyers: "What makes you think our working conditions are bad?"

Mr. Young: "I don't *think* they're bad, I *know* they're bad. In fact, they're so bad they're rotten."

Mr. Young is begging the question.

9. Sign in store pointing to ball-point pens: "One free when you buy a box of paper."

Customer: "Then I can't get one free unless I buy a box of paper."

The sign means, "If you buy a box of paper, then you get a free pen." The customer is saying, "If I don't buy a box of paper, then I can't get one free." The customer is substituting the inverse for the proposition.

10. Mrs. Horton: "Children today are certainly an ungrateful lot! They don't appreciate anything their parents give them!"

Mrs. Ingram: "I thought you were telling me just the other day about how good your married daughter has been to you—calling you often, asking if you'd like her to take you shopping, and all."

Mrs. Horton: "Well, she should be good to me, after all I've done for her." (Hint: There are two fallacies present here.)

Mrs. Horton is guilty of special pleading and ignoring a counterexample. Notice the similarity between this line of reasoning and Rod's line of reasoning in problem 6 above.

11. Advertisement: "If you would like to receive this beautiful gift absolutely free, let us come to your home to give you a free estimate on repairs."

Reader: "I'd like to have that gift. I'll let them come here and give me an estimate, and then I'll get the gift."

The reader is substituting the converse for the proposition.

12. Magazine article: "Those who think that the King of Outlandia allows more freedom in his subjects' choice of clothing than his predecessor should look more closely. The men and boys must all wear exactly the same uniform, and the women and girls have the choice of only two styles—either a trousers-and-shirt uniform, or a skirt-and-blouse uniform."

The article is avoiding the question of whether or not the current king allows more freedom in his subjects' choice of clothing than his predecessor. It gives us facts about the current king, but it tells us nothing about the predecessor, and so we have no basis for a comparison.

13. Announcer: "If you are to be sure of taking advantage of this fantastic offer, be sure to mail us your order tonight."
Listener: "O.K., I'll mail my order tonight, and then I'll be sure of getting in on it."

The listener is substituting the converse for the proposition.

14. Mr. Greene: "I'm all for going along with the latest scientific knowledge, but I think we ought to return to the public whipping post for these juvenile delinquents."
Mr. Oliver: "But research has shown that public punishment does more harm than good."
Mr. Greene: "You'll never convince me that getting publicly beaten won't put a stop to some of this delinquency."
Mr. Oliver: "Would you feel the same way if your own boy were found guilty of delinquency?"
Mr. Greene: "Just let me find out that he's been up to no good. I'll take care of him, all right!"
Mr. Oliver: "What makes you think that the public whipping post would stop some of the delinquency?"
Mr. Greene: "All we'd need is that whipping post and about ten roughnecks publicly whipped, and that would put an end to some of it!"
(Hint: There are three fallacies present here.)

Mr. Greene's first and second statements make him guilty of special pleading. (He claims he goes along with scientific knowledge; yet, he doesn't want to go along with it in the case of the whipping post.) Mr. Greene is guilty of avoiding the question in his third remark, and he is guilty of begging the question in his last remark.

_____

15. At the beginning of this chapter (page 17), two examples of arguments were given, the second of which involved fallacious reasoning. What fallacy was involved?

_____

Special pleading.

_____

# Chapter 5. Recognizing Assumptions and Implications

A person's thoughts are revealed to us by what he says and by what he openly implies, of course; but they are also revealed to us by what he implies indirectly and by what he indicates that he considers too obvious to mention. For example, suppose I say to you, "You ought to get rid of your dog. His continual barking is driving the whole neighborhood nuts." Among the open implications are:

1. Getting rid of your dog is better than driving the whole neighborhood nuts.
2. No one in the neighborhood likes your dog's continual barking.
3. It is all right to get rid of your dog.

Among the indirect implications and ideas too obvious to mention are:

1. You have a dog.
2. You have neighbors who can hear your dog barking.
3. It is undesirable to drive the whole neighborhood nuts.
4. You should be considerate of your neighbors.

A critical reader not only reads what the author says, but he also looks for open implications, hidden implications, and ideas the author considers too obvious to mention. These hidden implications and too-obvious-to-mention ideas can be called *hidden assumptions*, for the author assumes them to be true without bothering to tell us.

Since the author's assumptions might be quite different from our own, we may easily misinterpret what he says unless we learn to identify these assumptions. Only then can we intelligently agree or disagree with, can we intelligently believe or disbelieve, can we understand the author.

I. Here is a short passage—John 3:16–18—from the Bible (3) which is followed by several statements. Mark each statement "yes" or "no" to show whether or not this passage indicates the author assumed the statement to be true. An answer of "no" will mean only that the passage does not indicate the assumption was made and will not necessarily mean that the passage disagrees with the given assumption.

For God so loved the world that he gave his only begotten Son, that who-soever believeth in him should not perish but have everlasting life. For

God sent not his Son into the world to condemn the world, but that the world through him might be saved. He that believeth on him is not condemned; but he that believeth not is condemned already, because he hath not believed in the name of the only begotten Son of God.

| | |
|---|---|
| 1. God exists. | yes |
| 2. God had a Son. | yes |
| 3. God did not have a Daughter. | no |
| 4. God did have a Daughter. | no |
| 5. God loved the world very much. | yes |
| 6. God sent his Son into the world for a purpose. | yes |
| 7. There is such a thing as everlasting life. | yes |
| 8. Each man has a free choice of believing or not believing. | yes |
| 9. The choice of whether or not to believe is difficult to make. | no |
| 10. It is desirable to believe on the Son of God. | yes |
| 11. It is undesirable not to believe on the Son of God. | yes |
| 12. If a man is good enough (kind, charitable, etc.), he is not condemned even though he does not believe on the Son of God. | no |
| 13. A person's good works count for nothing in deciding whether or not he is condemned. | yes |
| 14. Once a man knows that everlasting life is so easy to attain, he will believe on the Son of God. | no |
| 15. Some people don't believe anything which they haven't personally seen. | no |

II. As you read the following passage from *The Scarlet Letter* (4), decide what Hawthorne is implying as well as what he is saying.

It is a good lesson—though it may often be a hard one—for a man who has dreamed of literary fame, and of making for himself a rank among the world's dignitaries by such means, to step aside out of the narrow circle in which his claims are recognized, and to find how utterly devoid of significance, beyond that circle, is all that he achieves and all he aims at.

1. Hawthorne says in the first clause, "It is a good lesson." Briefly, what does he mean by the word "it"?

a. For an author to learn a hard lesson.

b. For an author to learn that his writing is unknown outside his own little circle.

c. For an author to learn that his nonliterary achievements and aims are regarded as insignificant.

d. For an author who has been given literary recognition by some people to learn that other people do not regard his accomplishments and goals as extraordinary.

---

d. Not a, for the clause "though it may often be a hard one" refers to "lesson," not to "it." The key to the "it" is in the clause "in which his claims are recognized." The claims referred to in this clause are literary fame and being ranked with the world's dignitaries. Then "the narrow circle in which his claims are recognized" would be the set of people who have treated him as though he were a famous dignitary because of his literary accomplishments, and "beyond that circle" would be all other people. Therefore, he is saying that it is a good lesson for an author who has been treated as a famous dignitary by some people to learn that other people don't think he's done anything unusual (answer d). Answer b implies confinement to the author's circle of personal acquaintances (not b). Answer c misses the point that even his literary achievements and aims are considered as unnoteworthy by the "other people" (not c).

---

*Problems 2–9:* Mark each of the following statements "yes" or "no" to indicate whether or not Hawthorne has assumed the statement to be true in the passage quoted above. Again, a "no" answer indicates only that Hawthorne has not made the assumption, not that he disagrees with it.

| | |
|---|---|
| 2. A good lesson is a hard one. | no |
| 3. A hard lesson is a good one. | no |
| 4. A good lesson may be a hard one. | yes |
| 5. A humbling experience may be a good lesson. | yes |
| 6. An author's claim to fame is recognized only within a narrow circle. | yes |
| 7. Some people consider authors' achievements to be insignificant. | yes |
| 8. Some people consider authors' future aims to be insignificant. | yes |
| 9. Some people consider authors to be insignificant. | no |

III. The following letter appeared in "The Public Letter Box" of *The Detroit News* (5), p. 6-B, on March 20, 1967:

> To the Editor:
>
> Jimmy Hoffa's reign of terror was due to the fact that a Teamster could not, or dared not, say anything to him or his cohorts because he would get them fired.
>
> On the other hand, Hoffa didn't care how much he penalized industry by high wages. He knew by getting higher wages for his members he could keep them in line. So they went along—and so did inflation.
>
> The attorneys who kept him out of jail for so long should be disbarred. If he had known that he couldn't get an attorney to fight for him in his shady deals, he would not have gone so far.
>
> I am a member of three unions.
>
> [Name withheld]

1. What was the writer's purpose in including the last sentence of his letter?

The purpose was to show the reader that the writer is a union man, not a company man, complaining about a union official.

2. Does the writer assume that Teamster members valued their jobs above any disagreements they may have had with Mr. Hoffa?

Yes. See the first sentence of the letter.

3. Does the writer assume that Teamster members were more concerned with better wages for themselves than they were with whether or not Mr. Hoffa's methods merited their approval?

Yes. See the second sentence of the second paragraph of the letter.

4. Does the writer assume that if an attorney's client is found guilty, then the attorney should not file appeals in order to try to keep him out of jail?

Yes, per the first sentence of the third paragraph. Since Mr. Hoffa's attorneys kept him out of jail so long by filing appeals, either the writer has made the general assumption indicated by question 4 or he is guilty of special pleading (page 19), for he has made the assumption in Mr. Hoffa's case.

5. Does the writer assume that Mr. Hoffa wouldn't have done what he did if he thought he couldn't find an attorney to plead his case?

Yes. See the second sentence in the third paragraph.

6. Does the writer assume that everyone accused of a crime should be allowed to be represented by an attorney?

No. This assumption is inconsistent with the third paragraph of the letter, which apparently assumes that anyone involved in a shady deal is not entitled to be represented by an attorney. If we agree that a crime is a shady deal and that the accusation of a person involves him, then either the assumption in question 6 is a direct contradiction of the letter, or the writer is guilty of special pleading.

IV. The following letter appeared in the "Dear Abby" column (by Abigail Van Buren) of *The Detroit News* (5), p. 4–G, on February 15, 1967. Mark each statement following the letter either "yes" or "no" to indicate whether or not the writer implied it to be true.

Dear Abby:
I have worked for a large firm for many years and it makes me cringe to see the amount of stealing that prevails under the heading of "expense accounts." Some of the expense accounters put their wives' gas tickets in with their own—"Car Expense."
Some take their wives out for a birthday or anniversary celebration, along with a few other friends—"Business" entertainment.
Some buy a bottle for a friend and help him drink it—"Promotion."
The list could go on and on. These fourflushers are worse than thieves, since they are biting the hand that feeds them. I get so mad I could cry.
Infuriated

| | |
|---|---|
| 1. If you're going to steal, you should be open about it. | no |
| 2. Employees who include personal items on expense accounts are worse than thieves. | yes |
| 3. A thief does not bite the hand that feeds him. | yes |
| 4. It is wrong for a man to take his wife out for a birthday or anniversary celebration. | no |
| 5. It is wrong for a man to pay his wife's gasoline bills. | no |

6. It is wrong for a man to pay for his wife's gasoline at the same time that he pays for own.                                                      no
7. It is worse to steal from your employer than it is to steal from a stranger.                              yes
8. Some stealing is more morally wrong than other stealing.                                              yes
9. It is wrong to drink with a friend.                    no
10. It is wrong to buy a bottle for a friend and help him drink it.                                            no

Other exercises throughout this book will give you much more practice in recognizing the assumptions and implications made by authors.

# Chapter 6. Recognizing Intent, Attitude, Tone, and Bias

The preceding chapters have shown that before a reader can effectively evaluate what he has read he must consider the source from which he is reading, he must learn not to misread the author's words, he must recognize some of the more common informal fallacies in thinking, and he must learn to recognize assumptions and implications made by the author. In addition to all of these things he must also learn to recognize the author's intent, attitude, tone, and bias.

Answers to questions like these will indicate the author's *intent:* What did he hope to accomplish by writing this? Did he hope to amuse, to ridicule, to arouse sympathy or pity, to convince the reader of something, to deprecate someone or something, to refute an opponent, to prove something, to tell a story, to state facts, to state opinions, to spread gossip, to accuse someone of something, to moralize, to teach?

Answers to questions like these will indicate the author's *attitude:* Does the author consider this topic to be a serious problem for future consideration, a serious problem for immediate action, a problem which could be serious if not solved? Does he consider the topic to be interesting or dull, heavy or lighthearted, serious or nonsense, important or unimportant, worthy or unworthy of his attention? What are his personal feelings about the subject—is he happy, sad, neutral, angry, disgusted, irritated, sympathetic, revengeful, crusading, tolerant, disillusioned, enthusiastic? How does the author feel about his readers? Is his writing directed toward mental inferiors, superiors, or equals? Novices, masters, or in-betweens?

The *tone* the author uses in his writing will be determined in part by his intent and his attitude. His *tone* can be recognized by answers to questions such as these: Is he being serious, light-heartedly humorous, ironic, sarcastic, logical, emotional, condescending? Is he trying to impress the reader with his erudition? Does he use words whose connotations are filled with innuendoes not otherwise implied?

An author's intent, attitude, and tone will often indicate whether or not he is *biased* in his discussion. For example, when an author says that someone is being pig-headed we have no doubt that the author is expressing an opinion, not a fact. If he chooses to back up this opinion with facts, then we, too, might agree with his opinion, but in the meantime the author's choice of words has told us that he is biased about his subject. If an author's intent is to convince us of something, then we can take for granted that he is biased toward that something; nevertheless, his writing may be relatively unbiased in the sense that he may honestly try to present both sides of the story and then try to convince us that his side has the more merit. Answers to the following questions will help us recognize an author's bias in writing: Considering the topic as a whole, what factors would be *potentially* biasing no matter who wrote about them? Does the author appear to be one-sided about any of these? Is he being objective, or subjective? Is he stating fact, or opinion? How well are his opinions substantiated? Or are they unsubstantiated? How factual are his "facts"—are they solid facts, misrepresented or distorted facts, or merely opinions? Does the tone of his writing suggest that he may be biased?

The previous paragraphs are misleading if they make it appear that intent, attitude, tone, and bias can be conveniently separated at will into four distinct categories, for such a simple separation is not always possible. For example: The fact that an author finds it necessary to explain the obvious may indicate something about both his attitude toward his readers and the tone he takes with them. The type of publication in which his writing appears or the fact that he is an authority in his field may suggest something about all four factors. Although the question, "Did he hope to ridicule?" appeared in the paragraph about intent, a "yes" answer would certainly also indicate something about the author's attitude, tone, and bias. Consequently, although the above four paragraphs may seem to separate the four factors, this separation is more artificial than genuine and you should not think that such a breakdown is necessary or even always possible.

The questions following the selections in this chapter are designed to help you learn to recognize an author's intent, attitude, tone, and bias, as well as to reinforce the concepts discussed in previous chapters.

| | |
|---|---|
| The author's *intent* has to do with his (purpose, viewpoint) in writing, or what he intends to accomplish by his writing. | purpose |
| His *attitude* has to do with the way he (presents the facts, feels) about his subject or his audience. | feels |
| His *tone* has to do with (his knowledge of the subject, the way he chooses to express himself). | the way he chooses to express himself |
| His *bias* has to do with whether or not he is writing (objectively, clearly). | objectively |

| | |
|---|---|
| Getting a "yes" answer to a question such as, "Was the author malicious?" will (enable, not enable) a critical reader to decide that that question applies to just one of the four categories; but when asked a question such as, "What was the author's attitude?" the critical reader (will, will not) be able to answer. | not enable<br><br><br><br><br>will |

The first three of the following selections are interrupted several times by questions and statements. Questions and statements follow the other selections. Answer the *questions* asked. Each *statement* indicates a possible assumption made by the author of the selection, and you are to decide whether or not it appears that the author made the assumption indicated by the statement. If you believe that the author probably did make that assumption, then mark the statement "APM" (assumption probably made); if you believe that he probably did not make that assumption, then mark the statement "APNM" (assumption probably not made).

I. The following letter appeared in "The Public Letter Box" of *The Detroit News* (5), p. 18–A, on February 20, 1967:

To the Editor:
When are the newspapers going to expose all of these blasted insurance companies?

1. What appears to be the writer's attitude toward insurance companies?
*a.* Disgusted
*b.* Amused
*c.* Neutral
*d.* Arbitrary

*a.* His use of the words "expose" and "blasted" preclude his being neutral (not *c*) and make it highly unlikely that he is amused (not *b*). We cannot judge whether or not we think he is being arbitrary on the basis of his first paragraph (not *d*).

2. If the newspapers were to print the facts about insurance companies, the result would be unfavorable publicity for these companies.

APM. Again, notice the use of the words "expose" and "blasted."

3. Unfavorable publicity would result in the insurance companies' correcting some of the things wrong with them.

APM. Otherwise, there would seem to be little point in asking for the publicity.

4. It is the job of the newspapers to publicize unfair practices of big companies.

APM. Otherwise, there is no point in asking the question.

My home insurance company just notified me that it is placing a $50 deductible on my policy because I had five claims in three years. All claims were the result of kids busting windows, painting my house red during Halloween, and such things.

Why have insurance if you're not covered for such things? Why be penalized for something that isn't your fault?

5. What appears to be the purpose of this letter?
a. To inform the reader of the writer's experiences with insurance companies
b. To convince the reader that insurance companies are unfair
c. To warn the reader not to bother having insurance
d. To ridicule insurance companies

b. The writer wants the newspapers "to expose all of these blasted insurance companies," and the tone of the letter makes it appear that he believes himself to be the innocent victim of an unfair company. Although he tells us of his experiences, he does this to convince us that insurance companies are unfair (answer b), and the information about his experiences is not itself the purpose of the letter (not a). Since his company paid five claims in three years it is unlikely that he is trying to warn us not to have insurance (not c). His tone is one of complaint, indignation, and disgust, rather than of ridicule (not d).

6. I am in no way responsible for the damages to my home by the kids.

APM. Notice the question, "Why be penalized for something that isn't your fault?"

7. Did the writer's insurance company cancel his insurance on his home?

No. The insurance company placed a $50 deductible clause in his policy.

8. Did the insurance company notify the writer that they would in the future no longer cover damages to his home arising from similar circumstances ("kids busting windows," etc.)?

No. By placing a $50 deductible clause in the policy, the insurance company agreed to pay for damage in excess of $50.

9. What do you suppose is the writer's purpose in asking the question, "Why have insurance if you're not covered for such things?" What is your reaction to the writer's question?

The question is probably asked in order to further his argument that insurance companies are unfair. As it stands, the question is misleading and is a good example of innuendo, for it implies that the company has refused to insure him against such losses in the future; yet, we see from question 8 above that the company has not done this at all.

10. It is unfair to be penalized for something that isn't your fault.

APM. This is implied by the last question the writer has asked.

11. The amount paid by an individual for insurance should not be directly related to the claims he files against the insurance company.

APM. Since the writer has cited the $50 deductible decision of the company in his public letter of complaint, we can infer that he believes this to be an example of the company's unfairness. And, since his five claims in three years may well have amounted to more than he was paying for that portion of his policy, it is reasonable to infer that he believes the insurance company should absorb the loss rather than make any adjustment in his policy.

12. The question, "Why be penalized for something that isn't your fault?" applies to me, but it does not apply to my insurance company.

APM. Even though neither he nor the insurance company is at fault, apparently he considers the $50 deductible clause to be a penalty to him, but he does not consider it to be a penalty to the insurance company to continue without the $50 deductible clause. He is implying, "It's OK for my insurance company to be penalized for something that wasn't their fault, but it isn't OK for me to be penalized for something that wasn't my fault."

My car insurance has skyrocketed in the past five years, despite the fact that I didn't have one claim in years and years.

13. The amount paid by an individual for insurance should not be directly related to the claims he files against the insurance company.

APNM. We can infer that the writer believes his claim-free record should protect him from some of the increases in insurance costs. (Compare the writer's reasoning here with his reasoning about statement 11 above.)

14. Considering the basis on which insurance companies operate, what are two sound reasons to account for "skyrocketing" car insurance costs within the last few years? In answering this question, assume that the proportion of accidents to policyholders has remained constant.

If you gave as one answer, "Because there are more drivers (or "more cars") on the road," you have ignored the instruction following the question. As long as the proportion of accidents to policyholders remains constant, the number of drivers on the road does not matter. Some possible acceptable answers are: labor and material costs have increased, thus increasing the expense of repairs to cars involved in accidents; costs of new cars have increased, thus increasing the cost of replacing a car demolished in an accident; hospitalization costs have increased, thus increasing the costs of caring for accident victims; courts have been more and more liberal in awarding large compensatory sums to accident victims, thus increasing the costs of settling accident suits involving personal injuries.

It's interesting to note that my insurance agents no longer come to my home, as they did in the past. Instead, they always phone to give me the bad news. They don't dare step into my house any more—probably for fear I might shoot one of them in cold blood.

[Name withheld]

15. What does the writer imply in this last paragraph?

He implies that the insurance agents no longer come to his home because they are ashamed to face him or because they believe their companies are being grossly unfair and they are afraid to face him.

16. Where does this letter contain two instances of special pleading (page 19)?

See the answers to statements 12 and 13.

II. The following appeared in "The Public Letter Box" of *The Detroit News* (5), p. 22–A, on February 13, 1967, which was about 10 days after a series of heavy snowfalls in the Detroit area. DPW stands for Detroit Public Works.

To the Editor:
Citizens who have been criticizing the DPW for not clearing "impassable" residential streets of snow should take a good look around.

1. Is this letter going to criticize the DPW for not clearing residential streets of snow?

Probably not. When we tell someone to "take a good look around," we are usually indicating disagreement with him.

They will notice that in spite of all those "intolerable" conditions most of their hardier neighbors have their walks, driveways and most of the "impassable" streets in front of their homes clear of snow and ice.

2. What is the writer's purpose in enclosing the words "impassable" and "intolerable" in quotation marks?

These words were probably used by the critics of the DPW, and the writer uses quotation marks to show that he disagrees with the use of these words.

How lazy can human beings get? To expect the city to clear their streets is ridiculous. The very ones that cry the loudest are the greatest offenders. I suggest they get their shovels and scrapers and make like the other good neighbors.

3. The complainers have not attempted to clear the streets themselves.

APM. Notice the third sentence in this paragraph.

_____

4. The reason some residential streets are still unclear of snow is that the residents are too lazy to shovel the snow off the streets themselves.

_____

APM. Notice the question asked and the last sentence in this paragraph.

_____

Furthermore, citizens who own driveways and garages but still choose to park in the streets should be ticketed, warned or have their cars hauled away. They are a greater hazard to all their neighbors than they realize. Those who have had to back out of their driveways while the neighbors' car across the street prevents them from doing so safely know what I mean.

5. People always know when they are being inconsiderate.

_____

APNM. See the second sentence in this paragraph.

_____

6. Some people need to be reminded to think more of their neighbors' welfare and less of their own convenience.

_____

APM. See the first sentence in this paragraph.

_____

The city says it needs extra revenue. Well, here's one way to get a quick bundle legally without any fuss or bother or even the expense of those fact-finding committees. Let the Meter Maids [women who are employed by Detroit to ticket cars for parking violations] handle this one and by golly I'll bet before they get through they'll even buy them better-looking uniforms. We'll have a much better town for it.

[Name withheld]

7. We'd have a better city if the Meter Maids had better-looking uniforms.

_____

APNM. The use of the word "it" in the last sentence probably refers to ticketing the cars, rather than to buying uniforms for the Meter Maids.

_____

8. The Meter Maids do a good job.

_____

APM. Otherwise, there wouldn't be much point in suggesting that the Meter Maids handle the job of ticketing the cars.

_____

9. What appears to be the writer's intent in writing this letter?
a. To praise the Meter Maids
b. To defend the DPW
c. To stir the reader to action
d. To ridicule people who leave their cars parked in the streets

c. Although ostensibly written to the editor of the newspaper, this letter is primarily written to the DPW critics to tell them to shovel the snow themselves (last sentence of third paragraph) and to get their cars off the streets (fourth paragraph). He praises the Meter Maids only by implication and he mentions them only as a means to an end (not a). Not b, for he doesn't say whether or not the DPW is doing the job it is supposed to do. Not d, for his tone about people who leave their cars in the streets is not one of ridicule.

10. On what does the writer base his statement, "The very ones that cry the loudest are the greatest offenders"?

The letter doesn't tell us, but we are probably safe in assuming that the writer based this statement on his observations of his neighbors. If we are correct, then the writer's statement is an example of *proof by selected instances,* an informal fallacy in thinking which is explained below.

A *proof by selected instances* is a general conclusion drawn solely on the basis of a few (possibly just one or two) examples. Although such reasoning may lead to a correct conclusion, it also may not lead to a correct conclusion. As in the above writer's case, there are times when we are unable to observe all possibilities and so must draw a conclusion based on a few observations; but we should be aware that our observations may not have been representative of all possibilities.

Mark each of the following situations "yes" or "no" to indicate whether or not the conclusion represents a *proof by selected instances.*
1. Tommy, age four, sees a dog for the first time and the dog bites him. Tommy concludes that all dogs will bite him.

Yes.

2. Freddy, age five, wanders away from home and gets lost. He is found by a policeman and taken to the police station, where he is given ice cream and reassurance. Freddy concludes that all policemen are nice.

Yes.

3. Kathy, a ninth-grader who has always had A's and B's in arithmetic, signs up for algebra and just barely manages to understand what the teacher is talking about. Kathy concludes that she is unable to understand any mathematics easily except arithmetic.

Yes.

4. Mr. Johnson is a door-to-door salesman who finds housewives very rude. He believes that housewives are rude to all door-to-door salesmen.

Yes.

5. Mr. Johnson, the door-to-door salesman from problem 4, compares his experiences with the experiences of the other 1,500 door-to-door salesmen in his company and he finds that all these salesmen have found housewives to be very rude. He concludes that housewives are rude to all door-to-door salesmen.

Yes. Although his conclusion here is based on a wider range of experience than his conclusion in problem 4, he is still making a universal generalization about all door-to-door salesmen when he knows the experiences only of the salesmen in his own company.

6. Mr. Smith has lived in a remote mountain region amid poverty all of his life. He believes that everyone is poverty-stricken.

Yes.

7. For three years the Carsons lived next door to a family whose members all had yellow eyes. The family fought continually and let the property deteriorate. The Carsons moved to another home after first making very sure that no yellow-eyed people lived in the neighborhood.

Yes.

8. More than ever before, newspapers today carry stories of juvenile delinquency and teen-aged violence. Many adults have concluded that today's teen-agers are wild and irresponsible.

Yes.

9. Just graduated from high school, Sally was frustrated because she had

applied for several jobs and had been turned down by each prospective employer because she lacked experience. Sally concluded she'd have to lie about her lack of experience in order to get a job.

Yes.

10. Rick sees a flying saucer. He concludes that flying saucers exist.

No. (Notice that Rick made no generalization about *all* flying saucers.)

11. Rick sees a flying saucer with flashing lights. He concludes that all flying saucers have flashing lights.

Yes.

Following are more selections. Remember to answer the questions asked and to mark the statements "APM" (assumption probably made) or "APNM" (assumption probably not made).

III. The following editorial appeared on p. 6-B of *The Detroit News* (5) on March 20, 1967. The paragraphs are numbered to provide for easy reference.

### Venomous Speech—But Still Free

1) The TV news camera has recorded the smirk, the supercilious air of amusement and self-satisfaction at all the attention, displayed by the four young Detroit men who last week spread anti-Jewish leaflets around— inspired, it seems, by the arson destruction of Trenton's Beth Isaac Synagog.

2) They apparently don't and won't understand anything of the venomous nature of their "cute stunt."

1. What seems to be the writer's attitude toward the spreading of anti-Jewish leaflets by the four young men?
*a.* Amused approval
*b.* Amused disapproval
*c.* Serious approval
*d.* Serious disapproval

*d.* Notice the words "smirk," "supercilious," and "venomous," all of which connote disapproval (not *a* or *c*). Also notice the enclosing of the words "cute stunt" in quotation marks, which leads us to infer that the young men thought their actions to be a prank, but that the writer disagrees (not *a* or *b*).

The tone of paragraph 1 indicates he is definitely not amused, and this is verified by paragraph 2 (*d*, not *b*).

---

3) This void in their souls may suggest a commentary on the failure of our schools and churches to help many young Americans realize the monstrous implications of anti-Semitism, as they have likewise failed to foster an understanding of what bothers Negroes about White America. But that's another subject.

2. The schools and churches, not the parents, have the primary responsibility of teaching our young people to be unprejudiced toward other races and religions.

APM. The editorial mentions "the failure of our schools and churches" but doesn't mention parents. It is reasonable to assume that the writer would have mentioned parents if he felt they shared the primary responsibility.

---

3. The attitudes instilled in young people by their parents carry more weight than the attitudes instilled by schools and churches.

APNM. If the writer felt this way, it is unlikely that he would seem to place the primary burden on the schools and churches.

---

4. Is the writer implying that Trenton's Beth Isaac Synagog had a congregation largely comprised of Jewish Negroes?

No. The writer is saying that the schools and churches have failed in two respects: in teaching tolerance for another religion, and in teaching tolerance for another race. He is not implying that the two are connected in this case, as is evident from his sentence, "But that's another subject."

---

4) The arrogance of these four will be compounded, no doubt, by their escape from meaningful prosecution, since there is no state law against such hate-literature.
5) It's hard, save for those who agree with the tripe they peddled, to dispute Wayne County Prosecutor William Cahalan's belief that there should be a law. It is particularly hard, surely, for Richard Lobenthal, local director of the Anti-Defamation League of B'Nai Brith. But he does disagree.
6) "Freedom of speech in this country is something that must not be com-

promised, no matter how odious the statements might be," Lobenthal says. We are forced to agree.

7) A group libel statute seems at first blush to be an attractive answer for a decent society to scurrilous attacks on racial and religious minorities. Several states have tried to meet the problem this way.

8) But except as they tie prosecution and penalty to a finding that the utterance is reasonably calculated to cause a breach of the peace, such statutes are on very shaky constitutional ground. . . .

9) One of the prices we pay for our own freedom, then, is the annoyance of seeing foolish, even warped individuals free to disseminate odious ideas, so long as their activity cannot be shown to be the direct cause of violence.

10) Our best defense against them is the common decency and respect for one another which we like to think is the certain product of a free and fully informed people.

5. Were the four young men who distributed the anti-Jewish leaflets prosecuted for committing any crime or misdemeanor?

We can't tell. We are told that they escaped any "meaningful prosecution," which we can infer to mean prosecution commensurate with their actions (in the editorialist's eyes), but they may have been prosecuted for something relatively minor in connection with their actions, such as littering.

6. There should be a law against the distribution of hate literature.

APNM. In paragraph 5 the writer says that Lobenthal disagrees with Cahalan's belief that there should be such a law, and in paragraph 6 the writer says he agrees with Lobenthal.

7. We should not stop the distribution of hate literature unless such distribution can be shown to be the direct cause of violence.

APM. See paragraphs 9 and 10 of the editorial.

8. Allowing the distribution of hate literature is undesirable, but it is preferable to relinquishing any part of our freedom of speech.

APM. See paragraphs 6 and 9 of the editorial.

9. Where does this editorial contain an implied proof by selected instances (page 49)?

_____

The first sentence of paragraph 3 suggests that the failure of the churches and schools to teach these four young men means that many young people have not been taught.

_____

10. What appears to be the purpose of this editorial?
a. To point out that no great harm was done by these leaflets
b. To show that racial and religious prejudice will always be with us
c. To advocate that a law be passed against the spreading of such leaflets
d. To advocate that a law against the spreading of such leaflets not be passed

_____

d. The first three paragraphs are written as an introduction to the problem of whether or not there should be a law against the spreading of such leaflets and the rest of the editorial is devoted to discussing such a law. There would seem to be little point in devoting so much of the editorial to the discussion of a proposed law if the purpose of the editorial were either to point out that no great harm had been done (not a) or to show that we will always have some racial and religious prejudice (not b). That the writer is against passing a law to prohibit the spreading of such leaflets is made clear in paragraphs 5, 6, 9, and 10 (d, not c).

_____

11. How do you think most readers would react to this editorial?
a. With indifference
b. With thoughtful consideration
c. With anger
d. With disgust

_____

b. Although the writer makes it clear that he is angry and disgusted about the spreading of the leaflets, his attitude and tone in the rest of the editorial are reluctantly accepting of such actions as the price of freedom of speech for the rest of us. His words are not calculated to arouse in the reader either anger or disgust over the fact that such a situation must exist, but only a resigned annoyance (in paragraph 9). Because of his tone and the nonneutrality of most readers for the subject, it seems likely that the reader would think about what he had read (answer b), but not react to the editorial with indifference, anger, or disgust (not a, c, or d).

_____

12. How does the writer treat his subject?
a. Seriously

*b.* Ironically

*c.* Humorously

---

*a.* Although some irony exists in the situation—in order to protect the freedom of speech we must allow the persecution of people who are practicing the freedom of religion—the tone is serious, not ironic (*a,* not *b*). The writer's mention of amusement (paragraph 1) and "cute stunt" (paragraph 2) do not indicate that he treats the subject humorously.

---

IV. The following letter appeared in "The Public Letter Box" of *The Detroit News* (5), p. 20-A, on March 6, 1967. Cobo Hall is a large convention hall in Detroit; Garden City is a suburb of Detroit.

> To the Editor:
> If the United States mayors' convention were held at Cobo Hall, Garden City would no doubt manage to have one delegate in attendance. However, with this year's event being held in Hawaii, it seems necessary that the city send not only the mayor but also all four councilmen.
>      Travel expenses will come out of our tax funds. If this doesn't win us the trophy for the "Nation's Most Gullible City," we ought to run a close second.
>
> Helpless Taxpayer

1. Helpless Taxpayer's intent in writing this letter seems to be
*a.* to express the opinion that Garden City should win a trophy.
*b.* to point out the necessity of sending five city officials to Hawaii for a mayors' convention.
*c.* to advocate that the Garden City officials go to the convention at Cobo Hall instead of the one in Hawaii.
*d.* to express disapproval of the attendance of five Garden City officials at the mayors' convention in Hawaii.

---

*d.* The statement about the trophy is merely another way of expressing disapproval (*d,* not *a*). He did not point out any need to send five officials to Hawaii, for he said only, "It seems necessary . . .," and he did not back this up (not *b*). Answer *c* implies a choice of two conventions this year, but the letter does not imply this (not *c*).

---

2. To whom is Helpless Taxpayer *ostensibly* directing his letter?
*a.* The editor of *The Detroit News*
*b.* Taxpayers of Detroit

*c.* Taxpayers of Garden City
*d.* Officials of Garden City

*a.* Notice that it starts out, "To the Editor."

3. To whom is Helpless Taxpayer *really* directing his letter?
*a.* The editor of *The Detroit News*
*b.* Taxpayers of Detroit
*c.* Taxpayers of Garden City
*d.* Officials of Garden City

*d* via *c.* That is, H. T. is talking to other Garden City taxpayers about the Garden city officials, apparently hoping to let the officials know that their decisions have not gone unnoticed.

4. The writer's treatment of his subject is
*a.* Straightforward
*b.* Ironic

*b.* In ironic writing the words said are contrary to the meaning intended. Notice the contrast between his first two sentences. Paraphrasing these, we have, "If the convention were at home then one delegate would be enough, for he could bring back the knowledge he had gained to the others. But with the convention in Hawaii, naturally one delegate would not be able to bring back the knowledge to the other officials, so it is necessary for all of the high officials to go." We then wonder why five delegates are needed to do the job in Hawaii when it takes only one delegate to do the job in Detroit. The question follows, "What's the *real* reason all five high officials are going?" and the implied answer is, "To get a free vacation." From this line of thought we see that even though the writer *says* that the trip *seems* necessary, he *means* that the trip does *not* seem necessary. The writer again uses irony in the second sentence of the second paragraph: When we read, "If this doesn't win us the trophy for . . . ," the words "win us the trophy" connote a prize for high achievement, superior accomplishment—in this case, the prize for extraordinary perspicacity of the voters in electing officials so dedicated that they are willing to leave their homes and travel thousands of miles to attend a routine convention for the good of the city they serve. But the words inscribed on the trophy—"Nation's Most Gullible City"—are contrary to the connotations of "winning a trophy." We see, then, that although the writer has made his meanings clear to us, his treatment was not straightforward (not *a*).

Before we go on with more selections, let's discuss the various types of writing which serve to amuse us.

Humorous writing can include satire, irony, and sarcasm, but the usual meaning of "humorous writing"—and the meaning used in this text—restricts it to a lighthearted approach to life, an ability to laugh off minor (and sometimes major) irritations and incongruities without complaint, malice, or any other thought of somehow besting or reforming or exposing the opponent. It is always kindly and tolerant, usually warm and sympathetic, and it never passes judgment. Its purpose is to provide the reader with a laugh at no one's expense except his own or the author's.

Although both satiric and humorous writing hope to amuse the reader, their purposes are quite different, for satiric writing has the purpose of exposing foolish acts and vices in the hope that they will be ridiculed or censured. Humorous writing merely leaves us laughing at the situation, but satiric writing leaves us feeling that the situation should be corrected. Whereas the humor is usually obvious in humorous writing, it is often subtle in satiric writing.

In ironic writing the intended meaning is contrary to the ostensible meaning. Here, too, the humor is subtle rather than obvious. As in satiric writing, ironic writing leaves us with the feeling that the situation should be corrected, and both kinds of writing may give us the impression that the author is somewhat indignant about the situation. However, satiric writing usually implies the hope of reforming someone or something, whereas ironic writing is usually cynically submissive—"This situation is all wrong, but you can't fight City Hall." Humorous writing, too, can say one thing and mean another. The main differences among humor, satire, and irony are: Humor says, "What's all the fuss about?" and follows this with either, "Things are now the way they ought to be," or, in the case of things which obviously cannot be changed, "Let's change it and make it the way we want it." Satire says, "Look at how foolish or sinful these things are! Let's change them!" Irony presents a fictitious situation, implies, "This is what ought to be [done]," and *pretends* that the presented situation is the real one or the ideal one.

Sarcastic writing is brutal, bitter, cruel, vicious, and full of contempt. Its purpose is always to ridicule or hurt the subject, not merely to show disapproval, disagreement, or censure. It is barbed and merciless. The humor is wry and cynical—"We're only laughing to keep from crying." Sarcastic writing can be ironic, for it often says the opposite of what it means; however, ironic writing per se does not have the savage characteristics of sarcasm. In this text, sarcastic writing which is also ironic will be considered as sarcastic writing.

Designate the type of writing—humorous, satiric, ironic, or sarcastic—in each of the following selections, and support your answer.

1.

He's a great believer in the saying, "God helps those who help them-selves," so he steals whenever he can.

Humor. No judgment is passed on the man's misinterpretation of the saying.

2.

Why has everyone turned against him? He brushes his teeth after every meal, he uses Dial soap, he doesn't use "that greasy kid stuff" on his hair, and he uses Five-Day Deodorant every day. Of course, he *does* lie, cheat, and steal, but what's that got to do with it?

Satire. Although it pokes fun at the public's acceptance of widely advertised products (humor), it implies that this acceptance has gone beyond common sense. By this implication, it has passed from humor (which does not pass judgment) to satire (which does pass judgment).

3.

It's too bad that kids don't learn from their parents, because some parents are really magnificent examples for their kids. When the telephone rings they blithely say, "Tell her I'm not home," but of course the kids have to learn from someone else that there's nothing wrong with lying. They bla-tantly bring home pencils from the office, towels from hotels, and ashtrays from restaurants and brazenly display these "souvenirs" prominently all over their loot-filled houses; but of course the kids are too stupid to con-nect this with stealing. They brag elaborately about their own antisocial exploits as youngsters, but of course their kids aren't bright enough to think of applications of these ideas to the modern world. They proudly explain their intricate underhanded maneuvering to get ahead of the next guy at work, but of course their kids would never understand from this that it's all right to get good grades at school by cheating. Just think—all this extraordinarily superior teaching by parents, and yet their kids never learn from it. What a waste!

Sarcasm. We see here that the attack is bitter, brutal, and full of contempt, and the humor is wry and cynical. The writing is also ironic, but, as stated above, writing which is both sarcastic and ironic will be designated as sar-castic in this book.

4.

It has been well established that a worker's production and efficiency is increased when he is given periodic breaks from his work, but what happens when a worker is sent home early because of unusual circumstances such as temporary difficulty with equipment? In this case, the worker is likely not to have been allowed his relief time, and we think the unions have been remiss for not recognizing this inequity before now.

The unions intend to rectify this situation in the new contracts to be negotiated, however, for they are going to demand a stipulation that relief time lost by such means must be made up. For example, assume that a worker works 2 hours, takes a 15-minute break, works another 1¾ hours, breaks for lunch, and then repeats the morning schedule of work, break, work in the afternoon. If he is sent home after only 2 hours of work in the morning, then he has been deprived of 30 minutes of relief time that day. The union proposes that the new contracts stipulate that this lost relief time be made up during the next full workday.

This stipulation would then mean that if this worker were sent home after only 2 hours of work each day for 15 days, he has been deprived of 7½ hours of relief time. When he reports the next day for his regular 8-hour day, he must spend it entirely on a work break—7½ hours of accumulated time plus ½ hour for the current day. Surely the companies will realize that the workers are entitled to this consideration, for they will realize that the workers have gone 15 days without a relief period, without being given a break from the routine of their work, without the opportunity to pause so that they could return to their work with increased efficiency.

We applaud the unions for their recognition of this gross inequity in the present contracts, and we wish them luck in their efforts to convince the companies that the workers should have relief from working even when they're not working.

---

Irony. The situation as it would be under the proposed contract is explained and the writer pretends that the proposal is a good one. If we did not already suspect that the writer was being facetious in his agreement with the proposal, we are told that he considers it absurd by the last part of the last sentence—"the workers should have relief from working even when they're not working."

---

Since this book is not intended to be a definitive work on various types of writing, the above discussion of humor, satire, irony, and sarcasm was intended only to help you distinguish these types of writing from straightforward writing, and it is not expected at this point that you should be an expert at distinguishing among the various types of amusing writing. It is expected, however, that you recognize tongue-in-cheek writing for what it is and not confuse it with straightforward writing.

V. Early in 1967, a U.S. law was passed putting every state on daylight saving time during certain months unless a state's legislative body specifically exempted it from the law. The Michigan legislators were bombarded with arguments from farmers who didn't want daylight saving time, resort owners who did, mothers who didn't, golfers who did. During this controversy, the following letter appeared in "The Public Letter Box" of *The Detroit News* (5), p. 16-B, on February 26, 1967:

> To the Editor:
> Can I put in my two-cents worth on the daylight saving time question?
>     I have a solution which I think will please all factions—take one hour of daylight from the months of June, July and August, and add it to the days in December, January and February.
>
> [Name withheld]

1. The writer's tone is
a. Straightforward
b. Humorous
c. Ironic
d. Sarcastic

*b.* By suggesting a solution which is obviously impossible, he is saying, "What's all the fuss about? Let's change it and make it the way we want it!" He is not passing judgment either on those who want daylight saving time or on those who don't.

2. The writer's purpose appears to be to
a. amuse both sides.
b. admonish both sides.
c. provoke discussion of the impossibility of satisfying both sides.

*a.* His solution is amusing (answer *a*), and he does not imply that either side or both are wrong for their opinions (not *b*). Anyone who recognized the humor in his letter would also recognize the impossibility of satisfying both sides without having to discuss it (not *c*).

VI. The column of Jim Fiebig, "Mark My Words," appeared regularly in *The Detroit News* (5). The following appeared on p. 9-B on June 27, 1967. The paragraphs are numbered in this text to provide easy reference.

## The Hermit and the Hero

1) Imagine an ancient hermit wandering down from a Texas mountain into Houston last week, and coming upon Cassius Clay surrounded by wall-to-wall newspaper and TV men.

2) The old guy might ask some interesting questions:

3) ''Excuse me, but why is that man the center of attention?''

4) ''Because he won't go in the Army. You some kind of hippy or something?''

5) ''He must be very important. Is he a statesman or a scholar?''

6) ''Naw, man, he's the world heavyweight boxing champion. Who's your tailor anyway?''

7) ''What do you mean by 'boxing champion'?''

8) ''It means he's the meanest cat in the world, that's what. He can beat up any man in the world.''

9) ''But what has he done that's important?''

10) ''Important? He's won 29 pro fights, 23 of them by knockouts. Say, does that suit come with two sets of rope?''

11) ''I see. Because he is the ultimate in cats, because he 'knocks out' people, he has become famous in your country. And now, everything he does is of the utmost importance. Is that correct?''

12) ''Well, sure.''

13) ''Which is the road back to the mountain?''

1. Mr. Fiebig's intent in this column is to

a. report a conversation between a hermit and some newsmen.

b. expose the shallowness of some of the things we consider important.

c. express disapproval of Cassius Clay.

d. show that if we were hermits we wouldn't know what was going on.

---

b. The first two paragraphs tell us that this is a fictitious conversation (not a). The hermit's questions express his bewilderment over the importance accorded Clay—not Clay per se, but any man of Clay's accomplishments (b, not c). This article implicitly assumes that we already know that hermits don't know what's going on; otherwise, the conversation wouldn't make sense to us (not d).

---

2. What unspoken thought is implied by the hermit's last question?

---

Answers here will vary, but they should be along the lines of one of these: ''If this is what civilization is like, then I'm going back to my mountain.'' ''If this is an example of what this country considers to be important, then I'm going back into seclusion.''

---

3. Mr. Fiebig's tone in this column is

a. Straightforward

b. Humorous

c. Satiric

*d.* Ironic

---

*c.* This is an excellent example of satiric writing. Mr. Fiebig uses the hermit's questions to expose our shallow standards of what and who is to be considered important (not *a*). He lets us know that he disapproves (not *b*) by the hermit's last question. He does not pretend that this is the way the situation should be or that he approves of it (not *d*).

---

4. Does this selection succeed in doing what Mr. Fiebig intended it to do? Support your answer.

---

Yes. The statements and questions in paragraphs 5, 9, and 11 rather pointedly tell us that we treat as important *everything* a famous man does. This shows that we do not distinguish between the important and the unimportant aspects of a man's life, and we tend to treat a famous man as an authority in many fields when he is really an authority only in one.

---

VII. In early 1967, Michigan legislators were trying to find ways to raise additional money. One man wrote to the editor of *The Detroit News* (5) to suggest that taxes be levied on things that people didn't need. Among the taxes he suggested were an increase to 13 cents a package on cigarettes, a tripling of the tax on all alcoholic beverages, and a tax of $25 a year on every dog in the state except the leader dogs for the blind. Eight days later, on March 15, 1967, a woman replied in the *News*'s "The Public Letter Box," p. 20-B:

To the Editor:
In regard to the letter written by O. C. who feels that cigarets, liquor and dogs should have higher taxes put upon them.
   Well, I smoke, have a drink occasionally, and I love dogs—but, I don't particularly care for ice cream. I feel that Gov. Romney ought to levy a high tax on ice cream because it's fattening and it isn't necessary, or even good, for anyone to be fat.

[Name withheld]

---

1. The writer's tone in this letter is
*a.* Serious
*b.* Humorous
*c.* Satiric
*d.* Ironic

---

*d.* Since it is doubtful that the writer is serious about her proposal (not *a*), she is being ironic, for she has presented a situation and pretended to agree with it when she is, in reality, being facetious (answer *d*). Since her meaning is contrary to her words, satire is precluded (not *c*). Not *b*, for she has passed judgment on the taxes O. C. proposed.

---

2. The writer's intent in this letter is probably to show that
*a.* she thinks taxes should be levied on things that people *really* don't need, rather than on cigarettes and liquor.
*b.* some people really need cigarettes and liquor.
*c.* a tax based on O. C.'s criterion is impossible, since it would be impossible to agree on a definition of "things that people don't need."

---

*c.* By prefacing her suggestion with the disclosure that she smokes, drinks, and loves dogs, but doesn't "particularly care for ice cream," she is facetiously saying, "It's OK with me to tax things that people don't need, but only if *I* don't need them." This, in turn, implies that each person has his own definition of "things that people don't need" (answer *c*).

---

3. Most readers would probably react to this letter with _____ about the proposed tax on ice cream.
*a.* Disagreement
*b.* Amusement
*c.* Indifference
*d.* Thoughtful consideration

---

*b.* Most readers would probably recognize the irony in her proposal and so would be amused (*b*, not *c*). Having recognized the irony, they would know she was not serious about taxing ice cream (not *a* or *d*).

---

   VIII. In the August, 1967 issue of *Reader's Digest* (6), the article "Tyranny in the Internal Revenue Service," by John Barron, appeared on pp. 42–49. This article included subheadings indicating that there was much proof for the writer's charges, that the Internal Revenue Service (IRS) had unchallenged power, that the IRS was arbitrary in its treatment of taxpayers, that no one dared to challenge the IRS, that the IRS operated on a double standard, and that the IRS should not be allowed to go on as it was, uncontrolled. The following paragraph appeared on p. 48 under the subheading "A Double Standard":

   Honest citizens can derive little comfort, too, from the knowledge that IRS has issued a special ruling to reduce the tax that criminals owe on money they steal! Internal Revenue Bulletin No. 1966–42 of October 17, 1966, states: "Embezzled funds will be taken into account if a taxpayer chooses the benefits of the income-averaging provisions." So if a crook gets away with, say, $100,000, it will be okay for him to pay taxes on only $20,000 of stolen money a year over a five-year period.

1. Mr. Barron's primary intent in this paragraph appears to be to show that
a. the IRS gives criminals benefits not given to honest citizens.
b. the IRS gives criminals the same benefits given to honest citizens.
c. criminals do not have to pay income tax on all of their ill-gotten income.

---

a. We not only judge by what Mr. Barron says and how he says it, but we place much weight on the context. Considering the title of the article and the title of the subheading under which this paragraph appears, it seems that Mr. Barron wrote this paragraph as an example of a double standard (used by IRS) favoring tax delinquents and criminals (a, not b). Not c, for $20,000 a year times five years is still $100,000 to pay tax on.

---

2. Mr. Barron's attitude toward the ruling he cites appears to be one of
a. Indifference
b. Resigned tolerance
c. Righteous indignation
d. Approval

---

c. The clause "honest citizens can derive little comfort" tells us that Mr. Barron does not approve of what follows (not d). The exclamation mark shows that he is neither indifferent (not a) nor resignedly tolerant (not b).

---

3. Mr. Barron's tone in this paragraph appears to be
a. Serious
b. Ironic
c. Sarcastic

---

a. After judging Mr. Barron's intent and attitude, we can reasonably infer that he is serious in this paragraph (answer a). Mr. Barron does not use irony: in ironic writing the writer says one thing but means almost the opposite, and this paragraph apparently means what it says (not b). Not c, for sarcastic writing always ridicules something; as it stands, this paragraph may make the IRS bulletin appear to be unfair, morally wrong, and objectionable, but it does not make it appear to be ridiculous.

---

4. In this paragraph, Mr. Barron appears to be stating

*a.* Fact
*b.* Opinion
*c.* Both fact and opinion
*d.* Neither fact nor opinion

*c.* The first part of the first sentence—"Honest citizens can derive little comfort, too, from the knowledge"—is an opinion. The rest of the paragraph appears to be fact.

5. *Ignoring the opinion in the paragraph,* Mr. Barron's writing about the *facts* given appears to be
*a.* Objective
*b.* Subjective
Support your answer.

*b.* Two things in this paragraph tell us that the writing is subjective. First, the exclamation mark tells us that the writer considers the fact stated to be startling—a subjective reaction. Second, the wording of the last sentence implies personal feelings about the subject. (Notice the difference in connotations between the last sentence of Mr. Barron's paragraph and the following sentence, both of which give the same *objective* information: "This means that a man who embezzles money can elect to include one-fifth of the amount as income each year over five years instead of including the whole amount in one year's income.")

6. Judging from the answers to problems 2, 4, and 5, does Mr. Barron's presentation appear to be biased or not? Support your answer.

Yes. An unbiased writer does not use a tone of righteous indignation, and he usually does not write subjectively about *facts*.

7. At what kind of audience is this article directed?
*a.* People oppressed by the IRS
*b.* IRS people
*c.* Tax experts
*d.* Common everyday people

*d.* *Reader's Digest* is a magazine for the masses—the August, 1967 cover claims more than 28 million copies are purchased monthly—and so it must be assumed that its articles are directed toward the masses (answer *d*). Not *a,* for these people are already aware of the "tyranny in the IRS" and so do not have to be told about it. That neither *b* nor *c* is correct will be obvious to you as you continue reading these questions and answers.

---

8. Most embezzlers take money from the company where they work, so they will have their regular incomes as well as the embezzled funds. According to this paragraph, will an embezzler of $100,000 (who takes advantage of the quoted IRS bulletin) pay income tax on
*a.* only $20,000 a year over five years; or
*b.* $20,000 a year over five years plus his regular income each year?

*b.* Notice the words "of stolen money" in the last sentence.

---

9. Will most readers get the impression that an embezzler is not required to pay income tax on the embezzled funds unless he "chooses the benefits of the income-averaging provisions"?

Possibly, but probably not, for they would probably realize that the IRS is not about to say, "You don't have to pay on the income if you don't want to; but if you do want to, then you can use these provisions." If they do get this impression, then they are guilty of substituting the inverse for the proposition (page 26) of the bulletin: "Embezzled funds will not be taken into account if a taxpayer does not choose the benefits of the income-averaging provisions."

---

10. Will most readers get the impression that embezzlers get special consideration not granted to other taxpayers?

Probably. Considering the title of the subheading under which the paragraph appears—"A Double Standard"—and Mr. Barron's apparent intent in writing this paragraph and the fact that most readers are unfamiliar with IRS bulletins and "income-averaging provisions," they would probably not think of the possibility that such an inference was unjustified.

---

11. Is Mr. Barron's paragraph misleading to most readers? Support your answer.

I think his paragraph is quite misleading, for several reasons:
*a.* Most readers do not know that IRS bulletins are issued weekly (notice the number 42 of the bulletin quoted) and that these bulletins contain, among other things, numerous IRS rulings. Most readers probably inferred from the words "special ruling" that this ruling was something extraordinary rather than just one more ruling out of the hundreds issued each year.

*b.* IRS rulings are issued only for clarification purposes. From the context and the words "special ruling" most readers probably inferred that the IRS had either passed a new law or changed the present law; but, in reality, this ruling merely announced the IRS's opinion that the language of the present law on income-averaging did not exclude embezzlement income.

*c.* Per question 1 above, Mr. Barron's intent seems to be to show that the IRS gives embezzlers benefits not given to honest citizens; yet, the paragraph simply says that embezzlers are given the same benefits given to honest citizens.

*d.* Since this paragraph appears under the section headed "A Double Standard," it is natural for the reader to infer that this is an illustration of a double standard; yet, the paragraph does not illustrate a double standard at all.

*e.* It would not be unreasonable to infer from the last sentence quoted that the embezzler can spread the reporting of his extra income over this year and the next four years, thereby also postponing the payment of the applicable income tax. In reality, however, the law provides for the income to be spread over the current year and each of the *preceding* four years, making the total amount of tax due with the current year's return.

*f.* Mr. Barron's last sentence quoted is accurate only in *some* cases, most notably in the case of a person who had no other taxable income in the preceding four years. If the person did have other taxable income, then the amount to be spread would vary according to the average income, and it is entirely possible that an embezzler in a well-paid position with a company would receive no benefits at all under the income-averaging provisions of the law.

---

12. If we assume that Mr. Barron's last sentence was intended to be accurate only in some cases, then it is interesting to observe that—despite my protests that his paragraph is misleading in other respects—Mr. Barron has *not* misstated any facts. What is the moral of this observation?

*a.* We should be very careful of the inferences we draw.

*b.* An author's intent, attitude, tone, and bias can cause us to draw false inferences.

*c.* It is easy to draw false inferences when we are uninformed about the subject.

*d.* Even if we are reading a magazine which sells 28 million copies a month, we should remember to read it critically.

*e.* There may be a difference between the facts which are stated and the facts which we *think* are stated.

---

*a, b, c, d, e.*

# Chapter 7.
# Analyzing
# Arguments

You have been continually exposed to arguments in this book. Many kinds of questions have been included to make you think about whether or not statements and assumptions are justified, for if you develop the habit of questioning statements and assumptions, you will make more intelligent evaluations of the arguments presented.

There are many approaches to arguing, however, and we don't always thing of questioning some of the statements which should be questioned when we read an argument which especially appeals to us. Briefly, some of these approaches to arguing include the following examples.

*The sound of authority:* "At no previous time in our history have we ever . . ."; "Research has found this to be . . ."

*The authority of personal experience:* "Just the other day when I was on my way to work, I saw . . ."

*The authority of second-hand experience:* "At the office where my neighbor works, . . ."

*The authority of nth-hand experience:* "My neighbor has a friend whose sister-in-law's cousin said that he was . . ."

*The quoting of authorities:* "John Doe, eminent psychologist of Famous University, has said . . ."

*The unsubstantiated accusation or opinion:* "Teachers these days are more interested in money than they are in . . ."; "The revival of the guillotine would cut our crime rate so much that . . ."

*The innuendo:* "Are they afraid of the truth? Are they afraid to . . ."

*The logical approach:* "Now let's look at this from a common-sense viewpoint. We can . . ., in which case we will . . ., or we can . . ., in which case we will then . . ."

*The appeal to indignation or outrage:* "Are we going to stand by and let this happen after all the work we've done to try to prevent it? This is a direct slap in the face, and . . ."

*The appeal to pity:* "This poverty-stricken old arthritic woman, struggling to survive by scrubbing floors in offices at night, . . ."

*The emotive approach* (which also may include the appeals to indignation, outrage, and pity): "Even a two-year-old child would know better than to . . ."; "We are honor-bound by our long and noble tradition to see that we . . ."; "This so-called model citizen has not only succeeded in hoodwinking us, but he coldly and calculatingly has . . ."

Two things should be understood. First, the above list does not attempt to itemize all approaches to arguing; its purpose is simply to identify some of the approaches in order to give you a rough idea of how many might be used. Second, although any of the approaches above might be used to disguise a poor argument, none of them per se implies a poor argument. For example, it is much more sensible to appeal for blood donors on the basis of the need of bleeding victims of a horrible accident than it is to appeal on the basis that it won't do us any harm since our bodies will replace the blood within a short time anyhow. This can be illustrated by a comparison of the following two appeals:

1.

City Hospital asked today that persons willing to donate blood contact the hospital immediately. Donating blood is a painless procedure and takes only 20 minutes. It is also harmless, for the body automatically replaces the blood lost within a short time.

2.

At 10:07 this morning, the worst multiple-automobile accident in the city's history occurred when four cars collided head-on because of a malfunction of a stoplight at Highway and Main. Of the 15 passengers involved, three were killed, seven are on the critical list, and the other five are in serious condition. Of the survivors, one has lost both legs, one has lost an arm, two have each lost several fingers and toes, and one may be permanently blinded. All have suffered great losses of blood. City Hospital has issued an urgent appeal to the public for blood of all types immediately.

The purpose of this chapter is to teach you to analyze arguments. You will be presented with a selection and then asked questions such as, "Where does the writer back up his statement that . . . ?" "What does he imply when he says, '. . .'?" "What has his statement, '. . .,' to do with the argument?" It is hoped that asking you such questions will enable you to ask similar questions in your own reading.

| | |
|---|---|
| Since it is easier for most of us to think emotionally than it is to think logically, emotive appeals are likely to have (less, more) effect on us than logical appeals. | more |
| Emotive appeals (never, sometimes, always) disguise poor arguments. | sometimes |
| Because of the extra impact of _____ appeals they disguise poor arguments (less, more) readily than logical appeals. | emotive more |

Given a sound argument and the choice of arguing either logically or emotionally, the logical
approach is (never, sometimes, always) more          sometimes
effective than the emotive approach, and the
emotive approach is (never, sometimes, always)       sometimes
more effective than the logical approach.

The quoting of eminent authorities who support the viewpoint of the writer is (almost
never, sometimes, usually) a good way to win         usually
support for the argument, but the reader should
be sure that the person quoted is an authority
in the field being argued.

When a writer claims the support of an author-
ity we never heard of, we (should, should not)       should not
assume that the writer is being completely
honest with us.

We should be especially on the lookout for
(substantiated, unsubstantiated) opinions or ac-     unsubstantiated
cusations and for (innuendoes, logical ap-
proaches).                                           innuendoes

In order for you to obtain the fullest benefit from this chapter, it is important that you note your immediate reaction to each selection and then
compare this reaction with your reaction after answering the questions.
Each selection will be immediately followed with the question (and the answer to the question), "What is the question being argued, and what position
does the writer take?" So that you will be reminded to note your immediate
reaction, this first question will be followed by, "What is your initial reaction to this argument? That is, do you consider the writer's argument to be
good, indifferent, or poor?" No answer from me will follow this question, of
course. After the last question about the selection, you will then be asked,
"Do you consider the writer's argument to be good, indifferent, or poor?
Compare this answer with your answer to question 2." Again, no answer
from me will be given. The paragraphs of each selection are numbered in
order to provide for easy reference to them.

I. In *The Detroit News* (5) column "Mirror of Your Mind," by Joseph Whit-
ney, the following appeared on p. 12-E on March 2, 1967:

1) Are Most People Honest at Heart?
2) Answer: Yes; this was pointedly displayed when a post-exchange clerk

at Wright Patterson Air Force Base, Ohio, was returning from a bank with $600 in change. Before reaching his destination, he received  a glancing blow from an automobile, the money bag fell to the street and coins scattered all over the area. Unhurt, the clerk and many onlookers set about recovering the coins. When the money was carefully counted at the air base, the tally came to an eye-opening $603.50.

1. What is the question being argued, and what position does the writer take?

Question: Are most people honest at heart? Position: Yes.

2. What is your initial reaction to this argument? That is, do you consider the writer's argument to be good, indifferent, or poor?

3. Why does the writer tell us about the clerk's experience?

He tells us this in order to back up his answer of "yes."

4. Name all of the ways in which the writer backs up his argument.

He backs up his argument only by telling about the clerk's experience.

5. Has he established that his answer is correct?

No. He claims that most people are honest, but he gives only one example of group honesty and no examples of individual honesty.

6. What fallacy in reasoning has the writer used?

Proof by selected instances (page 49).

7. Do you consider the writer's argument to be good, indifferent, or poor? Compare this answer with your answer to question 2.

II. The following letter appeared in "The Public Letter Box" of *The Detroit News* (5), p. 4-A, on February 25, 1967:

1) To the Editor: This letter is an effort to reduce highway slaughter which has reached such proportions that more people are being killed on the highways than in Vietnam.
2) There is a simple solution which, if adopted, would eliminate a good

50 percent of the accidents; namely, the drunks. It is roughly estimated that a 50 percent reduction in fatal accidents would save the lives of 25,000 annually.

3) I suggest that the courts be instructed to impound for 30 days all cars of convicted drunk drivers after the first offense and permanently after the third offense. The second offense would be handled according to particular conditions.

4) Anyone caught loaning or selling a car to a convicted drunk would be dealt with exactly as the offender. The car would be impounded.

[Name withheld]

1. What is the question being argued, and what position does the writer take?

_____

Question: What should be done to reduce highway slaughter? Position: See paragraphs 3 and 4 of the letter.

_____

2. What is your initial reaction to this argument? That is, do you consider the writer's argument to be good, indifferent, or poor?

_____

3. What is the purpose of paragraph 1?

_____

The purpose is twofold: to tell us that highway slaughter is a major problem and to tell us that he thinks he has a solution to this problem.

_____

4. Where does the writer use emotive appeal in paragraph 1?

_____

He uses it in two places: First, the word "slaughter" connotes much more than the word "deaths"; second, the public is currently very concerned about the number of deaths in Vietnam, and the writer's comparison of highway deaths and Vietnam deaths is striking.

_____

5. How does the writer back up his statement, "More people are being killed on the highways than in Vietnam"?

_____

He doesn't.

_____

6. Should he have backed up the statement referred to in question 5?

_____

Possibly, but this information has been so widely publicized that it might almost be considered common knowledge.

_____

7. What is the purpose of paragraph 2?

_____

This is a build-up to show that his solution would be an attack on one of the major causes of highway deaths.

_____

8. What does the writer mean by a "good" 50 percent?

_____

He means "at least" 50 percent.

_____

9. What does the writer mean by the first sentence in paragraph 2?

_____

Apparently he means that drunk drivers *cause* about 50 percent of the accidents. His solution is a step toward eliminating drunk *drivers,* and he claims his solution would eliminate about 50 percent of the accidents. Therefore, he must not be referring to drunks in general—for example, pedestrians or passengers. Similarly, he must mean more than that drunk drivers are merely *involved* in 50 percent of the accidents, for if they were not at least part of the *cause,* then his solution would not eliminate the accidents.

_____

10. Where does the writer back up the first sentence in paragraph 2?

_____

He doesn't.

_____

11. Should he have backed up the first sentence in paragraph 2?

_____

No or yes, depending on whether or not you already knew that drunk drivers cause at least 50 percent of all accidents.

_____

12. How does the writer back up the second sentence in paragraph 2?

_____

He doesn't.

_____

13. Should he have backed up the second sentence in paragraph 2?

_____

I think so. Three questions occur to me about this statement: (1) Where did he get his figures? (2) How rough and how estimated is "roughly estimated"? (3) Who did this estimating?

_____

14. Suppose we accept both sentences in paragraph 2 as true. Then we have to accept that his solution would eliminate all drunk drivers who cause accidents and, consequently, at least 50 percent of the accidents. Does it follow that his solution would reduce highway deaths?

_____

No. He has not connected drunk drivers with *fatal* accidents. His writing leads us to *infer* a connection, but I believe that if he thought drunk drivers were the cause of at least 50 percent of the *fatal* accidents, he would not have omitted the key word "fatal" in the first sentence of paragraph 2.

15. In paragraph 3, the writer lists a three-step "get tough" procedure for handling convicted drunk drivers. Exactly how is the driver to be handled after the second offense?

We can't tell, for we don't know what he means by "would be handled according to the particular conditions." He is too vague about this.

16. Assume for the sake of argument that drunk drivers cause at least 50 percent of the *fatal* accidents. According to this letter, how many of these are caused by drunk drivers who have not been previously convicted of drunk driving? How many are caused by drunk drivers who have been previously convicted of drunk driving once? Twice? Three times?

The letter gives us no clue to any of these answers.

17. Again assume that drunk drivers cause at least 50 percent of the *fatal* accidents. Assume also that a driver who has had his car impounded will not drive someone else's car. What else must we assume in order to be assured that the writer's solution will eliminate this portion of the fatal accidents?

We must also assume that a fatal accident is never caused by a drunk driver committing his first, second, or third drunk-driving offense. In other words, the writer's solution provides that a drunk driver's car is possibly permanently impounded *after* the second offense and definitely permanently impounded *after* the third offense. This leaves him free to cause fatal accidents (1) if he has never before been convicted of drunk driving, or (2) if he has been convicted of drunk driving but has not yet reached the permanent-impounding stage.

18. Does the writer claim that the drunk drivers who cause 50 percent of the accidents have previously had at least two convictions for drunk driving?

No.

19. Does the writer claim that drunks who cause 50 percent of the accidents have these accidents within 30 days after being convicted of drunk driving?

No.

_____

20. Then how does the writer establish that his solution will result in eliminating the accidents caused by drunk drivers?

_____

He doesn't. He takes for granted that getting rid of drunk drivers with three
convictions (in some cases, two convictions) will result in getting rid of all
drunk drivers who cause accidents.

_____

21. Would the writer's solution result in decreasing the number of accidents
caused by drunk drivers?

_____

Probably, for it seems likely that at least some accidents are caused by drunk
drivers with three convictions and that some of these drivers wouldn't drive
if their cars had been permanently impounded.

_____

22. What is the purpose of paragraph 4?

_____

Paragraph 4 answers the natural question following from paragraph 3: "So
you impound his car permanently. So what? What's to prevent him from bor-
rowing a car or buying another one?"

_____

23. According to this letter, how could we be sure that we were not selling
our car to a convicted drunk?

_____

The writer does not suggest an answer to this question.

_____

24. If we loaned our car to a convicted drunk but had never done this before,
for how long would our car be impounded?

_____

Probably for 30 days, since the writer suggests we "be dealt with exactly
as the offender." On the other hand, he might mean that if the drunk driver
had already had two convictions and we loaned him our car, then our car
would be permanently impounded. He could be clearer about this.

_____

25. If we sold our car to a convicted drunk, how would we be treated?

_____

We can't tell. The writer says that *the* car would be impounded, meaning
the car that was sold, but this would have no effect on us as the seller.

_____

26. Do you consider the writer's argument to be good, indifferent, or poor?
Compare this with your answer to question 2.

_____

III. In June, 1967, Detroit policemen were asking for more money. At that time the salary for Detroit patrolmen ranged from about $7,400 starting to $8,300 maximum. The following letter appeared in "The Public Letter Box" of *The Detroit News* (5), p. 10-B, on June 22, 1967:

1) To the Editor: The policemen of Detroit should hang their heads in shame. They feel they require a minimum salary of $10,000 a year to support their families properly.

2) Have they ever stopped to consider what Wayne County Road Commission employees earn? As an equipment operator I for the road commission, my husband (and many others like him) has an hourly salary of $3.135, a weekly salary of $125.40, or a yearly salary of $6,520.80.

3) For this paltry stipend these men daily risk life and limb to maintain our expressways and other streets. This work includes sweeping the freeways, dropping salt during a heavy snow, repairing these roads when heat buckles the pavement, repairing guard rails, etc.

4) The entire time this work is being performed, motorists are whizzing past at speeds up to (and in many cases more than) 70 miles an hour.

5) If any individual is searching for a cause to champion, this is most certainly a worthy one. Our husbands surely deserve much higher compensation for these vital and dangerous services they render to the public.

6) After reading this I wonder how many policemen can honestly stand up, face the public and claim they are underpaid.

[Name withheld]

1. What is the question being argued, and what position does the writer take?

Question: Are Detroit policemen underpaid? Position: No.

2. What is your initial reaction to this argument? That is, do you consider the writer's argument to be good, indifferent, or poor?

3. Assuming that the readers of this letter were aware of the range of salaries of Detroit patrolmen, what is the purpose of paragraph 2?

The purpose is to show that Wayne County Road Commission (WCRC) employees are paid less than Detroit policemen.

4. What is the purpose of paragraphs 3 and 4?

The purpose is to show that the WCRC employees are exposed to danger daily.

_____

5. What is the purpose of paragraph 5?

_____

The purpose is to tie paragraphs 2–4 together by following them with an obvious conclusion.

_____

6. Considering the writer's position on the question being argued (from question 1 above), what is the overall purpose of paragraphs 2–5?

_____

According to paragraph 6, the overall purpose of paragraphs 2–5 is to show that WCRC employees are paid less money and are exposed to more danger than Detroit policemen.

_____

7. Does the writer believe that the WCRC employees are adequately compensated for the work they do, considering the risks they take?

_____

No, per the second sentence of paragraph 5.

_____

8. Suppose someone writes this: "I don't need a new car, my car is in much worse shape than yours, and we both give our cars the same amount of use. Therefore, you don't need a new car." What's wrong with this argument?

_____

Nothing.

_____

9. Suppose someone writes this: "I need a new car, my car is in much worse shape than yours, and we both give our cars the same amount of use. Therefore, you don't need a new car." What's wrong with this argument?

_____

According to the assumptions, it is entirely possible that both of our cars are rattletraps and that we both need new cars. The assumptions establish that I need a car worse than you do, but they do not establish that you don't need a new car, too.

_____

10. So what does question 9 above have to do with the letter we're supposed to be analyzing?

_____

The reasoning involved in the letter is exactly the same as the reasoning involved in question 9: "I deserve a raise, my pay is much lower than yours, and we both want a decent standard of living. Therefore, you don't deserve a raise." The assumptions may establish that I deserve a raise more than you do, but they do not establish that you don't deserve a raise, too.

11. Do you consider the writer's argument to be good, indifferent, or poor? Compare this answer with your answer to question 2.

IV. The following letter appeared in "The Public Letter Box" of *The Detroit News* (5), p. 16-B, February 19, 1967:

1) To the Editor: Just how long are the citizens of Detroit going to put up with ruthless criminals roaming the streets looking for new prey?
2) Even in broad daylight people are afraid to venture out of their homes and are not even safe inside them. Let's get some laws passed that protect the citizens—not the criminals—and give the police full power to use them.
3) I suggest the whipping post be revived and the judges should sentence criminals to a number of lashes according to the crime.
4) The criminals will have something to remember and will not want to come back to the post in a hurry.
5) They show no mercy to anyone and should have none shown them. Their punishment would be of their own making.

Irate Citizen

1. What is the question being argued, and what position does the writer take?

Question: What should be done to protect the citizens of Detroit from criminals? Or: What should be done to make the streets of Detroit safe for its citizens? Positions: Pass laws to protect the citizens and revive the whipping post.

2. What is your initial reaction to this argument? That is, do you consider the writer's argument to be good, indifferent, or poor?

3. What expressions in this letter let us know that the writer is making an emotive appeal?

There are several: "Just how long are the citizens of Detroit going to put up with . . . ?"; "ruthless criminals roaming the streets"; "ruthless criminals . . . looking for new prey"; "even in broad daylight people are afraid"; "people are afraid to venture out of their homes"; "people are . . . not even safe inside [their homes]"; "let's get some laws passed that . . . [don't protect] the criminals"; "they show no mercy to anyone."

4. Does the writer believe that the whipping post is a cruel punishment?

Yes. He says in paragraph 5 that the criminals should have no mercy shown them, implying that he believes the whipping post to be cruel.

5. Then how does he justify the use of such a cruel punishment?

He justifies it by saying, "Their punishment would be of their own making."

6. What does the writer suggest be done to protect the people and make the streets safe for them?

As answered in question 1, he believes two things should be done: pass laws that protect the citizens, and revive the whipping post.

7. What does the writer have in mind when he refers to laws "that protect the citizens"?

We can't tell, for he has given no example of such a law. We could probably think of several laws which he *might* mean, as, for example, a "stop and frisk" law. But we can't be sure, for many upstanding citizens are against such laws and the writer may be among these citizens. This phrase, "Let's get some laws passed that protect the citizens—not the criminals," without any examples of what is meant is an excellent illustration of a potentially dangerous appeal to emotion: the writer has used a catch phrase to arouse us to action, and we're all set to go without knowing exactly what it is that we hope to accomplish.

8. According to this letter, how would reviving the whipping post protect the citizens and make the streets safe for them?

Per paragraph 4, criminals punished at the whipping post would be deterred from further crime.

9. Does the writer imply that criminals will be deterred from crime because of the knowledge that if they are
*a.* caught, they will be publicly whipped; or
*b.* caught again, they will be publicly whipped again?

*b.* Paragraph 4 implies that the *experience* at the whipping post will be the deterrent.

10. The writer implies that a criminal would find a public whipping more odious than a jail sentence. How does he back this up?

He doesn't.

11. A big part of the problem of crime in city streets is that the criminals hit and run and cannot be found. What solution does the writer propose to this part of the problem?

None.

12. Another part of the problem of crime in city streets is that guilty persons are sometimes freed, thus being free to commit more crimes. What solution does the writer propose to this part of the problem?

None, except his ambiguous statement, "get some laws passed that protect the citizens—not the criminals."

13. Do you consider the writer's argument to be good, indifferent, or poor? Compare this answer with your answer to question 2.

V. The following letter appeared in "The Public Letter Box" of *The Detroit News* (5), p. 16-B, on February 26, 1967:

1) To the Editor: I watched my nine-year-old son struggle with this so-called modern math.

2) It made me sick to see how messed up the education of our children is getting. No wonder children have troubles with that crazy, idiotic modern math.

3) How are youngsters supposed to learn modern math when the teachers admit they don't know it and have a hard time with it?

4) I, for one, think our children are getting the poorest education in our history for the high taxes we pay. If our educators would cut out all the social activities maybe our children would learn something.

5) Between movies, gym, puppet shows, talent shows, music, etc., they manage somehow to squeeze in a lesson or two. No wonder there are so many dropouts.

Irate Parent

1. What are the two questions being argued, and what positions does the writer take?

Question: Should our schools stop teaching modern math? Position: Yes. Question: Should our schools eliminate social activities? Position: Yes.

2. What are your initial reactions to these arguments? That is, do you consider the writer's arguments to be good, indifferent, or poor?

3. What is implied by the use of the words "so-called" in paragraph 1?

The words "so-called" always imply doubt that the thing following is properly named. For example, "this so-called hero" implies, "We call him a hero, but I doubt that he should be called a hero." When the writer says "so-called modern math" in paragraph 1, he is implying, "We call this subject 'modern math,' but I doubt that this is really modern math."

4. Why does the writer doubt that modern math is properly named?

I give up. He doesn't say.

5. What is the writer's attitude toward modern math?

Apparently he is disgusted with it. Certainly he doesn't like it.

6. What is the answer to the question asked in paragraph 3?

The answer is that they aren't supposed to learn it under those conditions.

7. Paragraph 3 is a good example of innuendo. The writer doesn't say positively that teachers don't know modern math and have a hard time with it, but he does insinuate it by asking a hypothetical question as though the insinuation were a fact. How does he back up this innuendo?

He doesn't.

8. Do you think that he has either been personally told by teachers, or has been told by others who have been told by teachers, that some teachers don't know modern math and have a hard time with it?

Probably, for this is not uncommon.

9. Do you think that he has either been personally told by teachers, or has been told by others who have been told by teachers, that no teacher knows modern math and all teachers have a hard time with it?

No.
_____

10. Which group of teachers do you think he means in paragraph 3—*some* teachers, or *all* teachers?
_____

By saying "*the* teachers," he implies "*all* teachers," but I think he means "*some* teachers," for I doubt that even an "irate parent" would be so upset that he would think that not one teacher understands modern math.
_____

11. In the first sentence of paragraph 2 he says that the education of our children is getting messed up. What does he mean?
_____

Judging from the context of paragraphs 1–3, he probably means that the children are being told to learn things which are not understandable.
_____

12. How does the writer substantiate his allegation in paragraph 2 that modern math is crazy and idiotic?
_____

He doesn't. Even if we were to agree that nine-year-olds can't learn it and teachers don't understand it, we would not have agreed that it is therefore crazy and idiotic.
_____

13. Suppose the writer's insinuation in paragraph 3 about teachers' knowledge of modern math is justified. Does this prove that modern math should not be taught?
_____

No. It proves only that the teachers should be taught how to teach it.
_____

14. In paragraph 4 the writer says he thinks "our children are getting the poorest education in our history for the high taxes we pay." How does he back up this opinion?
_____

He backs it up only by his statements that the children do not understand the modern math. Since he wants to cut out all the social activities, it is obvious that he is comparing today's academic education with the academic education given by our schools in the past; however, the fact that today's curriculums include social activities does not support the statement that today's academic education is poorer.
_____

15. What two things does the writer imply in the last sentence of paragraph 4 and the first sentence of paragraph 5?
_____

He implies that the schools consider the social activities as more important than the academic activities, and the academic subjects are taught on an "if we have time we'll study today" basis rather than on a regular basis.

16. How does the writer substantiate these two implications?

He doesn't substantiate either of them.

17. Are the two sentences (named in question 15) expressions of fact, or of opinion?

Both are expressions of the writer's opinion.

18. What does the writer imply in his last sentence?

He implies that the students become dropouts because the school has too many social activities and not enough academic learning.

19. How does he substantiate this implication?

He doesn't.

20. Judging from your own observations, do you believe that most dropouts left school because there were too many social activities and not enough academic learning?

I have never seen a student quit school because there were too many social activities and not enough academic learning. On the contrary, many students have indicated that the only reason they stay in school is because of the social activities, and they consider the academic learning as the price they must pay for the fun of the social life.

21. Do you consider the writer's arguments to be good, indifferent, or poor? Compare these answers with your answers to question 2.

VI. For several days in July, 1967, *The Detroit News* (5) ran a series of articles, "Parents Unwanted," about the policies of adoption agencies and the troubles encountered by couples who want to adopt children. The following letter appeared in "The Public Letter Box" on p. 14-B on July 23, 1967:

1) To the Editor: Hurray for the greatest series I have ever read, "Parents Unwanted" by Ruth Carlton. I hope every agency concerned with adoption reads it.

2) So far as I'm concerned, people who head up these agencies sit and play God and then pass judgment. They are very smug when they interview you.

3) Who are they to sit and judge us to see if we are fit to be parents?

4) Any child is better off in a home than an institution.

5) If a person even goes down and applies that should speak for itself. Many people cannot accept the idea of taking another person's child. Questions like "Is your wife a good cook?" or, "What did you see in your husband when you married him?" don't make sense.

6) I wonder how many parents who have natural children ask themselves 100 questions before creating them. These agencies should stop being smug because only society will suffer, not the agencies.

7) Children who grow up in institutions become psychological misfits. Then they are turned out into society.

8) Let the people who are pleading to be parents, be parents. I know. I have two adopted children and love them dearly.

[Name withheld]

1. What is the question being argued, and what position does the writer take?

Question: Should any couple who wants to adopt a child be allowed to do so? Position: Yes.

2. What is your initial reaction to this argument? That is, do you consider the writer's argument to be good, indifferent, or poor?

3. Does the writer's approach to the argument include
a. the emotive approach? Support your answer.
b. the appeal to indignation or outrage? Support your answer.
c. the sound of authority? Support your answer.
d. the authority of personal experience? Support your answer.

a, yes (paragraphs 2–8).
b, yes (paragraph 3 and the last part of paragraph 5).
c, yes (paragraphs 4, 6, and 7).
d, yes (paragraph 8).

4. On what does the writer base the opinion expressed in the first sentence of paragraph 2?

According to paragraph 8, she probably bases it on her personal experience.

She gives us an idea of her concept of "playing God and passing judgment" in the second sentence of paragraph 2 and the last sentence of paragraph 5.

5. Is the second sentence in paragraph 2 an expression of fact, or of opinion?

Opinion.

6. What is the answer to the question asked in paragraph 3?

The answer is that they are the people who are responsible for the welfare of the children entrusted to them.

7. Is the statement in paragraph 4 an expression of fact, or of opinion?

Opinion.

8. Where does the writer substantiate this statement?

She doesn't. (The first sentence of paragraph 7 does not support this statement. See the answer to question 21 for a discussion of this sentence.)

9. What is implied by the first sentence in paragraph 5?

If a person is willing to make the effort to go to an adoption agency and apply for a child, then that in itself should indicate that he is willing to provide a good home for the child.

10. How does the writer back up this implication?

She backs it up by her next statement: "Many people cannot accept the idea of taking another person's child." The two statements together imply, "If a person goes down to apply, he is willing to take another person's child, and if he is willing to take another person's child, then he is willing to provide a good home for the child."

11. What two things are implied by the first sentence in paragraph 6?

First, that natural parents don't ask themselves these questions. Second, that since natural parents don't ask themselves the questions in paragraph 5, adoptive parents shouldn't have to, either. Another way of stating this latter implication is, "What's good enough for natural parents is good enough for adoptive parents."

12. Does the writer also imply that natural parents *shouldn't* ask themselves the questions asked in paragraph 5?

Yes. By saying in paragraph 5 that these questions don't make sense, she implies that no one should ask them.

13. How does she back up the implication that natural parents shouldn't ask themselves these questions?

By saying in paragraph 5 that these questions don't make sense.

14. How does she back up the last implication stated in answer 11?

She doesn't.

15. Is the last sentence in paragraph 5—"Questions like, . . ., don't make sense"—an expression of fact, or of opinion?

Opinion.

16. How does the writer back up this opinion?

She doesn't.

17. The writer says twice that the adoption agencies are smug—once in paragraph 2 and once in paragraph 6. How does she back this up?

She backs it up by citing some of the questions asked.

18. Is the first sentence in paragraph 7 an expression of opinion, or of fact?

Opinion.

19. Where does the writer back up this opinion?

She doesn't.

20. Does the writer believe that children who grow up in homes do not become psychological misfits?

Apparently. If she believed otherwise, she would probably believe that it wouldn't make much difference whether they were raised in an institution or in a home. However, her letter makes it obvious that she believes it does make a difference where children are raised, so she apparently believes that children raised in homes do not become psychological misfits.

21. What has the first statement of paragraph 7 to do with the writer's argument?

Nothing, unless we assume that both the statement and its inverse are implied: "Children who do not grow up in institutions do not become psychological misfits." Here we are caught in a predicament: Since inverses may not be substituted for propositions (page 26), this would be a poor assumption for us to make. On the other hand, if we do not make this assumption, the statement has no bearing on the writer's argument. We can resolve our difficulty by passing the buck to the writer and assuming, since both the proposition and its inverse are needed to further her argument, that *she* thought that by writing the proposition she was automatically implying its inverse, too.

22. Do you consider the writer's argument to be good, indifferent, or poor? Compare this answer with your answer to question 2.

# Chapter 8.
# Applying
# What You've
# Learned

At this point you should have a much clearer idea of how to read critically than you had when you started reading this book. You should also be fairly adept at practicing the items listed in Chapter 1. Although previous chapters were designed to give you practice in developing specific skills, this final chapter hopes to provide reinforcement for nearly all of them.

Now it's nice in theory to be able to read a book like this one and learn that you're supposed to be recognizing certain things in writing, asking yourself certain questions, and reading more critically as a result. But there is nothing to guarantee that your learning from this book will carry over when you pick up something else to read. Part of the difficulty in carrying over our learning seems to lie in the fact that a book may have *some* examples like the ones we run into every day, but there are not usually enough to allow us to absorb what we've learned and apply it.

It was thought that the learning from this book might be more likely to transfer to your other reading if you were given intensive exposure to a particular news event from many angles, just as though you were reading articles from several issues of your own newspapers or news magazines. Consequently, although the materials in previous chapters covered a variety of subjects, the material in this chapter is confined to just one subject— the Detroit riot of July, 1967.

On Sunday, July 23, 1967, the nation's worst riot in modern history started in Detroit, Michigan. Detroit's two major newspapers, *The Detroit News* (5)— an afternoon daily—and *Detroit Free Press* (7)—a morning daily—provided their readers with superior journalism.

Items which appeared in these newspapers included on-the-spot reporting in the middle of the action scenes, interviews with the people involved, descriptions of conditions, summaries of the riot so far, human interest stories, reports of disagreements among politicians, editorials, and letters from the public to the newspapers, as well as news from police headquarters, the mayor's office, Washington, D.C., and many other sources.

These items are the basis for this chapter, for they offer varied kinds of writing, and, consequently, they require varied degrees of critical reading.

As you read these excerpts, look for facts, of course, but look also for moods, pictures, feelings, and opinions. Try to distinguish between opinions strongly supported by facts and opinions which, although possibly supported by some facts, fall more into the realm of speculation than the realm of fact. Look for figures of speech; look for innuendoes; look for bias on the writers' parts; look for faulty reasoning; look for conflicting viewpoints.

Many questions could be asked which are not asked after the selections in this chapter. For example, questions like the following could be asked after *every* selection: What was the writer's main purpose in writing this article? What effect would this article have on most readers? Did the writer succeed in getting his point across? Which of the writer's statements appear to be facts, and which appear to be opinions? In order to avoid the endless repetition which would result from asking these questions after every selection, such questions are asked only after some of the selections. However, it is hoped that you will ask yourself such questions after each selection whether or not I ask them, too.

In other words, you should automatically be asking yourself questions such as those above by this time. The questions asked in this chapter hope to develop your skills more thoroughly. For example: when two or more articles about the same subject are presented, questions about the details are sometimes asked in order to point out that the articles may not agree about them; letters from the public about the same subject are presented in order to show that different people can draw entirely different conclusions from the same information; the idea that consideration of the context is vital to an understanding of what the author is saying will appear again and again; in some cases, different articles about the same subject are written from different viewpoints and have different purposes, and these are presented in order to illustrate again that the effect on the reader will vary according to the writers' viewpoints and purposes.

In order to give you an overview of the Detroit riot before attempting to break it down into some of its component parts, the text of "A Time of Tragedy," a special report published by *The Detroit News* (5) on Friday, August 11, 1967, is quoted here in its entirety. The numbers preceding the paragraphs were not included in the report, but they are included here in order to make later reference to specific paragraphs easier. Since this report will be referred to throughout the rest of this book, it is suggested that you keep a bookmark in it so that you may locate it easily. The report is prefaced by an editorial comment:

## About This Report

1) "A Time of Tragedy" is a glance back at a big story no one ever wants to cover again. It is the story of a violent birth and frightening life of the

worst civil riot in modern U.S. history as reported and photographed by Detroit News staff members.

2) Working in sometimes dangerous and always hectic circumstances, the men and women who put out The News assembled a volume of coverage unprecedented in Detroit journalism.

3) Their work, as a kind of "instant history," formed the basis of this 16-page special supplement, written by reporter Jon Lowell, who himself covered much of the story.

4) But we owe a debt, too, to the freelance photographers who supplied us with many of the pictures for this report.

5) One photographer, a large and courageous Negro, reported an interesting incident. He was at the scene of the beginnings of the riot on 12th Street, photographing a Negro leader who was obviously directing the crowd. . . .

6) Police asked the photographer to move back to avoid the crush. In doing so, he stumbled over a fire hose.

7) The riot leader turned in his direction: "Look, baby," he shouted to the crowd, "that poor black photographer has been knocked down by the police!"

8) "I stumbled over my big feet," the photographer shouted back. The crowd's anger diminished—for the moment.

And here is the report:

## It Was a Quiet Sunday Morning; Most of Detroit Was Asleep
### By Jon Lowell, Detroit News Staff Writer

9) For most Detroiters, including those who lead the fifth largest city in the United States, there were no dark clouds . . . no quiet rumblings of a storm.

10) When the summer lightning that has stalked our land—riots—finally burst upon Detroit it was on a warm summer Sunday morning in July.

11) Thoughts were of stumbling Tiger efforts towards a pennant, vacations just finished or about to begin, new efforts to ease the traffic jams on the expressway.

12) The flames were dying in Newark's ravaged riot areas and Detroit was the one place where it couldn't happen.

13) From the White House to the campus classrooms across the country, experts pointed to Detroit as the city that was doing things right.

14) In City Hall there were offices guiding an alphabet soup of programs aimed dagger-like at the heart of what authorities said causes riots.

15) Operating out of the mayor's office was a 24-hour intelligence network

pulled together to keep a continuing watch on the pulse of neighborhoods where even small trouble might start.

16) Police officials had been to Watts and the other battered communities where riots had desolated the streets. They had studied the mistakes made there and drawn plans to avoid them in Detroit.

17) Despite the inevitable bickering over methods, there was general agreement at all levels of leadership that Detroit should become a "model city." The term, in fact, had been invented here.

18) But summer lightning struck Detroit on Sunday, July 23, with a fury unprecedented in the modern history of our nation.

19) When it was over, whole blocks lay in rubble. Two weeks later, with the full toll still undetermined, 42 were known dead, thousands had been injured, more than 4,000 had been arrested, and some of the United States Army's finest fighting men had been called into the streets of Detroit to end the hours of madness.

20) The dream of a model city had been put to the torch by the people it was aimed at and a nation's government was still reverberating from the riot's echoes.

21) As August began, Watts' and Newark's were the bad riots—Detroit's was the worst.

22) For the people who live in nice neighborhoods, it started at the most unlikely hour on the most unlikely day anyone could think of.

23) Shortly before dawn on Sunday, the 10th precinct police cleanup squad raided an after-hours drinking club over the Economy Printing Co. at 9125 12th Street.

24) In the words of the head of the squad, Sgt. Arthur Howison, it was a routine raid in a neighborhood that was used to raids.

25) At night, 12th Street was "the turf" for prostitutes, pimps, junkies and gamblers. Sex, numbers and a drink after the 2 a.m. legal closing hour were all major industries there.

26) When police shoved their way into the club, the illegal industries were shutting down after a busy night.

27) Long-legged hustlers in hippy dresses, slick haired pimps in jitterbug suits and the usual assortment of drunks accepted the raid with resignation born out of long experience. Getting "busted" is part of life on 12th Street.

28) Three patrol wagons were called to transport the 85 prisoners down to the precinct station on Livernois.

29) Shortly before 5 a.m., the trouble started.

30) A rag-tag assortment of leftover Saturday night drunks and street people began gathering as the prisoners were being loaded.

31) Shouting, shoving and angry cries against "the Man" and "Whitey" began to fill the air. The crowd grew to about 200.

32) As the last of the prisoners were loaded, a bottle crashed through a squad car window.

33) "The balloon went up," as a weary mayor's aide was later to put it.

34) At 8:24 a.m. Sunday, the Detroit fire department got its first alarm of an arson fire. Someone had tossed a Molotov cocktail through a shoe store window at 12th and Blaine.

35) While people in the suburbs were getting ready for church, a mob raged uncontrolled in 12th Street.

36) Newsmen raced to the scene and were chased by angry Negroes. "It was the harriest thing I've been in since Korea," Detroit News reporter Joseph Wolff said after making repeated sorties into the neighborhood and outrunning howling mobs.

37) Free Press reporter Bill Serrin was led from the scene with his head gashed open by flying bricks and bottles.

38) Contradictions which may never be unraveled developed over what, precisely, were the police orders at this point.

39) Mayor Cavanagh says it was up to the police field commanders to determine moves. Officers at the scene were under the impression that they had orders not to fire and to avoid antagonizing the rioters.

40) They tried to seal off 12th Street, leaving the rioters loose inside.

41) At about noon Sunday, it appeared the strategy might be working. Things calmed down. Hopes rose that it might be a relatively minor ugly incident.

42) That bubble burst minutes later when the riot broke out again in full fury. Fire Chief Charles Quinlan already had been moving swiftly to get his department in shape to handle developments.

43) By drawing on fire companies across the city, he had formed an all-Negro fighting force, hoping the rioters wouldn't harass members of their own race.

44) Capt. Marcene Taylor, of Engine Company 13, a Negro, was made acting chief of the Fourth Fire Battalion.

45) Taylor led his men into the riot area early Sunday afternoon, but the plan didn't work.

46) "We seem to be their favorite target," Taylor reported back to Quinlan after his men were pelted with rocks, bottles and bricks.

47) The most carefully thought out emergency plans for the fire department just weren't designed to cope with what was happening.

48) "After 1:30 p.m. Sunday we threw away the book," Quinlan candidly admits.

49) Police Commissioner Ray Girardin was mobilizing his men for the

tactic that had worked so successfully a year earlier on the city's east side.

50) Police were to sweep the 12th Street area in force, breaking up mobs and hopefully snap the spine of the rapidly blossoming riot.

51) The sweep, so successful in 1966 that police around the nation had made detailed studies of it, had no effect whatever.

52) Like a human wave, the mobs parted before the police phalanx and then washed back in behind them.

53) Negro leaders were making frantic efforts to calm the crowds.

54) Congressman John Conyers took to the roof of a car with a bullhorn. He was chased from the area.

55) At 4:30 p.m. Sunday, the fire department telegraph clacked out the ominous code that had never been used since its invention during World War II.

56) Signal 3–777, instant recall to duty of all Detroit firefighters. In an amazingly short period, 95 percent of the department's personnel was on duty.

57) Earlier the firemen had been willing, but the already overtaxed Police Department simply couldn't cope with the situation.

58) At 1:42 p.m. came the chilling crackle over the fire radio:

59) "Emergency, emergency, give us police protection quick."

60) The call for help was from a fire company on 12th. The dispatcher's reply was terse: "Nothing available."

61) As afternoon pushed towards evening, sporadic reports of shooting began. Police riot command posts were in operation at Herman Kiefer Hospital and Police Headquarters.

62) Gov. Romney began ordering in more than 400 State Police troopers and the first of elements of the Michigan National Guard.

63) The authorities were moving swiftly in an attempt to snuff out the disorder, but the mood of the men at the top was clearly pessimistic.

64) The riot was spreading almost unchecked. The now familiar pattern exploded on Grand River.

65) All along the avenue, looters were smashing their way into stores.

66) The night was filled with the sounds of tinkling glass and laughter.

67) A man carried a couch out of a store. Another had a side of beef. Hopping gingerly through smashed storefronts, young and old, white and black, were dismantling stores piece by piece.

68) The arsonists moved in, putting the torch to looted stores.

69) The immensity of the riot quickly became apparent as police calls flooded into the command posts. Looting and arson had hit Livernois. A "second front" had opened up on the East Side, where Mack Avenue suddenly erupted into another battleground.

70) Detroit's inner city was out of control.

71) Negro store owners frantically scrawled "Soul Brother" on windows to alert Negro looters that theirs was a black man's business.

72) Gov. Romney had clamped on a 9 p.m. curfew, but it was to no avail as firemen had been forced to let some fires burned [sic] unchecked because of attacks by mobs.

73) By midnight, police had arrested more than 600 persons. The injured were flocking to inner city hospitals.

74) "It looks like a city that has been bombed," the governor remarked after a helicopter tour.

75) As the clock moved into the early hours Monday, still no one had died, but the mood of officials clearly pointed to the belief that death was only a matter of time.

76) At 3 a.m. Monday, a political drama began to show every sign of echoing through national politics for years.

77) Gov. Romney made a telephone call to United States Atty. Gen. Ramsey Clark to ask for federal troops.

78) The maneuvering which took place between that phone call and the time that crack paratroopers finally hit the streets of the East Side more than 24 hours later, remains a source of controversy on the highest levels of government.

79) President Johnson, Gov. Romney says: "Played politics" as the riot raged in Detroit. The governor, members of the Johnson administration claim, wavered on whether to actually commit the paratroopers in Detroit.

80) Whatever the reason, getting the airborne units into the riot-rocked East Side proved agonizingly slow.

81) The governor and Mayor Cavanagh made repeated calls to Washington. Congressman Charles Diggs and UAW President Walter Reuther asked for the troops.

82) There were debates between Washington and Detroit on the precise language the governor should use in calling the troops. The issue was: Should he "recommend" or "request"?

83) Airborne units began arriving at Selfridge Air Force Base in Mt. Clemens during the day Monday.

84) From Washington came Cyrus Vance, the President's personal emissary.

85) The debate on whether to use the federal troops continued.

86) Late Monday night, three units from the combined force of 101st and 82nd Airborne troops made their way to the State Fairgrounds at Woodward and Eight Mile.

87) The President went on television to announce that he was committing the troops, but in the process he belabored Gov. Romney by name for being unable to contain the riot with local action.

88) Soon before 3 a.m. Tuesday, airborne troops in full battle dress, incongruously riding DSR buses, moved through blacked-out streets to Southeastern High School.

89) During the day Monday, the riot had brought the city to an almost complete standstill.

90) People began to die in the riot Monday as chartered airplane loads of newsmen from all over the world arrived in Detroit to record the city's agony.

91) The first victim of riot bullets was 45-year-old Walter Grzanka, white, of 641 Charlotte, shot as he ran from a market on Fourth Street. Ten minutes later a bullet snuffed out the life of a white woman on Woodward.

92) Fires reached their peak Monday when the Detroit department received a staggering 617 alarms. By then, 44 other communities had volunteered men and equipment.

93) Guard riflemen were riding the trucks, sprawled on ladders and crouched alongside firemen.

94) The city was at war with the people who lived in it.

95) After dark, an ominous quiet settled over Detroit. It was broken by the wail of sirens, the crunch of police cars running over broken glass, the occasional crack of gunfire.

96) The National Guard was in the city in force, but it became obvious that the young "weekend warriors" weren't trained to handle the problems they were facing.

97) Later in the week, President Johnson was to order the Defense Department to set up new training procedures for the guard to equip them to handle future riots.

98) There were accidents as guardsmen took to the streets. They didn't have the intimate knowledge of their weapons that the razor-sharp paratroopers had. A fireman was creased across the head by a guard bullet. Guardsmen were riding out Livernois Monday night in a fire truck. The truck hit a bump and a rifle went off, blasting a hole in the truck's roof.

99) Guardsmen opened up on apartments with heavy machine guns. They were after suspected snipers.

100) There were arguments between police and guardsmen when police tried to get jumpy young riflemen to hold their fire.

101) Fireman Carl E. Smith died during a gun battle with a sniper at the station at Mack and St. Jean.

102) The looting and arson were dying off, but the deadly guerilla warfare with snipers was intensifying.

103) The contrast between the guard and the paratroopers was obvious to newsmen who saw both in action. Heavily leavened with veterans of both the war in Vietnam and the uprising in the Dominican Republic,

the airborne units showed few of the signs of nerves evident in the guard.
104) "A minimum of force," is how the paratroop officers summed up their strategy.
105) In sharp contrast Tuesday was the scene at an apartment building across from Southeastern High.
106) Where hours before guardsmen had assaulted the building with machine gun and other weapons fire, burly paratroop Col. A. R. Bolling took his brigade chaplain and went into the building to talk to residents.
107) Not long afterward, the apartment residents were offering the federal troops food and chatting amicably.
108) It was never established if there was, in fact, ever a sniper in that building.
109) By Tuesday night, the presence of the crack airborne troops had brought a tense calm over the East Side.
110) Foot and motor patrols by the paratroopers produced no incidents of serious proportions.
111) A paratroop officer nonchalantly told a reporter his patrol had been shot at a few times, but since his men couldn't spot the sniper, they hadn't fired back.
112) On the West Side, 12th Street was the scene of a raging gun battle. With the exception of tanks and armored personnel carriers, guardsmen and police were driven from some areas twice during the night.
113) At least two men, a state trooper and a Detroit policeman, were shot during the night as troops battled house to house.
114) "Help . . . Help me," a man's voice was heard calling at one point.
115) The voice finally stopped. The man was never found.
116) Tanks and personnel carriers whined through the blacked-out streets firing bursts from 50-caliber machineguns at roofs where they thought snipers lay in hiding.
117) Helicopters whirred overhead trying to spot anyone on a rooftop.
118) In one fire fight near 12th and Virginia Park, the battle began to take on a familiar pattern.
119) The crack of a sniper's rifle would echo down a dark street. Police and guardsmen would move along the houses. Rifle, shotgun and automatic weapons fire would smash into a building. Then the tanks, with their heavy machineguns, would smash into a building.
120) In an apartment on the West Side, someone lit a cigaret.
121) Mistaking the flash of the light for muzzle blast from a gun, men poured intensive fire into the apartment, killing a 4-year-old girl.
122) It was a chilling night of combat.
123) Reporters hiding behind trees and cars during the fighting were, days later, trying to talk out the unreal reaction to seeing an M-48 tank clank down a Detroit street.

124) For the reporters, getting into the middle of gunbattles on the city's streets was becoming a way of life.

125) Sniper fire spread from the 12th Street area into the heart of one of the world's major business complexes.

126) Within sight of the General Motors Building, a business woman from Connecticut was gunned down in The Harlan House motel as she watched the fighting from a hallway window.

127) The death toll crept toward 30 as troops and police killed three suspected snipers.

128) When dawn came, a restless truce seemed to envelop the area.

129) Volunteer programs to assist the estimated 5,000 persons left homeless were moving into gear as snipers launched a totally unexpected daylight assault on the police command post at Herman Kiefer.

130) Gunmen also took potshots at firemen battling a blaze at Grand River and 14th.

131) Damage estimates topped the $200 million mark during the day.

132) In the already hard-hit riot areas, reports of price-gouging by some groceries triggered swift action by the city.

133) In a hastily called City Council session, members passed a special ordinance to control profiteering by merchants in the riot neighborhoods.

134) By this time paratroop officers, off the record, were being sharply critical of guard tactics in dealing with snipers.

135) The airborne officers, below the top command level, argued that the guard didn't need the heavy machine guns being used.

136) "The airborne didn't bring any machineguns and we don't want them," a lean, crewcut captain said.

137) They pointed out that guard troops, when caught in sniper fire, were dropping behind vehicles and trees to exchange fire with the snipers.

138) The most effective method, paratroopers said, was to rush the buildings, seal off the exits and then make a room-to-room search.

139) "You've got to know which building they're shooting from first," a guard major said.

140) By now, the ban on the sale of alcoholic beverages was pushing thirsty Detroiters to venture well beyond their normal haunts in search of a cold glass of their favorite potion.

141) Bars and liquor stores in St. Clair County were swamped with new business. One store owner said that parched Detroiters were paying him for beer and taking it directly from a truck into their car trunks.

142) The ban on gasoline sales was also challenging the resourcefulness of some Detroiters.

143) Wednesday produced three deaths that could become one of the haunting tragedies of Michigan's long history.

144) Three Negro youths were found shot to death in an annex of the

Algiers Motel on Woodward at Virginia Park. Police found the bodies after a call from the motel. At first they were listed as suspected snipers who had been gunned down by police or guardsmen, but the men who killed them didn't wait around to identify themselves.

145) A Negro ex-paratrooper and Vietnam veteran located in Kentucky by News reporter Joseph Strickland, said that the youths were slain in cold blood.

146) Robert Lee Greene, 26, told authorities he saw a National Guard warrant officer take two of the youths into rooms at the motel annex where they were later found shot to death.

147) No guns were found to substantiate the belief that they were snipers. Greene and two white girls said that the raiding party beat and threatened to kill them.

148) Officials—from the FBI to local authorities—have been conducting an intensive investigation into these three mysterious deaths.

149) Arrests Wednesday topped the 3,000 mark and overflowed anything resembling a conventional jail.

150) By the time the riot had subsided, prisoners were being housed in Jackson State Prison, Milan Federal Penitentiary, county jails in Southeastern Michigan, DSR buses, the police gymnasium and in makeshift bullpens in police garages.

151) Recorder's Court judges and the Wayne County prosecutor's staff worked in shifts around the clock processing the flood of prisoners. Bonds averaged $10,000 and up for looters, ordered in an admitted attempt to keep those arrested from getting back on the streets during the riot. Suspected snipers faced bonds as high as $200,000.

152) By the weekend judges began releasing those without prior police records on personal bonds.

153) In an effort to create a makeshift prison more habitable than the police garages, the bathhouse on Belle Isle underwent a frenzied remodeling, and when people were moved in Saturday, it resembled a prisoner-of-war compound.

154) Efforts to restore law and order began to take effect, and the senselessness of it all began to become cruelly apparent.

155) Negro arsonists had concentrated on white-owned businesses, but in the process, the fires had spread and burnt down the homes of still uncounted number of their fellow Negroes.

156) The flames incinerated the businesses, homes, and future of those who could affort it least.

157) The "have nots" hadn't really set fire to the power structure after all. The violence of their revolution had wreaked most of its wrath upon those the riot leaders claimed they were fighting for.

158) Detroit was thrown face-to-face with a word that tolled for other places and other times.

159) The word was REFUGEE.

160) It smacked of poignant pictures of other wars in other lands.

161) A small Negro boy stood, stunned, in the charred wreckage of his home. It was a moving mockery of the words painted carefully on 12th Street. The slogan stood out bleakly on the pavement in violet paint in an aerial picture taken while stores burned on either side of 12th.

162) Black Power proclaimed the sign on 12th.

163) It was a sign the little boy will probably spend a lifetime trying to understand.

164) As the early hours of Thursday rolled in, Detroit's riot appeared to be dying painfully.

165) Lt. Gen. John L. Throckmorton, the paratroop officer who took overall command of the military operation when the National Guard was federalized, issued the order to sheathe bayonets.

166) A no-nonsense military man from a military family, Gen. Throckmorton had moved firmly, but played the whole operation in as low a key as circumstances would permit.

167) When the new week dawned, President Johnson would name Gen. Throckmorton as the new commander of the 250,000-man Third Army.

168) Thursday produced a false start on ending the stringent restrictions over the city. Gov. Romney lifted the 9 p.m. to 5:30 a.m. curfew. But by 7 p.m. that same evening he was forced to reinstate the curfew when hundreds of carloads of sightseers jammed the 12th Street area.

169) Police and military officials were appalled when some people brought their children into an area that was still to have sporadic trouble with snipers during darkness.

170) That night, guardsmen continued to search every car that attempted to drive through the riot area.

171) Even for people who were long distances from the disaster zone, the week was filled with fear. Rumors flew with a fierce intensity describing shopping areas like Northland and Eastland in flames, gangs of rioters heading into comfortable neighborhoods of expensive homes, and agitators heading for outstate Michigan cities.

172) By week's end, trouble had flared in a number of other cities, but there was no evidence to link it to troublemakers from Detroit.

173) Pontiac, Flint, Grand Rapids, Muskegon and other cities reported flareups of varying seriousness. In Pontiac, State Rep. Arthur Law, Pontiac Democrat, killed a young Negro with a shotgun. Law said the youth had started into his store through a window which had been broken moments before by a hurled trash can.

174) In Grand Rapids, a strict curfew halted trouble in the state's second largest city after some arson and looting.

175) Front pages around the world chronicled Detroit's agony, and many of the world's leading newspapers, magazines and television networks sent reporters on the scene.

176) As early as Thursday, city and state leaders began turning to the problem of planning for the future. Mayor Cavanagh and Gov. Romney appointed a blue ribbon committee headed by department store magnate Joseph L. Hudson Jr. to plan for the aftermath. UAW President Walter Reuther pledged the help of his huge union in the cleanup task. Industry weighed in with offers of help.

177) On Friday, the last major fire of the week of rioting broke out on 12th between Hazelwood and Taylor. In an already heavily damaged block, another store collapsed in rubble.

178) That evening, the President again went on national television to address the nation on the situation in Detroit and elsewhere.

179) He appointed an 11-member commission to study the causes and implications of the riots and also proclaimed Sunday as a "National Day of Prayer" for reconciliation between the races. He announced the order for retraining of the guard on riot control.

180) On that day, funeral services were conducted for Patrolman Jerome J. Olshove, the only Detroit police officer killed in the riots. Olshove died in a fight with looters.

181) At last, over the weekend, a fearful city began returning to normalcy.

182) On Monday the governor allowed the bars to reopen and the people of Detroit were left to talk about what happened.

183) They had not endured a battle between white and black like that which ripped the city in 1943.

184) What they had been a part of was the new litany in rioting, a battle against authority, whatever skin color it had.

185) Like those that disemboweled the summers that came before, Detroit's July disaster had followed a familiar pattern, with the fuse lighted by a minor encounter between police and citizens. It had gone from looting to arson to sniping on a scale never before seen in the nation.

186) During an appearance on a nationwide television show, Mayor Cavanagh zeroed in for an angry blast at Congress. It's [sic] members, he argued, were refusing to face the problems of the cities. Then Gov. Romney, in a television address to the state Sunday night, placed his emphasis in two areas.

187) The State, he said, must place law and order first and punish those who had fouled their own city.

188) But, with the hard line against the rioters, came stern warnings from the governor against any backlash by white residents.

189) The people of Michigan and the state's legislators, he said, should be prepared to back more efforts for equal job opportunity, strong support for open housing, and more money for the Michigan Civil Rights Commission.

190) Detroit had endured a tragedy of still unmeasured proportions but there was one tentative answer—a new beginning.

191) It lay in the city's motto.

192) "Resurget Cineribus," the motto reads in Latin.

193) "It shall rise again from the ashes," is the translation.

194) It offers a place to start.

1. Was the photographer mentioned in paragraphs 5–8 a newspaper photographer or a free-lance photographer?

We can't tell from the information given; he might have been either one.

2. In paragraph 14, what is meant by "an alphabet soup of programs"?
a. Programs which were often duplicated by other programs
b. Programs which were in a mixed-up mess
c. Programs from "A" to "Z"
d. Programs mixed and thrown all together in the hope of solving a problem

c, in view of Detroit's reputation as a "model city." We should reject choices a, b, and d because each of these connotes an inefficient and haphazard operation, whereas the writer says these programs were "aimed dagger-like at the heart of what authorities said causes riots."

3. In view of the context before and after paragraph 18, what is meant by paragraph 18?
a. The riot struck after a violent thunderstorm.
b. The riot struck with no forewarning.
c. The riot struck after storm warnings of widespread discontent had been ignored.
d. The riot started after blocks of buildings had been leveled by a violent lightning storm.

b. Paragraph 10 clearly tells us that the writer's use of the words "summer lightning" refers to riots (not a or d). Statement c assumes the existence of storm warnings of discontent, which is a flat contradiction of paragraph 9.

4. Referring to paragraph 23 for the starting time of the riot, what is meant by paragraph 22? People who live in nice neighborhoods

a. are in bed then.

b. think of Sunday as a quiet, peaceful, day.

c. think that everyone not required by his work to be out just before dawn on a Sunday is home.

d. think that if trouble were going to start, then it would start at some hour other than around dawn.

—————

*a, b, c, d.*

—————

5. What is meant by the expression "that bubble burst" in paragraph 42?

a. The people inside the roped-off area broke through the police cordon.

b. The hope that the outbreak was quelled was dashed.

c. Efforts to calm the crowd were unsuccessful.

d. The fire department was unable to extinguish all the fires.

—————

*b.* The words "that bubble burst" refer to the hopes expressed in paragraph 41. These hopes were of a general nature, whereas statements *a* and *d* refer to specific events. Statement *c* contradicts the second sentence in paragraph 41.

—————

6. What is meant by the first sentence of paragraph 54?

—————

The sentence means that Conyers climbed to the car roof and talked to the crowd through a portable loudspeaker.

—————

7. What is meant by the expression "a second front" in paragraph 69?

—————

The word "front" is used here in the military sense, so the expression "a second front" means that the crowds rioting on the west side did not advance to this area, but a different riot broke out here.

—————

8. In paragraph 96, what is meant by the expression "weekend warriors"?

—————

These men were trained on weekends but not during the week.

—————

9. Read the first sentence of paragraph 99 again. Who had the machine guns —the guardsmen or the people in the apartments?

—————

The guardsmen.

—————

10. Per paragraph 106, did Colonel Bolling enter the building hours before

guardsmen assaulted it, or did the guardsmen assault it hours before he entered it?

---

The context makes it clear that guardsmen assaulted the building hours before Colonel Bolling entered it.

---

11. Paragraph 116 refers to tanks and personnel carriers. Which of the law enforcement agencies is the author talking about at this point—the police and the national guardsmen, or the U.S. paratroopers?

---

The police and national guardsmen. The writer switched from talking about the paratroopers on the East Side to talking about the police and national guardsmen on the West Side in paragraph 112.

---

12. Paragraphs 134–139 state that some of the paratroopers were criticizing the tactics used by the national guardsmen. Paragraphs 137 and 138 list a specific criticism and a suggested alternative method, to which a guard officer replies in paragraph 139. Presumably this reply is meant as a defense of the guard tactics. What is wrong with this defense?

---

First we must notice that his reply implies that he agrees with the suggested tactics whenever he knows where the snipers are. If the guardsmen knew where the snipers were, then the defense falls through, for they did not use the suggested tactics. If they did not know where the snipers were, then they were needlessly endangering innocent lives by shooting blindly in return, and this, too, seems indefensible.

---

13. Assume that paragraph 172 is true. Then paragraph 172 proves that
a. Detroit's troublemakers were not organized.
b. there was no connection between the trouble in Detroit and the trouble in other cities.
c. Detroit's troublemakers did not cause trouble in the other cities.
d. none of these

---

d. Paragraph 172 says nothing about whether or not Detroit's troublemakers were organized (not a). The fact that there was no evidence of a connection does not prove the nonexistence of a connection (not b or c). If you thought that either b or c was proved, you are guilty of the fallacy of proof by failure to find a counterexample (page 10).

---

Because of the many articles chosen to give details of the riots, it is felt that to give the sources of these articles in the text would detract you from the material at hand; consequently, bracketed numerals refer to sources and these sources are listed in numerical order at the end of this chapter. However, dates of the articles are given in the text in order to help you relate them to the time of the riot. Whenever paragraphs of the special report are referred to, it is suggested that you skim them in order to compare the information there with the information in the article quoted. As you read the selections in this chapter, remember that the riot started on Sunday, July 23rd, and try to imagine that you are a Detroiter reading these articles on the dates they appeared.

Following are more details (7/24/67) about the precipitating incident described in paragraphs 23–31 of the special report:

1) Raids by "The Man" are part of the fabric of life in the tough, tense world that makes up the nights and days on 12th Street.

2) But there was one change yesterday in the normal routine the Detroit police use in raiding after-hours drinking establishments.

3) The change may be what triggered the melee in front of 9125 12th.

4) Normally, police prefer to load the people arrested in such raids into patrol wagons by pulling the wagons into an alley behind the building involved.

5) Yesterday morning they had to pull the three wagons onto the street on 12th. By the time they had finished loading the 73 persons arrested, an angry, bottle and rock throwing mob of 200 had gathered.

6) In the nice neighborhoods, it would be nearly impossible tc draw a large crowd at 5 a.m. on a summer Sunday morning.

7) But 12th Street isn't a nice neighborhood.

8) By day, 12th is a congested, narrow avenue with little between storefront and curbstone.

9) The Virginia Park area where the trouble first boiled into the streets is part of Detroit's 10th Police Precinct. An estimated 145,000 people are jammed into its 6½ square miles.

10) The main artery of the precinct is 12th and the precinct has the highest crime rate in the city.

11) During the daylight hours, the 12th Street area is the kind of place people dream of getting out of.

12) At night, too many of the people who did get out come back.

13) They come back for lures like a young girl standing with a hip cocked on a street corner. It's $10 for 10 minutes and it is one of 12th Street's major industries.

14) Blind pigs like the one that was raided are another big business on 12th.

15) They are the places where the "shooters," the big spenders, the night

people have their fun.

16) There are drinks, gambling and an occasional girl.

17) Sgt. Arthur Howison, the man who leads the Livernois Station clean-up squad that made yesterday morning's raid, has plunged through countless doors into blind pigs in the 12th Street area.

18) He doesn't understand what happened.

19) "It was just an average raid. We arrested the people and made out the papers. There was absolutely no trouble with the people we arrested," he said.

20) But by the time Howison and the other police officers could get the people from the blind pig into the wagon, angry Negroes were starting to vent their complex web of hostilities.

21) "Just as we pulled away a bottle smashed a squad car window," the sergeant said.

22) From that point on, 12th Street's swinging Saturday night became Sunday morning's horror. [1]


1.  How many persons were arrested in the raid?

---

73, according to paragraph 5 above.

---

2.  How many people were in the crowd which had gathered?

---

About 200, per paragraph 5 above.

---

3.  Were the people who were arrested unruly?

---

No, per paragraph 19.

---

4.  Why was this night chosen for the raid instead of some other night?

---

No answer in this article.

---

5.  What was the address of the place which was raided?

---

9125 12th St., per paragraph 3.

---

6.  How long had the police known about the operation of this blind pig?

---

No answer in this article.

---

7. How long had the police had this blind pig under surveillance?

No answer in this article.

8. How many trips were made in order to get all the people arrested to the station?

Paragraph 5 leads us to believe that only one trip was made—three wagons pulled up and were loaded.

9. Were any prisoners loaded in police cars instead of in the patrol wagons?

Paragraphs 5 and 19 lead us to believe that all prisoners were loaded into wagons.

10. Did the riot have anything to do with race?

No answer in this article.

11. What is the writer's purpose in including paragraphs 1 and 6–19 in this article?

He is trying to give his readers a brief picture of the neighborhood in which the raid occurred.

12. What was "the change" in normal raiding routine referred to in paragraph 3?

Per paragraphs 4–5, the patrol wagons were loaded in front of the establishment instead of behind it.

13. Why did the police load the patrol wagons in front of the building instead of in the back as they usually did?

No answer in this article.

14. What does paragraph 11 mean?

The area is a very undesirable place to live.

15. What does paragraph 12 imply?

Their presence helps keep the illegal businesses operating.

---

16. What is the major industry referred to in paragraph 13?

---

Prostitution.

---

17. Had Sgt. Howison led many raids on blind pigs in that area?

---

Yes, per paragraph 17.

---

18. Assuming that the 10th Police Precinct services an area bounded by a square, which of the following would more accurately describe this square?
a. Each side of the square is about 6½ miles long.
b. Each side of the square is about 2½ miles long.
c. We can't tell from the information given in the article.

---

b. Per paragraph 9, this precinct has an area of 6½ square miles, which would mean (if it is a square) that each side is about 2.55—or about 2½—miles long. If the article had said "its 6½ miles square" instead of "its 6½ square miles," then each side would be 6½ miles long.

---

19. Paragraph 10 says that the 10th Precinct has the highest crime rate in the city. Exactly what does this mean in terms of violence in that area?

---

The exact meaning is unclear. We are likely to infer that there is much violence in the precinct, but such an inference could be wrong, for we don't know whether or not the writer includes misdemeanors in the word "crime." (It might be that misdemeanors are included, in which case such offenses as parking violations and not having proper garbage containers would be included, neither of which connotes violence.) On the other hand, if the writer has included only felonies in the word "crime," then we still cannot be sure that violence is connoted, for not all felonies are crimes of violence. (For example, Detroit considers prostitution to be a felony after the first offense.)

---

The following article (7/24/67) gives more information about the raid, along with information about the early hours of the riot:

1) From a dingy, second-floor apartment in the heart of the city's high crime area, the ugly ripples that would become Detroit's first major racial disturbance in 20 years spread like tiny tongues of gasoline, volatile and slippery.

2) The events that brought the city to the edge of crisis Sunday began more than six weeks ago when the 10th Precinct's clean-up squad first identified an illegal after-hours liquor operation in the apartment at 9215 Twelfth St.

3) On the second floor of that building, in a vacant office, one of the dozens of blind pigs that operate in the 10th Precinct had found a home. It was placed under surveillance for the next six weeks.

4) Traditionally, Saturday night is a blind pig's biggest evening and the decision to raid was made on that basis. At 3:50 a.m. Sunday morning, Sgt. Arthur E. Howison and his squad entered the building and arrested more than 80 patrons who were drinking.

5) Squad cars and paddy wagons from the 10th Precinct made repeated runs, transporting those arrested to the precinct station to be booked and taken downtown. The process took time—too much time, it would seem later.

6) Howison's squad cleared the building at 4:45 a.m., 55 minutes after it had arrived. Attracted by police cruisers, a crowd had gathered on the sidewalk to taunt officers, mock friends now under arrest, giggle with girl friends.

7) As Howison recalled later: "They were across the street and bunched up on both sides of the building. We had no trouble with our prisoners. Just these loudmouthed onlookers who had no business being there started shouting."

8) As the last of the prisoners were loaded into cars, someone . . . picked an empty bottle off the street and from the protection of the crowd, hurled it toward the building. The bottle flashed in a lazy arc and smashed through the rear window of the squad car.

9) The crowd cheered. An incident had begun.

10) Within moments, it seemed, the crowd began to break apart and flow like a wave down Twelfth St. More bottles flew, windows smashed and the first hands reached behind the broken glass to steal.

11) At 5:10 a.m., the 10th Precinct received the first of the calls from the Twelfth St. neighborhood. Why are all the burglar alarms ringing, the callers wanted to know.

12) The number of calls grew quickly, then impossibly. More men were dispatched in cruisers to the area. Their reports were relayed to head-quarters. A major outbreak seemed imminent.

13) At 5:20 a.m., Police Commissioner Ray Girardin was called at home and told of the developing crisis. He immediately called Mayor Cava-nagh.

14) About 6 a.m., Girardin was at work in his third-floor office, conferring with staff officers. A battle plan began slowly, hesitantly, to emerge.

15) Meantime, the looting on Twelfth St. had increased. At 6:30 a.m., the first fire—in a Twelfth St. shoe store—broke out.

16) For more than 1½ hours, firemen fought the blaze without incident. But the fire trucks awoke those who were asleep, drawing larger crowds, and producing more rumors.

17) At 8 a.m., firemen returned to the scene to fight a fire started in rubbish that now littered the street. This time, they were stoned.

18) Police shifts in Detroit change at 8 a.m. and the 10th Precinct's crews were in the process of checking out and checking in for an hour or more. The ripples spread. . . .

19) From 8 a.m. until noon, there was a lull along the Twelfth St. area as the crowds wandered aimlessly, shouting at police, breaking a few bottles, spreading rumors among themselves.

20) The rumors grew, among them, that a pregnant Negro woman had been beaten by white officers, that another Negro had been stabbed by a police officer. Neither story was true.

21) At 11:30 a.m., Rep. John Conyers appeared to address the crowds. He was shouted down. More bricks were thrown.

22) Throughout the morning, police officers were under strict orders not to shoot, not to provoke incidents, to make as few arrests as possible. Later, their restraint would be sharply criticized by Negro leaders insisting that law and order should have been maintained at any cost.

23) But the police, fearful of contributing to the volatile situation, did not act. Impressed by their strength, the crowds began to move again.

24) Throughout the afternoon, knots and gangs surged both north and south along Twelfth St., past the rows of shabby storefronts, off onto the sidestreets, finally into private homes, looting.

25) Most were young—less than 20. Storefronts were smashed, fires set, the pleas of parents and adults disregarded.

26) By 3 p.m., Mayor Cavanagh had made his decision. Since mid-morning he had been in touch with Michigan State Police and Gov. Romney's office. At 8:30 a.m., all police leaves had been cancelled and 12-hour shifts ordered. But it was obvious that Detroit police were too few to combat the spreading strife.

27) Cavanagh called in the State Police shortly before 3 p.m. When the looting grew, he decided to use his last and ultimate weapon against civil strife—the Michigan National Guard.

28) At 6:13 p.m., the first of more than 4,000 guardsmen arrived in the city, deploying from Central High School to spread through the riot-torn area.

29) Police barricades were ordered, a curfew announced, bars and public places closed. The violence now raged beyond the Twelfth St. area. [2]

For the first ten questions, see the first ten questions (page 105) following the source [1] article. Compare the answers there with the answers which follow.

1. More than 80, according to paragraph 4.
2. No answer in this article.
3. No, per paragraph 7.
4. Because it was thought that business would be heavier than during some other night, per paragraph 4.
5. 9215 Twelfth St., per paragraphs 2 and 30.
6. "More than six weeks," per paragraph 2. If the length of time was considerably longer than six weeks, we could justifiably feel that paragraph 2 is misleading, for paragraph 2 is part of a news article, and we quite reasonably assume it has been included in order to give us definite information.
7. Six weeks for sure, per paragraph 3. Although paragraph 3 does not say that the building was not also observed after that "next six weeks," we would feel that the article had been misleading if, in fact, the surveillance continued for much longer than this.
8. Although the article doesn't give an exact number, paragraph 5 says "repeated runs" were made, telling us that more than one trip was necessary and leading us to believe that at least three trips were made.
9. We infer from paragraph 8 that some prisoners were loaded into cars, rather than patrol wagons. We reasonably assume that these were police cars.
10. Yes, per the words "racial disturbance" in paragraph 1.

11. Which started first—the looting, or the arson?

The looting, per paragraphs 10, 11, and 15.

12. Were the firemen hindered in trying to extinguish the fires?

Apparently not during their work on the first fire, per paragraph 16, but the article is vague about this. It is possible that their work was hindered *after* 1½ hours. They were hindered in fighting the second fire, per paragraph 17.

13. Read paragraphs 15–17 again. There appears to be conflicting information here. What is it?

We are told that the first fire broke out at 6:30 a.m. If the firemen fought the fire "for more than 1½ hours" then they were still there until sometime after

8 a.m. Yet we are told that they *returned* "to the scene" at 8 a.m., which implies that they had left the scene sometime before 8 a.m.

___

14. Who gave the police orders not to shoot?

___

No answer in this article.

___

15. Why didn't the police act with sterner measures than they used?

___

Per paragraph 23, they felt that sterner measures would make the explosive situation even worse.

___

16. Read paragraph 23 again. By whose strength was the crowd impressed—the strength of the police or the strength of the crowd?

___

The strength of the crowd.

___

17. Paragraph 1 calls this a "racial disturbance." How is this description backed up?

___

It isn't. In paragraph 20 the writer cites two rumors, the first of which involves race, but there is nothing in the article to indicate that the looting and arson were either racially inspired or racially aimed.

___

18. Paragraph 27 says Mayor "Cavanagh called in the State Police shortly before 3 p.m." Had the mayor alerted the State Police before this time?

___

Yes. Paragraph 26 tells us that the mayor "had been in touch with Michigan State Police" since mid-morning.

___

The following article (8/3/67) raises several questions about the start of the riot and provides some answers:

1) Since the riot began near 12th and Clairmont in the early morning hours of Sunday, July 23, there have been disturbing rumors and questions about the blind pig raid which started it all.
2) For instance:
3) 1. Why did police pick a time when racial apprehension was high due to the violence in Newark—to raid the after-hours drinking place at 9125 12th, which had been well-known to police and countless other people for many months?

4) 2. Why did they do it on a Saturday night, when many Negroes would be on the streets in the area, looking for excitement?

5) 3. Why did they bring the prisoners out the front way, in full view of bystanders and passersby, instead of out the alley door?

6) 4. How and why did a full-scale riot grow out of a more-or-less routine blind pig raid?

7) 5. Could it be true, as rumored, the persons who wanted an excuse to start a riot helped police to set up the raid?

8) One of the major findings is that coincidence determined the time of the raid. A plainclothes officer finally managed to gain entry after repeated attempts in previous months failed.

9) The fourth question may never be answered completely.

10) The others are answered in a carefully detailed, five-page report compiled . . . from formal statements of all policemen who were directly involved.

11) In essence, this is what it says:

12) The place, which is upstairs over a vacant print shop, is well known to police. It was raided once before, about a year ago, and 14 persons were arrested.

13) It has been under surveillance often in the last year as an after-hours and unlicensed drinking spot.

14) The only reason that it had not been raided again was that police could not get an officer inside—an absolute requisite for gathering evidence that would stand up in court.

15) The Livernois Station "cleanup crew," headed by Sgt. Arthur Howison, had tried many times, with various combinations of white and Negro policemen and policewomen.

16) They were always turned away, even when they carried "membership" cards in the United Community League for Civic Action, a "nonprofit civic organization" chartered in 1964 from the same 12th Street address.

17) About 10 p.m. Saturday, July 22, Patrolmen Joseph Brown and Charles Henry—dressed in flashy civvies and armed with a new cover story—tried again.

18) Henry told the doorman that Brown was a visiting basketball star from Cincinnati who was looking for a little fun.

19) The doorkeeper gave them a fishy stare and told them to go away.

20) Brown, Henry, Howison and a fourth member of the crew, Patrolman Anthony Fiermonti, left and spent the next five hours checking other businesses in the precinct.

21) About 3 a.m. they returned. This time Brown and Henry, who are

both Negroes, were in Brown's own car. They watched a number of men and women enter and leave the blind pig.

22) About 3:45, they saw three unescorted women approaching. Henry struck up a conversation, joined the women and walked casually with them through the door on the ground floor, past the doorman and up the stairs. He was not challenged.

23) At a locked door at the top of the stairs, another man surveyed them through a peephole and let them in without trouble.

24) Once inside, Henry went to the bar and bought a beer for 50 cents.

25) According to prearranged plan, the rest of the crew waited for 10 minutes. Then Howison called the station to send a four-man cruiser, which is equipped with a sledgehammer and an ax.

26) Another four-man scout car eased up the alley to the rear exit, a large steel door secured with a heavy chain and padlock.

27) Howison also called for a prisoner van, commonly called a paddy wagon.

28) Then he and his men kicked in the front door, rushed up the stairs and burst through the door on the second floor.

29) Howison had expected to find 20 people inside at the most. Beside Henry, 85 men and women were crowded into the big room.

30) "I was amazed," Howison said.

31) He went to the telephone and called for two more paddy wagons.

32) The policemen started herding the prisoners down the front stairs because they couldn't unlock or break down the heavy rear door.

33) As they were loading the first wagon, between 10 and 20 "curiosity seekers" gathered in front.

34) The crowd gradually swelled, but at first both prisoners and onlookers "seemed to be jovial," the report said. Wisecracks were shouted back and forth between those on the sidewalk and the roisterers being loaded into the wagons.

35) All three vans took their loads to the station. One returned to pick up the last few prisoners. By that time the spectators numbered about 200.

36) Things suddenly got ugly. Two men in the crowd triggered the change of mood. They shouted:

37) "Look what they're doing to our people!" and "Damn whitey cops—let's go get 'em!" and other things less printable.

38) The two agitators were joined by others. Someone tossed a bottle, which smashed on the sidewalk at the feet of the policemen. They ignored it.

39) "They're scared," a man shouted.

40) "They're not going to shoot. They're afraid of us. Let's go get 'em."

41) More bottles flew through the air. One smashed the rear window of the cruiser.

42) Howison radioed for help. Another eight or nine scout cars arrived within minutes.

43) The mob, temporarily cowed, backed off. Police finished loading the last few prisoners and left the scene.

44) All except Brown. Still in civvies and not readily identifiable as a policeman, he took cover in a nearby home, hoping to retrieve his car when the crowd dispersed.

45) It didn't. It swirled and eddied into small knots. From some of the knots flew bottles and brickbats, and there was the crash and tinkle of glass in store windows. The riot was under way.

46) Brown called the station, told what was happening and made his escape in a taxicab. [3]

For the first ten questions, see the first ten questions (page 105) following the source [1] article. Compare the answers following with the answers according to sources [1] and [2].

1. 85, per paragraphs 29 and 47.

2. About 200, per paragraph 35.

3. Per paragraph 34, we know they were not unruly at first. Paragraphs 36–41 tell us the crowd became unruly but do not tell us whether or not the prisoners, too, rebelled.

4. Paragraphs 8 and 14, backed up by paragraphs 15–25, tell us that this was the first night (since the previous raid) the police had been able to gain entrance to gather evidence.

5. 9125 12th St., per paragraph 3.

6. For at least about a year, per paragraph 12.

7. Although paragraph 13 leads us to believe that it was under surveillance off and on over the period of a year, we can't tell for sure, for the phrase "often in the last year" could also be used to describe daily surveillance over a two-week period. That is, being under surveillance 14 times within two weeks is also being under surveillance often within the year.

8. Paragraph 35 leads us to believe that only two trips were made.

9. Paragraph 35 implies that all prisoners were loaded into patrol wagons.

10. Paragraph 37 tells us that some of the spectators felt that the arrests had racial overtones, but there is nothing to indicate that the rioting, which started after the police left, had racial connotations.

11. Paragraphs 3–7 ask five questions, of which paragraph 9 says the fourth may never be answered completely, and paragraph 10 says the others are

answered in a detailed report. Paragraph 11 leads us to believe that the essence of the report is given in the rest of the article. What are the article's answers to questions 1, 2, 3, and 5?

Paragraphs 8 and 14, backed by paragraphs 15–25 answer questions 1 and 2. Paragraph 32 answers question 3. Question 5 is not answered in this article.

12. Was the raiding squad surprised at the number of people in the blind pig?

Yes, per paragraphs 29 and 30.

13. Why was only one paddy wagon requested by Howison in his first call?

Per paragraphs 29–30, Howison thought there would be fewer prisoners than there were and that one wagon would be enough to hold all of the prisoners.

14. Assuming Howison was still in a car, paragraphs 35–42 tell us that a police wagon and at least nine scout cars were on the scene when the trouble started, but paragraph 43 tells us that the police left the scene. Since it takes at most one car to escort the wagon to the station, why didn't the other eight scout cars stay and try to stop the trouble before it spread?

Paragraph 43 tells us that the mob was cowed and backed off. Apparently the police thought that their staying would only antagonize the crowd and that the crowd, now less unruly than it had been, would disperse if they left.

You have now read four articles which include information about the start of the riot. Not all of these articles agree in all of the particulars. In some cases, there is information which is definitely conflicting. In other cases, some articles give us information which causes us to believe that information in other articles is misleading. The following list includes several aspects of the riot. For each item, decide one of three things: conflicting information (CI) is given about this aspect; misleading information (MI) is given about this aspect; the articles which mention this aspect agree on the particulars (agree).

| | |
|---|---|
| 1. The incident which caused the crowd to gather | agree |
| 2. The number of patrol wagons used to transport the prisoners | agree |

| | |
|---|---|
| 3. The number of trips made by the patrol wagons | MI |
| 4. The number of people in the crowd which gathered | agree |
| 5. The conduct of the prisoners while being loaded into the wagons | agree |
| 6. The conduct of the crowd while the prisoners were being loaded | agree |
| 7. The address where the raid took place | CI |
| 8. The length of time the police had had this place under surveillance | MI |
| 9. The length of time the police had known about this blind pig | MI |
| 10. The date and time of the raid | agree |
| 11. The time of the first fire in the area | CI |
| 12. The number of people arrested | CI |

13. Consider the answers to items 3, 7–9, 11–12 above. What two critical reading lessons are illustrated here?

First, don't believe everything you read (page 1). Second, once you decide on what you're going to believe, be careful of the inferences you draw from the given information (item 21, page 2).

The actions of the police during the early hours of the riot, discussed briefly in paragraphs 38–41 of the special report, caused much discussion and various reactions. Following are excerpts [4] and [5] from two articles (8/4/67 and 7/30/67):

1) . . . [Police Commissioner] Girardin insists today that the decision to use restraint with the looters in the first hours of the riot was a field decision.

2) And he is convinced that if the undermanned police had tried to stop the crowd, or had shot into it, they would have been massacred, and the riot toll would be in the hundreds.

3) Reinforcing this position, Girardin contends, is new "raw" evidence that snipers may have been planted along 12th Street, ready to fire if the police moved in on Sunday morning.

4) There have been rumors that the police were told not to shoot, and that this order originated with Girardin or [Mayor] Cavanagh.

5) "There never was an order from here or from the mayor's office whether

or not to shoot," Girardin insists. "This judgment is made by men on the street." . . .

6) Detroit has a patrol force of 3,300, but probably no more than 500 to 600 men were immediately available early Sunday.

7) At 8:30 a.m., the riot-trained commandos of the Motor Traffic Bureau, under the command of Inspector Paul L. Donley, were enroute to 12th and Euclid.

8) At 9 a.m. the crack TMU [Tactical Mobile Unit], with about 22 cars and three to four men to a car, was mobilized and held in reserve in case of outbreaks in other parts of the city.

9) Donley . . . radioed headquarters for orders and was told to stand by.

10) About 10 a.m., the 40 commandos were pulled back from 12th Street. Their unsheathed bayonets, and single-file determined stance, was considered provocative to the crowd.

11) Negro leaders, going up and down 12th Street in an effort to calm the crowd, by noon realized it was impossible.

12) Donley . . . was later to tell a Detroit News reporter: "If we had been permitted to go after the looters and troublemakers on 12th from the first, we might have stopped it right there." . . .

13) Girardin said . . . he later talked with officers at the scene who insisted that any attempts to stop the looters on Sunday morning would have been suicidal.

14) Girardin said there were "damn few policemen" immediately available.

15) He was reluctant to draw off men from the east side, fearing the west side trouble was only a diversionary tactic.

16) "No order was given from the mayor or me to shoot or not to shoot," Girardin said. "I don't know who gave the order in the field, but if there was one, it was a damn good one."

17) Someone who was by Donley's side during much of the early police work said the inspector repeatedly asked for permission to take more aggressive action.

18) At one point he reportedly told someone at headquarters: "I wish you guys would let us do something here."

19) This could have been directed at any of the deputy superintendents, the superintendent, or others above Donley.

20) This same source said, however, that while Donley wanted to take tougher action, he admitted it might have been the wrong move. . . .

21) During his initial press conference after getting briefings from the police, Cavanagh said law enforcement officials would use restraint but they would fire if necessary.

22) But "restraint" was the key word. City officials gambled—and lost—on the hope that a softer approach would slow down the crowd.

23) By early Sunday afternoon looting was spreading, fires were being set and firemen were being attacked. [4]

24) At night, the police tactics changed. Their orders—not to shoot unless absolutely necessary—remained the same, but the situation changed. Commissioner Girardin is emphatic on this point.

25) "Police orders have never been changed," he said. "Despite all the talk, the manual spells out when a gun can be used and not used. This manual is based on state law."

26) The law, according to Girardin, says a policeman may shoot only to protect his life, the lives of others, or to stop a fleeing felon when he can do so without endangering others.

27) Shooting at the looting mobs "would have been bad business for many reasons," Girardin said. "There were too many men, women and children around. The streets were jammed. Policemen would have been killed." [5]

28) Some police are unquestionably bitter, and still confused, about the cautious approach to the initial looting and crowd handling. But others feel they barely had enough men to protect themselves and firemen. . . .

29) Girardin was asked why police took so long to take action against looters and whether the arrival of the National Guard was delayed by a command dispute?

30) "In the beginning, we followed tactics that were successful in the Kercheval [a street on Detroit's East Side] disturbance last summer," he replied. "When the looting got going, we didn't have enough men to stop it until the State Police arrived."

31) As to the second question, he said that he knew of no delay.

32) The National Guard and State Police command had been alerted earlier. By Sunday afternoon, the order was given to mobilize and move in. [4]

1. Were the policemen under orders not to shoot during the early hours of the riot?

We can't tell from these articles. Commissioner Girardin said the police orders have never changed (paragraph 25), that neither he nor the mayor gave orders not to shoot (paragraphs 1, 5, 16), and that if such an order was given it came from the men on the scene (paragraph 1). However, Donley (paragraph 12) and "someone who was by Donley's side" (paragraphs 17–

19) claim that orders not to shoot came from someone at the station, not from the men in the field.

_____

2. Did the policemen who were on the scene think they should have been less cautious in their handling of the rioters?

_____

Opinions of these policemen seem to be divided, per paragraphs 13 and 28.

_____

3. Was Commissioner Girardin in favor of a cautious approach during the early hours of the riot?

_____

Yes, per paragraphs 2, 13, 16, and 27.

_____

4. Paragraph 15 says Girardin feared "the west side trouble was only a diversionary tactic." Does this imply that Girardin feared
a. the riot was planned and organized?
b. the west side trouble would develop into a major problem?
c. riot leaders hoped to have most policemen on the west side?
d. riot leaders planned a major offensive elsewhere?

_____

a, yes. An event is not described as a "diversionary tactic" unless two thoughts are present: this is not the main event; this is supposed to divert our attention from the main event. This, in turn, implies the existence of planners and organizers who hoped to divert the police.
b, no. A diversionary tactic is designed not to be a major problem itself but to create a problem only until the main offensive is under way.
c, yes. A diversionary tactic is designed to draw the physical presence of men to it so that the location of the main event will be undermanned.
d, yes, as discussed in the answers to a, b, and c.

_____

Following is an editorial (7/27/67) about the police methods used:

1) Let's talk about restraint, its uses and its limitations.
2) Restraint, calm appraisal, cool response, use of just enough force to contain an ugly crowd without pushing people into its ranks—these had worked in Detroit until now. They had worked exceedingly well.
3) Last summer's successful handling of the Kercheval trouble was the showcase example.
4) A lot of communities, most recently Newark, have provided showcase demonstrations of how charging in like Gangbusters, beating every head in sight, make things a lot worse before they get better, if they ever do.

5) There are those now, with magnificent hindsight, who say that it all could have been nipped Sunday morning by gunfire. For some it's not hindsight; that's their prescription for any and all situations.

6) They are wrong. We say they are wrong in full knowledge of the dimension of the Detroit disaster and of all the might-have-beens to be conjured up.

7) Restrained but firm response had worked in Detroit. It had contained and put down violence without the customary aftermath of resentment which breeds more violence. There was reason to hope Sunday morning that it would do so again.

8) What is a restrained but firm response? It is the use against a crowd of a police formation of adequate size to impress the crowd, well-trained in both crowd control tactics and self-discipline. It is using these men to clear the street calmly but inexorably, employing enough force to override any genuine threat of violence, but refraining from excessive or ill-tempered response to meaningless minor harassment.

9) It was tried on 12th Street Sunday morning, as it had been tried before. It failed Sunday morning on 12th Street, as it had not before.

10) Nothing succeeds like success. Had the 12th Street mob subsided, everyone would have rested easy—though most citizens would never really know how right the decision had been.

11) But nothing fails like failure. And the tactic did fail.

12) It is too early to assess accurately and fairly why it failed, though some thoughts suggest themselves. One is the lack of manpower sufficient to the task. Sunday morning is the city's—and the police department's—low ebb. By the time the right size and kind of force were mustered, the situation was close to the point of no retrieval.

13) There may have been mistakes made in how and when available forces were deployed and employed, and in judging the nature of this particular mob. It will take a calmer time to find out.

14) But if there were mistakes made, they were made by people a lot closer to the mouth of the potential holocaust they sought to avert than most of those who gather now to berate them.

15) And what they sought to avert was something worse than what did happen, as terrible as that has been. They sought to avert a murderous personal conflict between white and black, as in 1943, which could have been produced by too quick a trigger finger.

16) In that they succeeded. True, the riots, the looting, the burning evolved from essentially racial antagonisms, but it was all impersonal. White and black citizens did not in 1967, as they did in 1943, throw up barricades and seek to exterminate each other.

17) As difficult as it will be to bind the wounds Detroit had suffered, it

would have been more difficult still to bind the wounds Detroit could have suffered had these become "race riots," as distinguished from "racial riots."

18) Let the postmortem on the whole sad affair begin when time and attention permit and perspective governs. There is much the community needs to know. But there is much it needs to remember as well. [6]

1. Does the writer believe the approach used by the police was right?

Yes, per paragraphs 6 and 7.

2. The "Kercheval trouble" mentioned in paragraph 3 refers to a disturbance on Kercheval (a street on Detroit's East Side) which was stopped shortly after it started. What does paragraph 3 mean?

Paragraph 2 must be considered in interpreting paragraph 3. Then paragraph 3 means that restraint, calm appraisal, cool response, and use of a minimum force were so successful in handling the Kercheval trouble that they seemed to represent the best approach possible.

3. What is the writer's tone in paragraph 5 when he uses the expression "with magnificent hindsight"?

He is being sarcastic.

4. What does the first sentence in paragraph 5 imply? These people
a. probably knew from the start that a restrained approach wouldn't work with the rioters.
b. probably didn't disagree with the restrained approach until it didn't work, and now they're saying a firmer approach should have been used.
c. have shown themselves to be of high intelligence by recognizing that the restrained approach was ineffective.

b. The writer's charge of "hindsight" precludes his implying that these people knew how the situation should be handled from the beginning (not a), and his use of sarcasm precludes his complimenting these people (not c).

5. What does the second sentence in paragraph 5 imply?

These people advocate the use of gunfire to settle all disturbances.

6. Who are the "they" in the first sentence of paragraph 6?

The people who think gunfire should have been used Sunday morning.

7. What is another way of expressing the second sentence in paragraph 6?
*a.* We are fully aware of the extent of the damage in Detroit and the riot's implications, and we know it might have been different if gunfire had been used, but we still say these people are wrong.
*b.* We say these people are wrong because we know the dimension of the disaster in Detroit and because these people are using hindsight to tell us, "But it might have been different if . . ."
*c.* Knowing the cost of Detroit's riot in lives and property, we say these people are wrong to sit back and tell us how different things might have been if we had followed their advice.

*a.* Paragraph 6 does not tell us *why* the writer thinks these people are wrong (not *b*). The writer is objecting to the proposed solution of these people, not to their expressing their opinions (not *c*).

8. Considering the context of paragraph 10, what is meant by, "though most citizens would never really know how right the decision had been"?

Most citizens would not have known that the costs of a riot would be so great and that they had been spared those costs.

9. What does the last sentence of paragraph 13 imply?
*a.* We can't determine the answer now because the people involved are still too emotional about it.
*b.* We can't determine the answer now because the riot is still going on and we won't have time to talk about it until later.
*c.* We'll have to wait until a similar situation arises, but one in which the crowd isn't so unruly. Then we can try the same tactics again and see why they don't work.

*a,* or *a* and *b*. Answer *a* is supported by the writer's reference to the need for perspective in paragraph 18. Throughout this editorial the writer's theme is, "A restrained response has worked in Detroit before; why didn't it work this time?" Therefore, the writer is interested in finding answers so that a similar riot doesn't occur, and he is not advocating the use of a similar situation as an experiment (not *c*). Since the city was almost back to normal when this editorial appeared (paragraphs 164, 168, 176 of the special report), answer *b* is unlikely but acceptable if you also chose *a*.

10. Which of the following statements are implied in paragraph 14?

a. Most people who are criticizing the police were not as close to the scene of action as the people who made the decisions.
b. Most of the people who are berating the police are armchair critics.
c. If mistakes were made, they were honest mistakes.
d. The people who were at the scene should have left the decisions to others, so that the decisions would be more objective.
e. The people who made the decisions knew more about the situation than most of the people who are now criticizing them.
f. It's easy to criticize someone for a wrong decision when you don't know all the conditions considered in making the decision.

*a, b, c, e, f.*

11. What is the "something worse" referred to in paragraph 15?

A race riot. This is answered in the second sentence of paragraph 15—"a murderous personal conflict between white and black."

12. Was this a race riot in the usual sense—white against black?

No, per paragraph 16.

13. What does the second sentence in paragraph 16 mean?
a. White and black fought and tried to kill each other because of race hatred, but there was nothing personal about it.
b. The looting and burning was of stores owned by white people, but these stores were razed only because of this, not because the rioters had anything personal against the owners.
c. The rioting reflected a protest against a system of injustices, rather than against a race per se.
d. The rioters were expressing hatred of the white race in general, rather than of individual members of the white race.

c. The rest of paragraph 16 makes it clear that this was not a riot of black against white (not *a*). The rioters could not have been "expressing hatred of the white race in general," for this would have resulted in conflict between black citizen and white citizen (not *d*). Answer *b* does not account for the looting and burning of stores owned by nonwhites. Answer *c*, however, does account for this, for the rioters also deliberately burned down Negro-owned stores where they had been treated like second-class citizens.

14. Is the writer against people's discussing whether or not the police tactics were wrong? Support your answer.

No. In fact, he thinks discussions should be held (paragraph 18), but he also thinks the discussions should wait until people can be objective about them (paragraphs 12, 13, and 18).

15. Of what is the writer trying to convince his readers?
a. People who live in glass houses shouldn't throw stones.
b. It's senseless to talk about what might have been after it's too late to do anything about it.
c. People should wait until the riot is completely over before saying that the police were wrong.
d. None of the above.

d. The writer is saying, in effect, "The fact that the tactics used did fail doesn't necessarily mean that the tactics were wrong (paragraphs 11, 4, 6, 7), but we do need to know why these tactics failed this time (paragraphs 12, 18) when they had been successful before (paragraphs 3, 7, 9). Furthermore, even though these tactics failed to stop a riot this time, they did succeed in not provoking a race riot (paragraphs 15, 16)."

16. This editorial is an example of
a. an illogical argument about an illogical reaction.
b. an illogical argument about a logical reaction.
c. a logical argument about an illogical reaction.
d. a logical argument about a logical reaction.

c. As discussed in the answer to question 9 above, the writer's theme is one of questioning why the method used didn't work. He examines the method (paragraph 8), notes that it worked in Detroit before this time (paragraphs 2, 3, 7, 9) but failed this time (paragraphs 9, 11), suggests that the fault of the failure may lie somewhere other than in the method itself (paragraphs 12, 13), and proposes that further discussion be postponed until the situation can be viewed more clearly (paragraphs 12, 13, 18). Since this is a logical way to approach the problem, answers a and b are incorrect. If you chose d, you are probably thinking something like, "The method tried didn't work; therefore, it's logical to think that a different method should have been used." If you are thinking along these lines, then you are ignoring the fact that the method used *did* work in Detroit before but failed this time; it is, therefore, illogical to suggest that the method itself was wrong before finding out why it failed this time.

17. This editorial writer lists five things wrong with his opponents' viewpoint. Name four of these five things.

(1) My method had worked before (paragraphs 3, 7, 9), whereas your method had made bad situations even worse (paragraph 4). (2) You're using hindsight to criticize the action (paragraph 5) when you weren't even on the scene and so don't know what the situation was there (paragraph 14). (3) You're missing the point that the use of restraint was designed not only to disperse the crowds, but to prevent a race riot (paragraph 15), and you're ignoring the fact that the tactic used did succeed in doing this (paragraph 16). (4) The fact that my method failed doesn't mean that your method is the right one (paragraph 12). (5) You're jumping to conclusions (paragraphs 12, 13, 18).

Following are two letters (7/31/67 and 8/5/67) from citizens expressing their opinions of the police tactics used in the riot:

1) . . . [The instructions to] our police not to shoot looters and arsonists shocked me and my associates. Such namby-pamby handling of deliberate lawbreakers struck us as asinine and a dereliction of duties to the rest of us. 2) Some 95 percent of us behave ourselves. We work. We create jobs. We pay ever-increasing taxes to finance Alice in Wonderland projects. We pay for welfare costs to support those who cannot or will not work. 3) Doesn't our mayor believe our rights are important enough to make every effort to uphold the law and to protect our property rights? In my opinion, . . . [this instruction] was an insult to every decent citizen—and also to our police who are eager and able to do a job if their hands were untied.

[Name withheld] [7]

To the Editor:
Detroit police officers on duty on 12th Street in the early stages of the riots are to be commended for their restraint in not using firearms. Certainly, riots are not to be condoned—but neither is indiscriminate shooting into masses of fellow citizens.

[Name withheld] [8]

1. Do these two letter writers agree in their opinions of the tactics used?

No. The first believes them wrong; the second believes them right.

2. What is the purpose of the first writer's paragraph 2?
a. He is just blowing off steam because he is angry.

b. He is building his argument to show that the rights of the majority should be protected.

c. He is showing that the majority of citizens have already been unfairly treated.

d. He is showing that the majority of citizens did not take part in the riot.

b. In order to understand the purpose of including paragraph 2, we must place it in the context of the letter. His purpose is made clear by the question he asks in paragraph 3, and this question is reflected in answer b. The writer may be doing all of the things named in answers a, c, and d, but none of these is his *purpose* in including paragraph 2.

3. What, briefly, is the second writer saying?

a. Riots usually happen for a good reason, and shooting the rioters doesn't help the thing that caused the riot.

b. The police know better than the average citizen knows whether or not the rioters should have been shot.

c. It's bad enough to have rioting, but shooting into the crowds of rioters would be even worse.

d. When a major riot occurs, the police are wise to ignore the rioters.

c. Since the writer makes no mention either of the reasons for riots or of the reaction of the general public, answers a and b are incorrect. The first part of his second sentence conflicts with answer d.

4. What does the first writer imply in his paragraph 2 when he says "Alice in Wonderland projects"? The projects

a. are unrealistic and do not accomplish their intended purposes.

b. are fantastically wonderful, but they are expensive.

c. accomplish things which previous generations never dreamed of.

d. are elaborately planned and carried out.

a. In *Alice in Wonderland,* no mention is made of expensive projects (not b), the projects accomplished nothing (not c, but the second part of a is supported), the projects were seldom planned in advance (not d), and they were certainly unrealistic (first part of answer a).

5. Aside from the fact that the first writer believes the police tactics were wrong and the second writer believes they were right, these two letters reveal that the writers also differ in a basic assumption about these tactics. What is this difference? The first writer believes

a. the police had guns and didn't use them, while the second writer believes they didn't have guns at the scene of the riot.

b. the police wanted to shoot but were ordered by a higher authority not to do so, while the second writer believes that any such order came from the men at the scene.

c. it is important to consider that he pays for the Alice in Wonderland projects, etc., while the second writer apparently doesn't consider these as being relevant to the question at hand.

d. the police should have shot the rioters out of duty to the law-abiding citizens, while the second writer believes they should not have done their duty.

b. Answer c avoids the question (page 21), for it does not discuss the police tactics at all. Not a, for a contradicts the second writer's implication that the police had guns but exercised restraint in using them. Not d, for the second writer believes that the police *did* do their duty (by using restraint).

Paragraphs 65–66 of the special report mention the looters and their laughter. Here are excerpts from two articles (7/25/67) about the looting.

1) A Negro teen-ager slid out of a darkened jewelry store at Oakman near Grand River Monday, carrying a softly gleaming silver teapot.

2) "What are you going to do with that?" asked a passerby.

3) "Make some tea," he grinned. . . .

4) The daylight looters brazenly carried their booty across heavily traveled streets, smiling and nodding to office-bound drivers while burglar alarms shrilled behind them. . . .

5) At Grand River and Larchmont, four men carried a console TV halfway across the street, then gave up and left it in the center lane. They ran away laughing—leaving traffic to detour around the abandoned set. . . .

6) "It wasn't real," said one observer. "The looters didn't care who saw them. The drivers were embarrassed watching." [9]

7) The crowds were moving through the street, picking and choosing, their faces glinting with sweat and whisky and sometimes pure joy.

8) Summertime, and the living is easy. A small boy runs down the street and drops some of the new shoes he is carrying. "Make sure you got the right size, boy," a man yells, and there is laughter. . . .

9) Three young men sit on the sidewalk and try out guitars just acquired from a Twelfth Street music store. They take them out of black, imitation leather cases. A man strums a tune. He plays well. The music sounds fine and they laugh. . . .

10) A little farther down on Bethune a man was scratching his chin and gazing at the burned-out interior of what had been a neighborhood gro-

cery store. It was suggested that people would have a hard time finding food in the ensuing days.

11) His face broke into a broad grin.

12) "Naw," he said. "All you got to do is go over to Packers or the A & P and walk right in and take all you want. There's plenty of food."

13) Plenty of food, plenty of drink, plenty of singing and dancing and fine merchandise. If only just for today, there is plenty of everything. [10]

1. These excerpts give the reader the impression that, in general,
a. the looters were unconcerned about being caught looting.
b. the looters were happy.
c. only a few stores were being looted.
d. the police were unconcerned about the looters.
e. the looting was widespread.
f. the looters were unconcerned about the results of their looting.

a, b, e, f. Not c, for three reasons: various merchandise and locations are mentioned; the reaction to the inquiry about a shortage of food (paragraphs 10–12) indicates that the supply is unlimited; the looters' carefree attitude indicates that the looting is so widespread that the police cannot possibly catch all the looters. Not d because of the last reason mentioned: the police could be doing their best to stop the looting but be unable to stop it because it is too widespread.

2. It may be reasonably assumed by the reader that the reporters who wrote these articles
a. used typical examples of looters' words and actions in order to give the reader a general idea of the situation.
b. chose examples which were not typical but which would give the reader the impression that these examples were typical.
c. tried to gloss over the seriousness of the looting so that the public wouldn't be so angry about it.

a. The articles leave little doubt of the extent of the looting (not c). Although some newspapers do purposely distort the news, I presume that the news was not purposely distorted in this case (not b) for two reasons: first, I can see no purpose in such a distortion; second, the newspaper from which these articles were taken is a reputable newspaper.

3. Considering the nature of these excerpts, the fact that the reader was left with the general impressions discussed in question 1 above shows that the reader is

*a.* accepting as true everything he reads in a newspaper.

*b.* using proof by failure to find a counterexample (page 10).

*c.* using proof by selected instances (page 49).

*d.* not using his common sense in interpreting what he reads.

---

*c.* The acceptance of *a* as the answer to question 2 above necessitates the acceptance of answer *c* here. The reader can doubt the truth of parts of these excerpts and still have the *general* impressions discussed in question 1 (not *a*). The use of common sense does not preclude being left with these general impressions (not *d*). Answer *b* is inappropriate, for this is applicable only where a universal generalization has been made; these excerpts, however, are designed to portray the general mood of the looters, not to give us the impression that *all* looters shared this mood.

---

4. Judging from these excerpts, what was the purpose of these articles?

*a.* To report the news

*b.* To convince the reader of something

*c.* To describe a situation

*d.* To defend a viewpoint

---

*c.* These reporters neither stated nor implied their personal opinions in these excerpts (not *b* or *d*). Nowhere do these excerpts tell us that the looting was widespread or that the looters were happy and unconcerned, and yet (per question 1) these impressions comprised the information given by the excerpts (not *a*).

---

5. In paragraph 6, what did the observer mean when he said, "It wasn't real"?

---

The looters' lack of concern about being seen looting was too fantastic to be believable.

---

6. Which one of the following statements most accurately expresses the meaning of paragraph 13?

*a.* Live for today and let tomorrow take care of itself.

*b.* Never look a gift horse in the mouth.

*c.* God helps those who help themselves.

---

*a.* Also see the explanation of the answer to question 7.

---

7. What is implied by the last sentence in paragraph 13?

*d.* Today is a better day than yesterday.

*e.* It's good to be able to enjoy life and have nice things.

*f.* There won't be plenty of everything tomorrow.

*g.* Things are getting better all the time.

---

*f.* The expression "only just for today" in paragraph 13 implies that the prosperity will be short-lived (answers *a* and *f*), not that this is the start of something better (not *g*). Answers *c, d,* and *e* all imply an optimistic outlook for the future, conflicting with the implication of a short-lived prosperity. Statement *b* implies a reaction of, "Take it while you can get it, and don't worry about whether or not it will last," but since "a gift horse" is something which comes to the recipient with no effort other than passive acceptance, it is felt that *b* is the more appropriate answer.

---

The immediately preceding excerpts were chosen because they conveyed to the reader the carefree nature of the looters. Following are other excerpts from the same two articles. As you read them, decide what the reporters' purposes were in including these paragraphs in their articles.

14) Earl Chenault . . . works at the Ford Motor Co., but the plant is shut down today [because of the riot]. He talks of the black man's plight:

15) "People are bitter. White people gyp you all the time. I went to a gas station at Wyandotte and Michigan to get a tire changed. It was raining and the man wouldn't change it. Then he wanted to charge me $12 to change it because I'm a Negro. That kind of stuff is wrong. I've been looking for this riot to happen for years."

16) Chenault took the white reporter on a tour of the looted stores. . . .

17) He pointed to a furniture store that was blackened and fire-gutted. The charred and water-soaked ruins of sofas and chairs squatted in sad splendor among the broken glass of the show window.

18) "You go in there to buy furniture and those people would act like they were doing you a favor," Chenault said bitterly. "They send furniture down here that the white people wouldn't have and then they charge you double for it. It's too much." [10]

19) . . . Thousands of looters . . . descended like locusts on the city's stores Sunday and Monday, grabbing and running in a sometimes senseless, sometimes calculated snatch at the good things in life.

20) They took fur stoles and floor mops, diamond rings and dresses, wigs, hamburger, color TV sets, shotguns, cameras, records, cigarets, soda pop, lamps, toasters, shoes, underwear, guitars, two-pants suits, $8 Scotch and skinless hot dogs.

21) It began early Sunday in an orgy of flames and violence, a lust for destruction and revenge for wrongs that the rioters couldn't have named.

22) By Monday much of the violence was over, but the looting continued. . . .

23) And as the looting spread, so did the conviction that this riot had less to do with race than with color TV sets; less with Black Power than with something for nothing.

24) White men passing through some of the former riot areas were ignored or greeted with derision, but seldom menaced.

25) The looting, which had been incidental to the riot, became the chief reason for prolonging it. It was too sweet, too simple and too stupid not to join in.

26) Grand River became a grab bag from Oakman to downtown. Unabashed looters picked and chose amid acres of shattered plate glass. . . .

27) Twelve-year-olds carried armloads of clothes and gladiolas.

28) Men carried armloads of liquor.

29) Teen-agers carried new appliances with the price tags still dangling from them. . . .

30) Looters stripped roomfuls of furniture from Gorman's Gallery at 15700 Livernois.

31) They helped themselves at the S & H Green Stamp outlet at 7601 Second.

32) They cleaned out the cameras and hi-fis at the Federal Department Store at Harper and Baldwin.

33) Police rounded up hundreds of looters in vans and borrowed Greyhound buses, but had to ignore hundreds more.

34) Patrolmen filled station houses with truckloads of stolen liquor and TV sets to be used as evidence. . . .

35) Earlier, crowds that gathered to watch the flames in the Twelfth and Clairmount area began breaking into groceries to hand around beer, Cokes and cigarets and ended by hauling away whole larders from the shattered supermarkets.

36) A dozen men laid hands on the steel-barred gate of a Twelfth St. pawnshop.

37) The metal twisted free to let the yelling crowd inside.

38) Pawnshops became armories for the snipers who picked away at police and firemen from the rooftops.

39) Looters also pillaged the chic Avenue of Fashion on Livernois stretching north from W. Seven Mile.

40) Grinnell's lost every electric guitar and amplifier in stock and all its jazz records but none of its classics.

41) Looters skinned racks of mink, broadtail and Persian lamb at Ceresnie & Offen Furs. They even took the unsewn pelts from a workroom.

42) Walter's Apparel was stripped of $100-and-up dresses.

43) "This isn't a race riot, it's a riot of thieves," said a weary police sergeant.

44) It was.

45) Anarchic, irrational and unstoppable in a nightmare holiday of piracy and waste, the have-nots helped themselves to class and status.

46) Youngsters pecked like magpies at whatever was biggest, brightest, nearest—picking it up on Twelfth St. to drop it dirty and unused on Blaine.

47) Teen-agers sacked stores of clothes they didn't want.

48) Middle-aged men grabbed anything because nothing could really satisfy them.

49) Bold young men grabbed because this was their moment and though it wasn't going to last they weren't going to be sorry when it was over. [9]

1. What appears to be the reporter's purpose in including paragraphs 14–18 in his article? He was trying to show that
a. this was a race riot.
b. the looting was justified.
c. the looting was not widespread.
d. Negroes have been treated unfairly.

---

d. Not a, for if this had been a race riot, it is doubtful that a white reporter would venture into a riot-torn neighborhood, conduct an extensive interview with a Negro and be led by him unharmed through the riot area. Not b, for the fact that Negroes are discriminated against by some business people does not preclude them from dealing elsewhere, and we have no basis for assuming that the reporter is trying to justify the looting. Not c, for the fact that the reporter writes about only one area does not suggest that looting was not going on elsewhere.

---

2. What appears to be the reporter's purpose in including paragraphs 19–49 in her article? She was trying to show that
a. this was not a race riot.
b. the looting was unjustified.
c. the looting was widespread.
d. Negroes have not been treated unfairly.

---

c. The reporter does lead us to believe that this was not a race riot, and she may be implying that the looting was unjustified; however, this information seems to be included in order to substantiate the extent of the looting rather than as the main idea of the paragraphs quoted (not a or b). She says nothing about the treatment of Negroes (not d).

3. In paragraph 45, the reporter describes the looting as "a nightmare holiday of . . . waste." This implies that
*a*. the looters stole things they wouldn't use.
*b*. the goods were stolen by people who could afford to pay for them.
*c*. the store owners were suffering huge losses.

*a*. Paragraphs 46–49 elaborate on this statement. These paragraphs tell of the looters' taking things they wouldn't use (answer *a*) and did not mention the financial status of the looters (not *b*) or the store owners (not *c*).

4. Consider the implication from question 3 above, and compare this with this same reporter's statement in paragraph 40. Do these two statements conflict with each other?
*a*. Yes. Paragraph 45 implies the looters stole whatever they could, but paragraph 40 tells us that they ignored things they couldn't use.
*b*. No. Paragraph 45 says there was both piracy and waste. Some of the paragraphs before 45 tell of the piracy, while paragraphs 46–49 tell of the waste.

*b*. If you chose *a*, you have misinterpreted the writer's intent. She did not say that everything stolen was wasted, nor did she say that all merchandise in every store looted was taken.

5. The reporter who wrote paragraphs 19–49 leads us to believe that the riot was not a race riot. How does she do this?
*a*. By reporting the looting as though both races were doing it.
*b*. By planting the idea and giving an example, then quoting a policeman and agreeing with him.
*c*. By reporting the looting but not reporting any racial violence.

*b*. See paragraphs 23–24, 43–44. If you chose *a* you are inferring that the nonmention of the race of the looters implies that there was more than one race. If you chose *c*, you are using proof by failure to find a counterexample (page 10).

As indicated by paragraphs 76–88 of the special report, a major controversy among politicians arose as one result of the riot. Among the many articles chronicling this controversy were those with the following headlines:
7/24/67, "Romney's Troop Plea"
7/25/67, "Crisis Brought Quick Action at White House Meeting"
7/26/67, "Vance Defends Delay in Use of Paratroop Units"
7/26/67, "Romney Fumes at LBJ 'Inaccuracy'"

7/26/67, "Hart Rows With Griffin on Troops"
7/26/67, "President Plays Politics With Detroit—LBJ at His Worst" (editorial)
7/27/67, "LBJ's Faltering Aid" (editorial)
7/27/67, "City Begs Army to Get Tough"
7/29/67, "LBJ, Inadequate Again" (editorial)
7/31/67, "Text of Gov. Romney's Speech on Rioting"
8/1/67, "Romney Rakes LBJ for 'Riot Politics'"
8/1/67, "White House Is Silent After Romney's Attack"
8/2/67, "Riots Sweeping the Nation Should Be a Political Issue" (editorial)
8/2/67, "Reply to Troop Charge; LBJ Aide Snaps at Romney"
8/2/67, "Clark Denies LBJ Used Riot Politics"
8/6/67, "Was Face-Saving Basis for Guard Decision?"
8/6/67, "LBJ Offered Troops to New Jersey—but Not to Gov. Romney"
8/6/67, "LBJ Riot Role Hit by Griffin"
8/8/67, "Romney Backed; LBJ's Riot Role Criticized in Poll"

1. Several headlines refer to "LBJ." Who is LBJ?

Lyndon B. Johnson, President of the United States.

2. Although many of these headlines imply unfavorable reactions to LBJ's role in the riot, one headline indicates that its writer had a favorable reaction to LBJ's role. Which one is it?

The second headline. Answers such as "the third headline" or "the fifth from the last headline" are not acceptable, for these headlines do not indicate that the writers themselves had favorable reactions but only that *someone* did—Vance in the former case, Clark in the latter case.

The following excerpts (8/4/67) give an overview of the controversy. While reading these excerpts and trying to decide whether or not the charges of "playing politics" were justified, it is helpful to keep the following political affiliations in mind: President Johnson and Vice-President Humphrey, Democrats; Governor Romney, Republican and possible contender for nomination as presidential candidate in 1968; Mayor Cavanagh, Democrat; Cyrus Vance and U.S. Attorney General Clark, both appointed to their offices by President Johnson; Senator Robert Griffin, Republican; Police Commissioner Girardin, appointed to office by Mayor Cavanagh. As you read, also try to decide whether or not the writer believes the game of politics was being played, and, if so, by whom.

1) The dispatch of paratroopers to Detroit has become embroiled in a bitter personal feud between the Johnson administration and Gov. Romney. . . .

2) Various officials describe the same event, but with vastly different testimony as to what really happened.

3) Romney insists that Atty. Gen. Ramsey Clark indicated by 2 a.m. on the Monday of the riot that federal troops would be sent.

4) Clark now says Romney vacillated, and no firm request came until 10:56 a.m. on Monday.

5) But aides to the governor and city officials insist that Romney and Mayor Cavanagh clearly stated their request for troops by the early hours of Monday, and believed they were on the way.

6) The troops were not actually on the streets until an agonizing 24 hours later.

7) By then, the situation in Detroit had developed an unswervable downhill momentum.

8) The riot destruction and killing might have been lessened significantly with faster action. . . .

9) The circumstances surrounding the federal troops has triggered a wave of angry recriminations and debate between national figures that promises to carry over into the 1968 presidential year.

10) By late Sunday evening, it became apparent to city and state officials that federal troops might have to be called in.

11) Mayor Cavanagh called Vice-President Hubert H. Humphrey around midnight, told him the situation had rapidly deteriorated and troops were needed.

12) Humphrey advised Cavanagh to talk with Atty. Gen. Clark. The mayor called him. Romney also talked with Clark and discussed the need for federal troops. He was told they were available if he asked for them.

13) Robert J. Danhof, Jr., legal adviser to the governor, said Romney, Cavanagh, Girardin and other state officials in Girardin's office then discussed the situation . . . and decided at least 5,000 federal troops were needed.

14) Sometime after 3 a.m., Romney called Clark again and told him the troops were needed.

15) An aide to Cavanagh said both the mayor and the governor believed they had an "oral agreement" from Clark that troops would be sent. They scheduled a 5 a.m. press conference to announce this.

16) Before the press conference, the governor indicated to his aides that he had assurances from Clark that the troops would be sent.

17) But the early morning press conference was interrupted. Clark was on the phone, telling Romney that he must declare a "state of insurrection" in order to have the President send federal troops.

18) Romney had conferred with Danhof who hastily checked the federal statute and the insurance clauses. He advised the governor not to declare an "insurrection." It would wipe out all insurance claims.

19) In the early morning hours from 5 a.m. until 8 a.m. telegrams were drafted in which troops were "recommended." Clark insisted Romney must "request" troops.

20) Romney reportedly slammed down the phone, but later framed a telegram in which troops were urgently "requested."

21) This was acceptable to Clark, although the telegram read: "There is no evidence that any organized state of insurrection presently exists against the government here; there is also no evidence that it does not."

22) The telegram reached President Johnson at 10:56 a.m. Monday and six minutes later . . . 4,700 paratroopers . . . began their airlift to Selfridge Air Force Base [about 20 miles from Detroit].

23) . . . Cyrus R. Vance, former deputy defense secretary, . . . was to act as the President's adviser at the scene.

24) Romney received a call from Vance that he would be in Detroit at 1:30 p.m. The governor had just left for some needed rest, but changed his shirt and came back to Detroit Police Headquarters.

25) Vance finally met Romney at Police Headquarters at about 3:45 p.m. Afterward Romney told Danhof that "they are still pressing me on this insurrection thing" but he refused to budge.

26) Everyone generally believed that the paratroopers now coming to Selfridge would soon be out in the streets. This was not the case.

27) Vance toured the area, then at a 7 p.m. press conference Monday said: "We hope very much that the situation will quiet down by tomorrow and people will return to work. It is always best to use local police and state troops if possible to contain the situation. We have seen it work in the past in other situations, and I believe the same thing pertains here."

28) Cavanagh interjected: "I don't want to appear to be an ungrateful host to our distinguished guest but I still share the conviction expressed earlier today that I would like to see the commitment of federal troops at this point. . . ."

29) Romney limited himself to a statement that the situation now seemed "hopeful," and listed the availability of federal troops, better organization of the National Guard working with the police, and the availability of the State Police.

30) Some interpreted this as a lessening in his demand for immediate federal troops. But his aides said privately, this was not so. . . .

31) Romney was later to indicate, heatedly, that he never deviated from his demand of early Monday morning that federal troops hit the street.

32) By 11:22 p.m. Monday, even Vance had been won over. He told the President and Mr. Johnson went on national television shortly before midnight to announce his order to send the troops into the city.

33) The President linked the move with the "inability" of Romney no

fewer than seven times during his brief speech. Romney was furious at the political innuendo. . . .

34) On Tuesday, Romney declined to comment on Mr. Johnson's television address other than to say he had "always urged immediate use of federal troops."

35) But by Wednesday, the lid blew off the troop "dialog." Senator Robert Griffin . . . blasted the White House for letting the troops remain idle for 11 hours from the time they arrived at Selfridge.

36) The Michigan Republican said Vance arrived two hours late on Monday and "it was immediately apparent to those on the scene that Mr. Vance was not ready to commit troops when he arrived."

37) Vance told a press conference later he had not held back on sending in the troops until all National Guard and state and local enforcement units were used.

38) Then last Sunday, the White House leaked a story that Romney had vacillated nearly 20 hours before deciding he wanted the troops. Romney, obviously angry, told a press conference the next day: "I think the President of the United States played politics in a period of tragedy and riot."

39) The governor said the delaying of federal troops Monday night hurt efforts to control the riots. He blamed federal authorities for the lag.

40) Romney said Clark first promised the troops Monday at 2 a.m., then demanded a written request.

41) "I had the impression that the attorney general was making more of a political request than a legal request," Romney added.

42) The governor accused the White House of "quibbling" over the use of "request" for "recommend."

43) Romney also said many community leaders had forcefully told Vance that the troops were needed immediately when the presidential representative arrived.

44) "We pleaded with him to get the troops out into the streets," he said.

45) Mr. Johnson said "he saw nothing to be gained by trying to justify or explain" his presidential decisions after Romney's critical remarks were made known to him.

46) But Tuesday, Atty. Gen. Clark "reluctantly" replied to Romney, denying that the White House played politics. The first firm request for troops he received from Romney was at 10:26 a.m. the Monday of the riot, he insisted.

47) Clark released the log of series of phone calls made between himself and Romney on the Monday morning of the riots.

48) Romney does not dispute the chronology of the phone calls, just their substance. He insists that his demand for federal troops was firm early in the conversations. Now Clark said it was not. [4]

1. With whom does the writer appear to side on the question of just when the U.S. troops were requested—Clark, who claimed that no firm request was received until 10:26 a.m. Monday (paragraph 46), or Romney, who claimed that the need for troops was made known in the early morning hours of Monday (paragraph 48)? Support your answer.

He appears to side with Romney. Notice that the writer usually qualifies his statements by saying that someone else said the thing reported—for example, see paragraphs 3, 4, 5, 13, 15, and 20. In paragraph 14, however, the writer makes the flat statement that Romney told Clark at "sometime after 3 a.m." that the troops were needed. Even though "sometime after 3 a.m." could be *any* time after 3 a.m., paragraph 15 narrows down this time for us to "sometime after 3 a.m. and before 5 a.m."

2. To whom was Romney's telegram requesting troops sent?

Apparently to Clark, per paragraphs 21 and 46.

3. Assume for the sake of argument that Romney did make a firm request for federal troops sometime between 3 a.m. and 5 a.m. Monday. Per paragraph 22, President Johnson did not receive Romney's telegram until 10:56 a.m., and the troop shift began 6 minutes later. Do these excerpts imply that LBJ knew before 10:56 a.m. that federal troops had been requested?

No. We are told that calls were made to the Vice-President and the U.S. Attorney General, but the article does not imply that calls were made to LBJ or that LBJ was informed of any calls. Clark's statement in paragraph 17 does not imply that he was relaying a message from LBJ, for part of Clark's duties include interpreting federal laws. That the troop shift started 6 minutes after LBJ received the telegram does not indicate that LBJ knew about the request beforehand: the riot was national news, and any of a number of people— including Clark and LBJ—may have anticipated such a request and told the troops to stand by for immediate departure.

4. Some of the articles whose headlines are quoted above tell us that the federal troops started arriving at Selfridge Air Force Base about 3:00 p.m. Monday, but that they didn't get on Detroit's streets until about 2:30 a.m. Tuesday. According to article [4] above, there are two sides to the story of the reason for the delay. Briefly, what are these two sides?

One side said that Vance wanted to tour the area to make sure that the local forces couldn't handle the situation (paragraph 27) and that Romney "vacillated nearly 20 hours before deciding he wanted the troops" (paragraph 38). The other side said that Vance was requested immediately to deploy the troops to Detroit's streets (paragraphs 43–44), but that "it was immediately apparent . . . that Mr. Vance was not ready to commit troops when he arrived" (paragraph 36).

---

5. In paragraph 36, who or what is "The Michigan Republican"?

Senator Robert Griffin, referred to in paragraph 35.

---

6. Paragraph 38 says, "the White House leaked a story." What is meant by this?
a. The White House held a press conference.
b. Reporters learned of this story from the White House by accident.
c. The White House intentionally released the story, but the release was unofficial.

c.

---

7. According to this article, why did Romney refuse to declare a state of insurrection in his request for federal troops?
a. As a national figure, such an admission would hurt his chances to be nominated as a presidential candidate.
b. He didn't agree that such a declaration was necessary in order to get the troops.
c. He didn't want the people who had insurance to be denied their claims.
d. None of the above.

c, per paragraph 18. Most insurance policies contain clauses absolving the companies from liability for losses in the case of insurrection. Not a, for no such implication appears in the article. Although Romney's refusal to declare a state of insurrection makes it obvious that statement b is true, the article does not give this as his reason for refusing (not b).

---

8. Remembering that the federal troops were at Selfridge but not yet on Detroit's streets, read paragraphs 29–31 again. State two interpretations of Romney's statement per paragraph 29, the first of which is a lessening of the demand for immediate use of federal troops on Detroit's streets, and the second of which is not a lessening of this demand.

First interpretation: "The situation looks hopeful. The riot seems to be dying down, but if it flares up again, we have local and state police, national guardsmen, and federal troops all available when we need them." Second interpretation: "Now that we have state and local police, national guards-men, and federal troops all available, we should be able to stop this riot within a short time. The situation looks hopeful."

9. Paragraphs 19–20 tell of the dispute over the use of the words "recommend" and "request." What is wrong with Governor Romney's accusation in paragraph 42?

The word "quibble" connotes that the matter discussed was unimportant or minor. If Clark had not previously made his position clear and if the telephone conversation of paragraph 20 involved only a short discussion about the two words, then nothing is wrong with Governor Romney's accusation. However, if Clark did make his position clear before or if the telephone conversation involved a lengthy discussion about the two words, then Romney is guilty of special pleading (page 19), for then he, too, would be quibbling over the use of the two words.

10. What does the first sentence of paragraph 48 mean?

Romney agrees on the times the phone calls were made, but he disagrees about the main things said.

The public's reaction to the delay in getting and using federal troops and to the destruction caused by the riot was varied, as is shown in the following letters to the newspapers, which are only a few of the many published. As you read these letters, notice that two people may have exactly opposite reactions to the same news. The names of the writers of the letters are not included here.

Letter 1 (8/1/67):
1) To the Editor: I was horrified that the President . . . would stoop to play politics while a city burns. Such behavior is abominable and an utter disgrace.
2) Holding back federal troops stationed nearby for 11½ hours, to make political hay, is inexcusable. [11]

Letter 2 (8/1/67):
3) To the Editor: I fail to understand the motives of Cyrus Vance. It took him an exceptionally long time to decide to use federal troops here.
4) His methods of deployment left me wondering what his objectives were. . . .

5) . . . Could he have been helping the President in what seems to be a political game? [12]

Letter 3 (8/1/67):
6) To the Editor: This letter should be entitled, "Pussyfoot in Cinderland."
7) Sift one integrated city with good race relations, civil rights and job opportunities. Add a dash of American moral spirit. Stir in a pussyfooting mayor and a politicking President. Roast in high flames for several days. [13]

Letter 4 (8/2/67):
8) It is rare indeed when the loss of a billion dollars can be laid at the doorstep of one man, but we have such a rare case in Mayor Cavanagh.
9) Perhaps we should add his advisers, whoever they may have been. Certainly they were not responsible Negroes, who—as one man—would have said, "Shoot!" [14]

Letter 5 (7/31/67):
10) The rioting and looting is the fault of Mayor Cavanagh who with his dove attitude gave the hoodlum element a foothold in Detroit. Governor Romney went along, as any good politician would. Then President Johnson's aide, Cyrus Vance, came to town with his holier than thou attitude about not using government troops till just one more life was lost. . . .
11) Once pirates were shot dead on the spot. Today our officials wait to see if the offender has a voter's card. [15]

Letter 6 (8/2/67):
12) Amid all the political name calling, I wonder if the public has paused to remember and reflect. I seem to remember a televised news conference in which Gov. Romney and Cyrus Vance agreed that federal troops were not needed. . . . In that same news conference, Mayor Cavanagh demonstrated his intellectual clarity and foresight by . . . disagreeing and calling for immediate use of the troops. Cavanagh did not allow his personal and political troubles, nor his ambitions, to cloud his judgment.
13) The voter should remember Romney's lack of foresight and hindsight when preliminaries roll around. A man who cannot remember what he said a week ago certainly isn't presidential material.
14) Neither is President Johnson to be exonerated. One is led to wonder about the character and mentality of a man who uses death and destruction as a political bandwagon. . . .
15) And a note to those people who think that Cavanagh was remiss in his duty by not proclaiming a "Shoot-to-Kill" condition when the rioting started. The question that should be put to these people is this: "What

value do you put on human life? The price of a TV set or even a pocketful of shoe laces?"

16) Mayor Cavanagh, in my opinion, was the only person who showed any intelligence, foresight, or compassion during this incident. . . . [16]

Letter 7 (8/1/67):

17) To the Editor: It was poor political policy for President Johnson to attack Gov. Romney during his speech on TV on the riots here.

18) Romney's ability cannot be questioned. He stepped in and took over in a bad situation when other leaders showed an inability to cope with the disaster.

19) Inability was shown by the President's representative, Cyrus Vance. Federal troops should have been dispatched at once when they had been requested from Washington. The troops should not have been allowed to stand idle at Selfridge Air Force Base for so many hours.

20) If President Johnson had not delayed so long the riots could have been ended much sooner with less loss of life and fewer injured. [17]


1. In answering the following questions, keep in mind that to "not blame" someone—which can be accomplished simply by not mentioning him—is not the same thing as to "exonerate" him—which cannot be accomplished without mentioning him. However, if we do exonerate someone, of course we do not blame him. For example, suppose someone says only, "Vance is primarily to blame." Then he has not blamed LBJ, but neither has he exonerated LBJ. On the other hand, suppose he says, "Vance is to blame, and LBJ is not to blame." Then he has not blamed LBJ and he has exonerated LBJ; he has also neither blamed nor exonerated Romney. Which of the letters above

a. exonerated Vance?

b. blamed only Vance, with no references to LBJ?

c. blamed only Vance directly, but indirectly blamed LBJ?

Letter 2

d. blamed both Vance and LBJ directly?

Letters 6 and 7

---

*e.* blamed LBJ only?

Letter 1

---

*f.* exonerated LBJ?

---

*g.* blamed LBJ and Cavanagh?

Letter 3

---

*h.* blamed only Cavanagh?

Letter 4. Although paragraph 9 includes the possibility of blaming Cavanagh's advisers, paragraph 8 makes it clear that even then Cavanagh is to be held responsible.

---

*i.* exonerated Cavanagh?

Letter 6

---

*j.* blamed Cavanagh, Vance, and Romney directly, and LBJ indirectly?

Letter 5

---

*k.* blamed Vance, Romney, and LBJ?

Letter 6. The reader may think that paragraph 14, which states that LBJ is not to be exonerated, shows neutrality about blaming LBJ—as though the writer is saying, "I don't know whether or not to blame LBJ." However, having mentioned LBJ, the writer must be considering and rejecting him when he says in paragraph 16 that Cavanagh is the only person who acted wisely. Thus, the writer is blaming all those he has mentioned except Cavanagh.

---

*l.* blamed Romney only?

---

*m.* exonerated Romney?

Letter 7

*n.* charged, either directly or indirectly, that the federal troops were delayed because the game of politics was being played?

Letters 1, 2, 3, 5, 6. Letter 2 implies this in paragraph 5. Letters 1 and 3 make the charge directly. Letter 5 makes the charge indirectly in paragraph 11. Letter 6 makes the charge by implication in the last sentence of paragraph 12: by saying what Cavanagh did not do, the writer implies that Romney (and possibly Vance) did do these things. (The charge of "political name calling" in paragraph 12 does not imply that federal troops were delayed because of politics. The charge in paragraph 16 that LBJ did not show intelligence, etc., is not a charge of playing politics.) Letter 4 is excluded because it does not imply political connections. Letter 7 mentions politics only in connection with LBJ's TV speech, not as an implication that political considerations delayed the federal troops. (Paragraphs 19 and 20 imply poor decisions, but they do not necessarily imply political decisions.)

2. Considering the first sentence in paragraph 10, two things are wrong with the political connotations of the second sentence. What are they?

First, it is not true that "any good politician would" go along with giving "the hoodlum element a foothold in Detroit" or with the mayor's "dove attitude"; on the contrary, many good politicians are elected to office because they oppose a dove attitude or because they campaign on a theme of "let's clean up the city." Second, Cavanagh is a Democrat and Romney a Republican, and the situation stated in the first sentence, if true, would provide an excellent opportunity for opposition along political party lines.

3. Paragraph 11 implies that officials today are too easy on piratelike offenders because they fear political repercussions from the offenders if they treat the offenders with more firmness. What is basically wrong with this implication?

Piratelike offenders comprise only a small minority of the voters; consequently, if the nonoffenders feel that the officials are not doing their duty, the political repercussions from the nonoffenders are likely to be much greater than those from the offenders. Therefore, the "too easy" treatment of offenders cannot be based on fear of political repercussions from them.

That the furor over the dealy in sending the federal troops did not just flare up and die immediately is shown by this editorial (8/12/67), which appeared over two weeks after the incident.

1) Did politicians fiddle while Detroit burned? Trying to find reasons for the delayed use of federal troops has so far been an exercise of more heat than light. But now Michigan's Republican senator, Robert Griffin, offers some illuminating material explaining the powers of the President in situations similar to Detroit's.

2) Griffin reviews the three "necessary" elements for the use of federal troops, as explained by President Johnson: first, a request by the state legislature or governor; second, certification of insurrection or domestic violence; and third, demonstration that local and state resources cannot control the situation.

3) However, Griffin points out these criteria do not square with the well-remembered use of federal forces in Arkansas and Mississippi, since neither their respective legislatures nor governors requested the presence of federal troops.

4) Furthermore, the section of the U.S. Code cited by the President as requiring a state to request assistance makes no mention of "domestic violence." It refers exclusively to a "state of insurrection."

5) Michigan's Gov. Romney deliberately refused to declare a state of insurrection in order to preserve insurance protection for those whose property was being destroyed. Yet, federal troops were eventually dispatched. How can this be reconciled with a code that specifies insurrection?

6) Griffin provides the answer: Another section of the code permits the President to use armed forces to put down "domestic violence"—and he can do so without a request from the state. This, of course, explains Arkansas and Mississippi.

7) This section should be read closely by Atty. Gen. Ramsey Clark, who seems to have confused the issue again in a letter to the 50 governors. He still argues the request for troops must originate with the state.

8) Thus the initial conclusion in Detroit's case is that the delay in sending troops was the result of legalistic confusion. The U.S. Code clearly permits the President to intervene and suppress domestic violence—which Detroit certainly had—without a request from the governor and without a declaration of insurrection. Since Romney did actually request troops, there should have been no White House delay.

9) But how can anyone justify "legalistic confustion" on these points of the law at this particular time? Newark had previously erupted. The President and the New Jersey governor had conferred about the ongoing riots

there. Surely someone researched the law on the use of federal troops! And surely someone in Washington remembered Arkansas and Mississippi! 10) If legal confusion is the "excuse" for delay in Detroit's case, the implications are embarrassingly clear. Either there is unbelievable incompetency in the attorney general's office, or Washington politicians did indeed fiddle while Detroit burned. [18]

1. This editorial claims that one of two conclusions must be reached in answering the question of why there was a delay in sending federal troops to Detroit. What are these conclusions?

This is answered in the last sentence of paragraph 10.

2. Legal confusion is mentioned four times in this editorial: "seems to have confused the issue" in paragraph 7; "legalistic confusion" in paragraphs 8 and 9; "legal confusion" in paragraph 10. What, specifically, is the writer referring to in these instances? Do not give a generalized answer such as, "He is referring to confusion about (or "misunderstanding of" or "misinterpretation of") the federal laws regarding the use of federal troops."

Paragraphs 4 and 6 of the editorial refer to two sections of the U.S. Code under which the President is permitted to use federal troops. One section requires a state to request assistance, and the other section allows the President to send troops without a request from the state. The writer is claiming that people who argue that the former, but not the latter, section applies in the case of riots like Detroit's are legally confused.

3. In paragraph 1, what is meant by "an exercise of more heat than light"?

More anger than information has been produced in discussions about the reasons.

4. Why is the word "necessary" enclosed in quotation marks in paragraph 2?

The quotation marks are used to show that the writer questions the use of the word. He is implying that President Johnson claimed three elements to be necessary when, in fact, not all *are* necessary.

5. Paragraph 3 refers to the "well-remembered use of federal forces in Arkansas and Mississippi." Why were federal troops sent to these two states?

Federal troops were sent to these two states in some of the years prior to

1967 for the purpose of assuring that the civil rights of Negroes would not be violated. Most notably, federal troops were sent to make sure that desegregation in the public schools would proceed without violence.

---

*Questions 6–9:* Paragraph 2 says that President Johnson specified three elements as being necessary in order for him to send federal troops, and it designates these three elements as "first," "second," and "third."

6. Regarding the first element, does the writer agree that a section of the U.S. Code requires a state to request assistance? Support your answer.

---

Yes, per paragraph 4. Although he says only that this section was "cited by the President as requiring a state to request assistance," the fact that he did not deny that this section contains this stipulation makes it reasonable for us to infer that he agrees that the stipulation is in this section.

---

7. How does the writer refute the claim that the first element is necessary?

---

In paragraphs 6 and 8 the writer says that the U.S. Code allows the President to use federal troops without a request from the state in the case of "domestic violence." (Paragraph 3 does not refute the necessity of the first element: We must assume that the President meant "legally necessary" when he said "necessary," for otherwise there would be no point in his talking about the stipulations of the U.S. Code. Consequently, the fact that Presidents may have sent troops to other states without having requests from those states does not obviate the *legal* necessity of such a request.)

---

8. How does the writer refute the claim that the second element is necessary?

---

He refutes it by implication, rather than by direct statement. Paragraphs 6 and 8 imply that the President can decide that "domestic violence" exists without having its existence certified. Paragraph 8 also says that this Code section does not require a *declaration* of insurrection, so we can reasonably infer that no *certification* of insurrection is necessary.

---

9. How does the writer refute the claim that the third element is necessary?

---

He doesn't. Since the writer doesn't mention this third element in his discussion of either of the two U.S. Code sections in question, it is possible that both sections include this element.

---

10. Which of the following statements are implied in paragraph 9?
*a.* The eruption in Newark justifies legalistic confusion at this time.

b. The use of federal troops in Arkansas and Mississippi justifies legalistic confusion at this time.

c. There is no justification for legalistic confusion at this time.

d. There has been enough use of and discussion about the use of federal troops in the past so that any confusion about the law should have been cleared up by this time.

e. The discussion between the President and the New Jersey governor served only to confuse the legal issues involved.

f. The U.S. Code is so complicated that the research on the use of federal troops proved only to be confusing.

g. The people who remembered using federal troops in Arkansas and Mississippi also remembered the legal confusion which arose from this use of the troops.

c, d. The question asked in paragraph 9 is meant to have the obvious answer of, "They can't possibly justify it." To prove that no justification is possible, the writer cites the case of the riot in Newark, New Jersey, implying that the President and the New Jersey governor had discussed the use of federal troops. He then implies that if there was any question at that time about the use of federal troops, these questions should certainly have been answered by the time of Detroit's riot—"Surely someone researched the law on the use of federal troops!" As a further proof that no justification is possible, the writer implies that even without research it should have been obvious that federal troops could be sent without a request from the state—"And surely someone in Washington remembered Arkansas and Mississippi!"

11. In paragraph 10, the writer mentions the attorney general's office. What connection does the attorney general's office have with the argument?

The U.S. Attorney General is responsible for the legal interpretation of the U.S. Code.

12. What was the purpose of this editorial?

a. To convince

b. To explain

c. To describe

d. To inform

a. If you chose b or c you are probably either thinking, "He is explaining (or "describing") his viewpoint," or, "He is explaining (or "describing") the law." He is explaining his viewpoint, but his purpose in explaining it is to convince the reader that he is right, not just to inform the reader of why he thinks as he does (not *d*). He has made allegations about the law, but he has not explained the law to us.

---

In paragraphs 55–60, 72, 74, 92, 101, 130–31, 155–56, and 177, the special report gave us an idea of the damage wrought by fires during the riot. From the many newspaper articles which were written primarily about the fires, the following excerpts have been chosen because they illustrate writing about the same event from various viewpoints.

The full impact of Detroit's fire situation will hit different readers at different points in their reading, of course, but once that impact is felt, the excerpts still to be read do not allow an impersonal assimilation of the additional information. It is in this respect that they are unusual, and they were chosen for their ability to impress the reader again and again with the awfulness of the situation. The dates the articles appeared are, respectively, 8/2/67, 7/24/67, 7/24/67, and 7/28/67.

Before reading these excerpts, reread the paragraphs named above from the special report (pages 93ff.).

1) Detroit fire inspectors Tuesday counted 387 buildings destroyed and damaged by fire during last week's rioting. . . .

2) A few more damaged buildings in isolated areas may increase the total beyond 387.

3) In many cases, fire inspectors were unable to tell what sort of business had occupied the burned buildings. Of those that could be identified, grocery stores and furniture stores were the most frequent victims.

4) One inspector who made a block-by-block check of some of the main riot areas around 12th street [sic] said he saw no furniture store untouched by fire.

5) There was also a disproportionate number of corner buildings burned— an indication that the arsonists were choosing targets to convenience rather than following a premeditated pattern. Corners are more accessible than mid-block locations.

6) [Fire Chief] Quinlan noted that there was "a separation of looters and burners. Many times, the looters were still working when the torches were set." . . .

7) There were 1,617 fire alarms in the city during the riot week—nearly double the average for the previous weeks in July.

8) The peak fire days were Monday, with 617 alarms and Tuesday, with 319.

9) The Detroit Fire Department used 108 pieces of its own fire fighting

equipment and borrowed 56 pieces from 41 suburban communities. Damage to fire fighting equipment was at least $100,000, according to Chief Quinlan.

10) The department is sticking to its earlier damage estimate of $250 million from fires alone. [19]

11) The fires were everywhere, not merely on 12th Street, where it began in a blind pig. . . .

12) The trouble spread west to Dexter and Grand River, south to the Boulevard, east to the freeway. There were fires that went untended for lack of fire equipment.

13) Which gives you an idea of how many fires had erupted subsequently on Mack, Sheridan, Gratiot, Kercheval.

14) At first the firemen had trouble from bottle throwers, troublemakers who wouldn't permit them to pursue their chores. Then as the night wore on, there was a countermovement of colored folks who began protecting the firemen. . . .

15) Back we came down a 12th Street you wouldn't believe. . . .

16) There was the center of the holocaust, now a simply blackened, charred street.

17) A sign kept winking off and on, in two parts Franklin's and then Cleaners, the only sign operating on the entire street.

18) Smoke lay everywhere and there were just the two words Franklin's and Cleaners winking on and off.

19) The national guardsmen kept looming up out of the smoke and the darkness.

20) As we passed the final fire, a couple of Negro youths were manning the fire hoses. They had been working for 3½ hours, relieving the crew.

21) "I don't know who they are. A couple of youngsters from the neighborhood," commented the exhausted firemen. [20]

22) The plane came through a sky that was alive with lightning and then it ran through fog and when it came out of it, Detroit was below. And everywhere, fire burned into the night sky. Bright fire. Bright fire wavering in the wind, then the wind stopping and the fire reaching higher.

23) On the right, an entire block in flames. Look out another window. One, two, three smaller fires. Look out the other side of the plane. Directly below was fire, strong fire, coming out of a wide base, climbing into the night.

24) Off to the left of that was another. Beyond that, still another. New patches of black smoke from the fires began running past the windows of the plane. And now you could see that the civil rights movement is becoming a rebellion. . . .

25) The cab [from the airport] took the Chrysler Freeway. The air was bitter with smoke and the sky was a red glow. Then the top of flames showed. The cab pulled over onto the side of the embankment.

26) Up on the top, on the corner of the Chrysler and Wilkins, a one-story drugstore was completely in flames. A telephone pole in an alley behind the store was covered with small flames. The wires were burning and the fire was skipping along the wires toward a second pole.

27) The firemen threw water at the store from the middle of the street. One fireman stood with his back to the fire and watched the street and the embankment. All firemen know of Newark, where one of their own was shot in the back while he was on the ladder. [21]

28) The Detroit Fire Department answered its first multiple-alarm fire of the riot at 1:38 p.m. Sunday.

29) Somewhere in Detroit, for the next 60 hours and 58 minutes, there was at least one fire being fought in the city at any moment.

30) Firemen who had been called back to duty Sunday afternoon did not get a break until Wednesday, when all who wanted to spend six hours with their families were given a chance to go home.

31) They fought more than 1,300 fires, including 50 that in more normal times would have been classified as multiple alarms.

32) Bricks, bottles, concrete blocks and snipers' bullets rained upon them while they worked.

33) An estimated $100,000 worth of equipment was damaged, lost and stolen during their four-day ordeal.

34) Some fire fighters were pinned down for more than an hour under their trucks, as they avoided bullets from nearby buildings and alleys.

35) One fireman, Carl Smith, 30, was killed by a shot in the head as he ran across Mack to join his comrades on Engine 13 near the corner of St. Jean.

36) Fire fighter John Ashby was blinded in both eyes, perhaps permanently, when a high tension wire struck his metal helmet while he was on an aerial ladder.

37) Ten other firemen were still hospitalized Thursday, with serious injuries including, besides burns and heart attacks, contusions from rocks and bricks and cuts from glass windshields that were shattered by bullets and stones.

38) Sixty more had been injured, 25 of them seriously, and released after treatment. . . .

39) Some [firemen] came back 300 to 400 miles Sunday, when they heard of the outbreaks, without being called. By early Monday morning the 450 men on duty had been supplemented by an additional 685. . . .

40) When the fires broke out Sunday afternoon the department used regular procedures. Then all off-duty firemen were called back and by 8 p.m., in Tighe's [secretary to the board of fire commissioners] words, "We had thrown away the book."

41) Firemen had virtually no protection Sunday night and Monday morning, when they came to realize that they, like firemen in other American cities, now had more to fear than fire.

42) Police, busy trying to contain looting in other areas, were unable to provide protection against cursing, rock-throwing mobs.

43) A Negro captain was put in charge of an entire battalion of fire fighters, but, as he had predicted, this failed to appease the crowds.

44) A white man who tried to help firemen was stabbed in the chest. As he bent to the ground he was stabbed again in the back.

45) Monday at dawn firemen hoped for a letup, but none came. At noon Chief Quinlan began negotiating to have National Guardsmen accompany his trucks. By nightfall, agreement had been reached, and the guardsmen were picked up.

46) Monday night sniper fire at stations on the East Side sometimes kept firemen from answering calls. Smith was killed.

47) All through the night firemen labored. Four times a woman's impassioned voice, promising protection for firemen by neighborhood vigilantes, begged them to come to Vicksburg and Linwood.

48) Four times, without a protector on the street, firemen were fired upon.

49) Chief Quinn [sic] ordered firemen to retreat immediately if they were fired upon at any time, anywhere. Two guardsmen were assigned to each truck.

50) Still the fires raged on. One ladder company called the central office:

51) "I've got five stores and an apartment building on fire. Can you send me a pumper?"

52) The answer was no, so the five men worked alone.

53) The sniping continued. Firemen would fight a fire on one side of the street while looters pillaged on the other. [22]

Although the writers of the above excerpts left the reader with the definite impression that the fires were widespread, we can see that most of these writers tried to do something more. Following are several statements about what some of their intentions may have been. For each statement, indicate the source—special report, [19], [20], [21], or [22]—which tried to do what the statement describes. The answer to some statements may be "none," and more than one source may be named for some statements.

1. He tried only to give the facts objectively.   |   [19]

|  |  |
|---|---|
| 2. He tried to describe the effects of the fires on the city's economy. | none |
| 3. He tried to give an idea of the desolate wastelands left by the fires. | [20] |
| 4. He tried to give an idea of the part played by the fires in the overall drama of the riot. | special report |
| 5. He tried to describe the fires so that the reader could visualize them. | [21] |
| 6. He tried to give an idea of the efforts of the firemen. | [22] |
| 7. He tried to depict the impossibility of fighting all the fires. | special report, [20], [21], [22] |
| 8. He tried to show that the firemen could have done better if they had tried harder. | none |
| 9. He tried to show that some of the people kept the firemen from doing their jobs. | special report, [20], [22] |
| 10. He tried to show that some of the people tried to help the firemen. | [20], [22] |

Both the special report (paragraph 101) and source [22] (paragraph 35 above) mention the death of fireman Carl Smith. The following article (7/30/67) also reports his death.

1) Fireman Carl E. Smith died doing his duty—a martyr to the forces of sanity in a city suddenly gone mad.

2) Saturday a grateful city with an aching heart paid its last respects to Carl Smith, 32, the avid, eager fire fighter, the guy they called "commissioner" down at Ladder Company 11 because he was quick to give orders.

3) Smith—husband of slim, light-haired Patricia Ann and father of crew-cut, 4-year-old Dwayne—was killed by a sniper's bullet Monday as he darted across Mack, trying to get back to his rig on the corner of Mack and St. Jean.

4) He had volunteered for duty. Officially, he was on the sick list, recuperating from an emergency appendectomy.

5) But he came, like hundreds of other fire fighters, because he knew they needed him to fight the fires of Detroit's disastrous riot.

6) Saturday, Carl Smith was laid to rest in Elmwood Cemetery, in the plot dotted with headstones carved with two trumpets, the fire fighter's symbol.

7) After services, . . . the funeral cortege moved downtown, past the black

draped rigs gleaming in the sun at Fire Department Headquarters, past the white gloved men, standing at attention.

8) Smith's flag-draped coffin rested atop a new pumper, No. 203.

9) Near the cemetery, an honor guard of nine red-suited firemen and six blue-uniformed American Legionnaires marched slowly, to the tap of muffled, black-draped drums.

10) More than 1,000 of Smith's comrades, a long blue line of fire fighters, marched to the cemetery and stood at attention.

11) Mostly, they came from Detroit. But there were men from Windsor, Southfield, Warren, Highland Park—all of the 40 or more communities that helped out in the emergency—Cleveland and New York.

12) Mayor Cavanagh, his face grim, his shoulders hunched, marched beside Fire Chief Charles J. Quinlan. There were common councilmen three, and other dignitaries.

13) The band played "Nearer My God to Thee" and they took Carl Smith's coffin down from the truck.

14) The minister spoke the comforting words: "The Lord is my shepherd. I shall not want . . ." "I am the way, the truth and the light . . ." They took the flag from Carl Smith's coffin and folded it in a triangle. Quinlan handed it to Mrs. Smith. Mayor Cavanagh shook her hand and said a few words.

15) But for the pretty young woman in the black dress there could be no comfort, not now. And for a little boy, all dressed up in a suit and a white shirt, there could be no understanding.

16) As the echo of taps died away, she sobbed and caressed a white star on the flag, and cried, "Oh, Carl! Carl!"

17) The little boy, only 4 and too young to understand, clutched at his mother's skirts. He looked up at her tear-drenched face and said: "Mommy . . . don't cry Mommy." [23]

---

The special report and the source [22] article both reported the (death, funeral) of Carl Smith, but most readers probably (did, did not) have much of a reaction to Smith's death after reading either of these reports.

> death
> did not

However, most people reading article [23] probably (did, did not) have some kind of emotional reaction.

> did

Since the average person also is not affected by reading simply that someone had a funeral, this difference in reactions (can, cannot) be ac-

> cannot

counted for by the fact that article [23] reported the funeral, whereas the other articles did not.

Therefore, if we are to discover the reason for our greater reaction to article [23], we (can, cannot) attribute the difference simply to the fact that this article provided more information.

cannot

Whereas the previous two reports of Smith's death merely reported that he died as the result of being shot by a sniper, paragraph 1 of article [23] sets the mood for an (emotional, impersonal) reaction by saying that Smith died doing his duty, that he was martyred while acting (sanely, insanely) in a city gone mad.

emotional

sanely

The emotional reaction is (lessened, increased) in paragraph 2 by the phrases, "a grateful city with an aching heart," and, "the avid, eager fire fighter."

increased

Paragraph 3 increased this _____ still further by telling us that Smith was married and had a four-year-old child.

emotional reaction

After reading this far in the article, it would be bad enough to be told that Smith had died as a result of smoke inhalation, severe burns, or some other cause which is considered to be an occupational hazard of _____; but then to be told that he was killed by a sniper as he ran toward (safety, his fire truck) leaves us feeling bitterness as well as (sadness, a lack of concern) about his death, for we now know that someone deliberately killed a man who was trying to help others.

firemen

his fire truck
sadness

But the writer taps our (emotions, thirst for knowledge) still further by telling us that Smith wasn't supposed to be (working, staying home) in the first place; he was on the sick list but he knew he (had recovered, was needed), and so he reported for duty (voluntarily, as soon as they called him).

emotions
working

was needed

voluntarily

At this point, we have a (condensed, detailed) picture of the man who was Carl Smith—a fireman, a man who loved his work, a husband, a father, a man recuperating from surgery who volunteered to help because he knew he was needed, a man who died trying to help others.

condensed

This is the kind of man who is (admired, disliked) by most people, and we no longer feel (sad, impersonal) about his death, for we feel that we knew him personally at least to some extent. Having conditioned us to think of Carl Smith as a hero, the writer is assured of our interest in knowing whether or not his funeral befitted him. With carefully chosen words, the writer describes the funeral cortege (in general terms, with many details), and we are left at the end of paragraph 14 with an overall sadness, but with a sadness which is somewhat (mitigated, made impersonal) by our knowing that his funeral was truly a hero's funeral.

admired
impersonal

with many details

mitigated

This mitigation is short-lived, however, for in paragraph 15 the writer involves us again by letting us know that the story of Carl Smith (is, is not yet) over.

is not yet

We are reminded that Carl Smith left a young widow and a four-year-old son.

The first sentence in paragraph 15 does not affect us as much as the second: the widow is an adult who understands that "these things happen," even if such words do not comfort her, but we are left with a feeling of terrible impotence by the (certain, uncertain) knowledge that no words exist which can make this four-year-old boy understand why someone killed *his* daddy.

certain

We can almost hear his questions: "But why did the bad man shoot daddy?" "Did the man hate daddy?" "Did daddy do something to the man?" "Did daddy do something bad?" And we know that the answers (will, will not) lead

will not

| | |
|---|---|
| to understanding. We are not left to dismiss the widow's grief so lightly, however, for paragraph 15 tells us of her anguished cries. | |
| And in paragraph 17, the writer exposes the irony in the situation by telling us that the small boy, about whom we have been (more, less) concerned than we have about his mother, tries to comfort his mother. | more |
| We see, then, that the manner in which an author writes (does not make much difference, makes a great deal of difference) in the emotional impact of the material. | makes a great deal of difference |

The special report tells us in paragraphs 156–63 (pp. 98–99) that the arsonists "incinerated the businesses, homes, and future of those who could afford it least," that they "hadn't really set fire to the power structure after all." The meaning of this general statement can be readily interpreted: "Maybe some of the big businesses and rich people were financially hurt by the fires, but not many were; the people affected the most by the fires had below-average incomes." Since most of us traditionally root for the underdog, this statement has some impact on us, but not much, for we tend to adopt the rather cynical attitude of, "Well, that figures. The little guy is always the one who gets it in the neck," and we let it go at that. However, a critical reader, having read the rest of the special report up to these paragraphs 156–63, will tend to think rapidly of some of the implications of this statement. Before starting to read the next paragraph, take pencil and paper and allow yourself 10 minutes to make a list of some of the possible implications of the statement, "The flames incinerated the businesses, homes, and future of those who could afford it least." For example, your list might include these items: "household goods destroyed"; "loss of business income while repairing store."

Did you make your list yet? If not, you're not following instructions. Now make out the list before you read any further.

Although most of the newspaper articles telling of some of the implications of the statement above were good examples of writing which produces an emotional impact, it was decided to approach this topic with the emphasis on facts rather than emotions. Consequently, although the excerpts below are direct quotations, most of them represent grossly butchered versions of the original articles, for, in general, they do not give dependable pictures of the individual articles, the purposes of the articles, the impacts of the articles, or the writing abilities of the authors.

Taken all together, however, these excerpts do give an accurate composite picture of the facts—and, occasionally, of the emotions—revealed in the many articles. Keep your pencil and a clean sheet of paper handy, and as you read these excerpts, make a new list of the implications of the statement, "The flames incinerated the businesses, homes, and future of those who could afford it least." When you are through reading these excerpts (and so are also through making the new list), compare the new list with the original list to see if your comprehension of the statement has been increased. The date of each article is given prior to the article.

7/24/67:

1) "They're burning themselves out." The policeman said it quietly and looked at the sky.

2) The smoke spread over miles of troubled city, but it was the people who sat on their porches and watched their own neighborhood burn who were hurt the worst.

3) They were the adults—Negroes who shook their heads and said: "Race has nothing to do with this." . . .

4) Up and down Twelfth, fires wiped out stores where local people had shopped for years. By evening, whole blocks had been destroyed and firemen gave up on the area. There was just too much.

5) Above many of the stores were apartments and they were destroyed by the dozens. The occupants had abandoned them early in the morning.

6) Near the end of the fruitless battle against the flames at Twelfth and Pingree, an angry man cursed the crowd and said: "How dumb can they get? Where are we going to get our food tomorrow, where are all these people going to work? It makes no sense. I feel like crying." [24]

7/25/67:

7) One woman cried. Unashamedly. She didn't care who watched her. . . .

8) She was wearing a housedress. Inexpensive, but clean and freshly ironed.

9) She was scared.

10) "Why, why, why," she kept repeating. Not to anyone in particular. To the whole world.

11) "I'm innocent. I didn't do anything. Why must I suffer like this.

12) "I don't mind for myself, but I've got two little babies at home. They're the ones who will suffer for this.

13) "They burned down the A & P and Packers stores last night. I went into a market today and asked for some milk for my babies.

14) "The man told me to get out of there. He wouldn't sell me anything. I couldn't steal like those others. If I did, I couldn't live with myself.

15) "What can I do? Where can I go? Please tell me what to do."

16) "I live on the fourth floor of the Jeffries project. Am I safe there? I can't take my babies out tonight. I can't leave the area. Buses aren't running tonight.

17) "Do you think they'll burn the apartments. Please, dear God, . . . tell me what to do?"

18) No one answered the plea. No one knew the answer. [25]

7/29/67:

19) . . . 35 families uprooted by the riot . . . [are] quartered in the city's emergency welfare shelter [at the hotel] while officials seek new homes for them. . . .

20) Volunteers are seeking magazines, toys and a television set to help ease the shock that still grips the riot refugees.

21) "We had to do something," . . . [one man] said. "Last night I heard children crying and kicking against the walls of the room. They are still frightened by what happened and have nowhere to go." . . .

22) "I saw the flames shooting up. . . . All I could do was grab the children and run out. We lost everything," [one mother said]. [26]

7/25/67:

23) Mrs. Jonas Smith sat on a neighbor's porch complaining because her baby's food was spoiling in the refrigerator.

24) "All our electricity is out," she said. "We don't know when it's going to come back on. I don't understand what's happening.

25) "Now people are coming in from over on the other side of town and I know things are going to get worse," she said.

26) "They're just hurting themselves." . . .

27) Mrs. Emma Jean Woolfork, who lived at 9815 Linwood before her small apartment was destroyed by a fire set in the store below, sat with her family on a grassy section across the street. . . .

28) The few possessions she managed to salvage were scattered about. [27]

7/25/67:

29) The Rev. John Green, who lives at 1710 Euclid between Woodrow Wilson and Twelfth, considered himself lucky. All the houses between his and 12th were burnt out except one.

30) "My house was saved, thank the Lord," he said. "An apartment building on the other side of the street was partly burned out. The third floor was destroyed. People in the building are salvaging whatever belongings

they can find, but there's no power, gas or water there. They are taking refuge in the houses that are still standing." [28]

7/25/67:

31) "I don't know how many burned out houses we saw last night," [Edward] Aye said. "We couldn't count them."

32) "After I packed up my family, we drove around from 10 p.m. to midnight looking for someplace safe to stop the car or someplace to stay. There weren't any safe places." . . .

33) "I came to Detroit from St. Louis because I heard about the good jobs here," he said. "I thought I'd have a chance. Now I'm thinking of leaving . . . going someplace like Philadelphia or maybe Indiana. We've gotta get away from this trouble. I just don't like this kind of stuff."

34) The Roys sat on a porch across the street from the gutted shell that was their home until the trouble started.

35) Mr. Roy, 79, is confined to a wheelchair. His wife, Luedilia, 80, uses a cane to get around. They had to be carried from their home Sunday night.

36) "Everything we had is gone," Mrs. Roy said. "I just got the two pieces on my back. Everything is gone. I don't know why this would happen. . . .

37) "Everything, everything is gone. We don't have any kids. That was all we had . . . and now it's gone." [29]

7/28/67:

38) "I'm wiped out," said Samuel Lipson, owner of a clothing and variety store that stood on 8541 Twelfth.

39) "I'm 63. At this age, I lost everything. I don't know what I'm going to do," he said. . . .

40) His insurance expired five weeks ago. The company refused to renew, claiming the risk of rioting during this long, hot summer was too great.

41) "We didn't expect any trouble," said Lipson. "As a matter of fact, I was consulted by different civic groups about whether we felt there was any trouble. In our opinion there wasn't a sign of it." . . .

42) Neither does Rubin Teicher [have a business any more], who operated Teicher's fruit market at 8531 Twelfth for 38 years. He lost $3,000 in stock and fixtures and there is no insurance.

43) "They say no insurance on Twelfth St.," he said Thursday. . . .

44) "I made a nice living, I saved a few dollars, I had no enemies. Now I am 65 and wanted to sell: I had a buyer. I had to settle with him Sunday," said Teicher. The riot settled it for him. [30]

8/12/67:

45) Mrs. Mary Travulsy, 65, today stands in violation of the law.

46) And, for this, she cried.

47) The gray-haired widow of a Lebanese immigrant, who uses a cane because of crippling arthritis considers the law of the city unjust. . . .

48) . . . [Since the riot, she and] her invalid daughter, Jenny, 37, bed-ridden for 21 years because of polio, . . . no longer have a source of income.

49) All the city cares about, the mother added, is that she do something about the two-story building . . . that was willed to her by her husband when he died six years ago.

50) The building contained a grocery, dry cleaners and two flats. Mrs. Travulsy rented all four units. She was receiving a total of $240 monthly in rents from them.

51) Together with a monthly social security check of $95, it provided enough of an income so that she and Jenny could live in their home at 23630 Joy.

52) During the riot an arsonist's torch destroyed the property.

53) Only a shell remains.

54) Mrs. Travulsy received a form letter from the city—a "notice of viola-tion" from the Department of Buildings and Safety Engineering. . . .

55) Mrs. Travulsy read the notice—and cried.

56) Her daughter phoned a wrecking company. A price of $1,800 to comply with the city's orders was quoted. . . .

57) There was no insurance on the building.

58) To the city's building inspectors, it was a routine matter. The public has to be protected from the menace of such ruins, they said.

59) . . . The city's chief building inspector said notices to owners of burned-out buildings warn them to remove the remains or repair them. [31]

Now check the list you made while reading the above excerpts against your original list in order to see if your comprehension of the statement, "The flames incinerated the businesses, homes, and future of those who could afford it least," has been increased. Following is a checklist for some of the implications you may have included. Each item is followed by one or more source numbers, but these are provided only for your convenience. If you already have the item listed, you can ignore the source number(s).

Before proceeding with the checklist, however, let's make sure you under-stand its purpose:

| | |
|---|---|
| The author of the special report made a state-ment saying that most of the people who were (physically, financially) hurt by the fires were | financially |

| | |
|---|---|
| people who (had, did not have) much before the fires. | did not have |
| The implications of this statement were (all, not all) immediately apparent to many readers. To help you realize that this statement's _____ were (all, not all) immediately apparent, you were asked to list as many _____ as you could think of (before, after) reading excerpts from various articles which followed. | not all<br>implications<br>not all<br>implications<br>before |
| You were then asked to (add to this list, make a new list) of implications (while, after) you read the excerpts. | make a new list/while |
| After you read the _____, you were instructed to compare your (revised list, new list) with the original list in order to see if your (comprehension, knowledge) of the statement made in the special report had increased. | excerpts<br>new list<br><br>comprehension |
| These lists were to be comprised of (detailed, brief) descriptions of how the fires affected people and their possessions. | brief |
| When compared with your original list, your second list will serve as a yardstick to measure your increase in _____ of the statement made in the special report. | comprehension |
| However, to see if you read carefully enough to recognize most of the items which should be listed, a checklist appears below, and you can use this checklist as a _____ to measure the amount of progress still to be made. | yardstick |
| Your list may include some items not included in the _____ below, but this (indicates, does not indicate) that your list is wrong, for you may have recognized an implication not _____ by me. | checklist<br>does not indicate<br><br>recognized |
| However, it is suggested that you reread the excerpt from which you listed that item to make sure your interpretation is correct.<br>On the other hand, the _____ below may | checklist |

include some items not included on your
_____ .                                                    list

If you recognize that the excerpts justify the inclusion of that item, then proceed to the next
item on the checklist; but if you do not recognize that the _____ justify the inclusion of    excerpts
that item, then refer to the source number(s) following the item on the checklist, for these
_____ will refer you to the ap-        source numbers
propriate excerpts.

Here is the checklist:
Incomes of people hurt apparently average or below average:   all excerpts
Both white and Negro people hurt:   24
Shopping inconvenience for the future:   24
Innocent people hurt:   all excerpts
No food available for purchase:   24, 25
Food on hand spoiled:   27
Homes destroyed:   24, 26–29
Jobs gone because places where employed were burned down:   24
Anger, despair, bewilderment over senselessness of rioting:   24, 25, 27, 29
Adults openly crying:   25, 31
Children crying:   26
Children suffering:   25, 26
Children left with permanent emotional damage (implied):   26
People fearful:   25, 26, 29
Negro image lowered in the eyes of some white people:   25
No place to go:   25, 29
Clothing, furniture, household goods destroyed:   26–29
All worldly possessions except clothing on body destroyed:   26, 29
Living in emergency shelters:   26
Living in neighbors' homes:   28
Utility services interrupted:   27, 28
Volunteers needed to help the displaced:   26
New homes must be found for the displaced:   26
Disillusionment after moving to Detroit for a better life:   29
Old people displaced with no relatives to help:   29
Businesses destroyed:   30
No insurance to help defray losses:   30
Retirement plans destroyed:   30
Source of income destroyed:   31
Hope for the future destroyed:   29, 30, 31

Additional expenses incurred besides complete loss of property:   31
People left financially unable to rebuild:   31
Welfare rolls permanently increased (implied):   29, 31
Neighborhoods destroyed:   28, 29
People trapped in riot area with no way out to safety:   25, 29

Although none of the excerpts mentions the following, your list might also include these items:
Development of unsanitary conditions caused by lack of water and fresh food
Loss of business income while repairing stores
Expense of repairing stores
New debts incurred in order to replace burned household goods, etc.
Price gouging by stores still open (verified in paragraph 132 of the special report)
Large families split up because one neighbor's home not big enough for all
Inability to buy children's school clothes because of other extra expenses from fire
Friends lost because of neighborhoods destroyed
Shopping inconveniences prolonged, perhaps permanently, because others will be fearful of locating businesses in the areas hit
Rates on insurance policies probably greatly increased—perhaps insurance unrenewable because of high risks involved
Continuing fear that the riot may be repeated
Mothers forced to work—probably as domestics—in order to help get family started again
Detroit hurt economically because skilled and other needed workers will be afraid to move to Detroit area

There are 48 items listed above. Score yourself as follows: 15 or less, you're not reading carefully enough; 16–21, poor; 22–27, fair; 28–33, good; 34 or more, excellent.

Following are two articles about a family affected by the fires. At the end of the first article (8/7/67), you will be asked some questions about the article's purpose, its emotional impact and the usage of quotation marks. At the end of the second article (8/13/67), several statements are made about the content of both articles, and you will be asked to evaluate the truth of these statements.

1) Willie Gibson's family has lost everything but hope.
2) But it's a determined hope that is rising from the ashes and terror of the Detroit riot.
3) Compared to the early morning hours of July 24, that's progress for the Gibsons who are among the many innocent victims of the disorder.

4) Midnight had exploded with snipers' shots, breaking glass and the stench of fire that Monday when the 31-year-old Ford Motor Co. foundry worker, his wife and four children were forced to flee from their blazing second floor flat at 7614 Kercheval.

5) By 4 a.m., the entire block of buildings and homes on Kercheval between Townsend and Baldwin was leveled by the flames. There was nothing left, not even hope. There was only fright, despair and smoldering debris.

6) Where did the Gibsons go? How did they start anew? What are they doing? How did they manage to eat and sleep with only $3 in funds? Where did they find hope?

7) Willie Gibson is a Negro, big in physique and outlook. So is his wife, Mildred, 48, who is stepmother to his children, Sandra, 11, Cynthia, 9, Bennie, 8, and Sylvia, 5.

8) "Now I can say that there's a brighter day ahead—I've got to," Mrs. Gibson said at the home of her sister, Mrs. Dewie McCloud, 3860 St. Clair.

9) She and her husband have been sleeping on a bed without a mattress in the basement at the McCloud home. The children are with Gibson's mother, Mrs. Centlia Mitchell, 2643 East Willis.

10) "The hardware store next door to us on Kercheval caught fire first," Gibson recalled. "We were all in bed, but I could smell the smoke and hear some shooting.

11) "When I ran outside and saw what was happening I ran upstairs and woke everyone up. We dressed fast and I had about $3 in my wallet.

12) "Then we got in my brother-in-law's car—he and his wife were staying with us—and we didn't know which way to go because we didn't know which way was safe."

13) His wife made an inventory:

14) "We're all together. We're all well."

15) She also estimated a loss ranging between $3,000 and $4,000 in clothing and furnishings destroyed in the seven-room flat which they were renting for $60 a month.

16) Besides that, she said, there are debts for a stove and a phonograph stereo set—"about $400 altogether on things we don't have any more but which must be paid." There was no insurance. There is no bank account.

17) Gibson said he averages $105 a week take-home pay. He was laid off for two weeks before the riot started because of a changeover at the plant.

18) The Gibsons are searching for a three-bedroom home which rents for approximately $65 a month, not including heat and utilities. They're willing to decorate and clean it, if necessary.

19) "There's one thing we've learned from this whole thing," Mrs. Gibson admitted. "That's the goodness of people, all kinds of people.

20) "They've been bringing us lots of things, mostly clothing. There's a

church over on Jos. Campau that gave us food, and there was another place for food run by the city over on Grand River and Joy. Block clubs also helped."

21) The Gibsons, who have "never been on welfare, and don't intend to be," have also asked the United Community Services for essential furniture to assist them once they find a home.

22) Convinced there's "a brighter day ahead," Mrs. Gibson intends to find work either as a domestic or a cook.

23) "That'll help us," she said. "And I hope I can find a job that'll let me be home by 4 in the afternoon when the children are back from school. My husband, he works afternoons."

24) While surveying their losses and problems, the Gibsons admitted that they are as baffled about the causes of the riots as many Detroiters.

25) "I don't know what caused these troubles," Mrs. Gibson said. "That's what I still keep trying to figure out."

26) "I never thought it would happen in Detroit," her husband commented. "Other towns, but not Detroit."

27) They both said that "a few hoodlums who don't care about anything" are responsible for starting the disorders.

28) "There's opportunity—especially in education, and education is what's needed to get a good job," said Gibson, who completed the 10th grade and then attended a trade school. "My children are going to get a good education."

29) Mrs. Gibson nodded. She was thinking of the children and so many things. She admits that sometimes she wakes up in the night unable to return to sleep and that it's not always possible to "throw these worries off my mind."

30) Sometimes she weeps to get rid "of that choked up feeling" and then remembers that there's "a brighter day ahead." [32]

1. Judging from the dates of the many excerpts quoted before article [32], the public was well aware that hundreds of families fled their homes because of the fires. What, then, seems to be the purpose behind this article, dated more than a week after the end of the riot and more than two weeks after its start?

The purpose behind this article appears to be to follow through on one of the families victimized by the riot in order to let the public know what was happening to such victims.

2. How would you evaluate the emotional impact of this article? That is, do you think this article affected most readers emotionally, or not? If so, to

what extent—a little bit, or quite a bit? For the purpose of this answer, assume the following: If you think most readers reacted only with something like, "Well, at least they have relatives they can stay with," or, "That's an interesting article," or, "What do they want to print stuff like that for?" then answer "no" to the second question above. If you think most readers reacted only with something like, "Gee, that's too bad," or, "I wouldn't want to be in their shoes," or, "I hope things get better for them," then answer "yes" to the second question and consider that the readers were emotionally affected a little bit. If you think most readers had an involuntary physical reaction—such as a lump in the throat, a sinking stomach, a pang in the heart, or tears—or reacted with, "I'm going to help them," then answer "yes" to the second question and consider that the readers were emotionally affected quite a bit.

The answer to this question is given following the next article.

3. In paragraph 16, why are there no quotation marks around the words, "Besides that," and, "there are debts for a stove and phonograph stereo set"?

In view of the third and fourth words of paragraph 16—"she said"—the lack of quotation marks indicates that the writer is paraphrasing Mrs. Gibson's words, rather than quoting her directly. Quotation marks are not used when a speaker is being paraphrased.

4. In paragraph 21, why are quotation marks around the words, "never been on welfare, and don't intend to be"?

Since the paragraph is talking about the Gibsons, these indicate that the writer is quoting the Gibsons.

5. In paragraph 22, why are quotation marks used for "a brighter day ahead"?

Since the paragraph is talking about Mrs. Gibson, these indicate that Mrs. Gibson is being quoted. See paragraph 8.

6. The quotation marks around the last sentence in paragraph 28 indicate that this is a direct quotation. Who made this statement?

Mr. Gibson.

7. Paragraphs 8 and 9 tell us that Mr. and Mrs. Gibson are sleeping in a

house on St. Clair, but the children are staying in a house on East Willis. Yet Mrs. Gibson says in paragraph 14 that the family is all together. Does this indicate a contradiction in the information the article gives us?

No. Mrs. Gibson could mean that even though they don't all sleep in one house, they are together during the day.

Now here is the second article, which appeared six days after the first article:

31) The Willie Gibsons lost their clothing and furniture in the Detroit riots but gained something more important—a deep belief in the fundamental goodness of people.

32) The Gibsons and their four children were burned out of their flat over a store at 7614 Kercheval in the early morning hours of July 24 at the height of the riots. They escaped only with the clothes on their back and $3 in cash.

33) On Saturday, the Gibson family moved into a neat three-bedroom, two-story house at 4751 Hurlbut.

34) Gibson proudly drove them over in a 1956 DeSoto.

35) Inside, the dwelling was almost completely furnished—chairs, sofa, bedroom furniture, a stove and a refrigerator.

36) All this was achieved because Detroiters of goodwill, both white and Negro, had read of the Gibson's plight in The Detroit News last Monday and decided to be their brother's keeper.

37) The house was made available by a Detroit woman who called the Gibsons, then staying with relatives, on the day that The News article appeared.

38) The Gibsons' rent for the home on a quiet, tree-shaded block is exactly what they were paying for the flat on noisy Kercheval.

39) The DeSoto—"its motor is sound as a dollar," said Gibson—was the the gift of a St. Clair Shores [a suburb of Detroit] man, Carl Babits, of 21201 11 Mile.

40) Mrs. Susie Smith, 5009 Seminole, donated a bedroom suite.

41) A dining room table and chairs and a buffet came from a Grosse Pointe Farms [another Detroit suburb] woman who asked to remain unidentified.

42) Dr. James A. U. Carter offered free medical care for the family until they get back on their financial feet.

43) There were numerous other gifts of clothing, kitchen utensils and cash.

44) The week of almost bewildering kindness was climaxed when dele-

gates to the national convention here of Sigma Gamma Rho, a sorority of Negro college and professional women, asked the Gibsons to appear at their meeting at the Sheraton-Cadillac Hotel.

45) There, as several hundred delegates looked on moist-eyed, Mrs. Annie Neville, of Rocky Mount, N.C., gave the Gibsons a $500 check.

46) "Our heart goes out to you and all other innocent victims of these civil disturbances," said Mrs. Neville, a warm, grandmotherly woman. "We want you to consider that you have been adopted by our organization.

47) "In addition to this check, chapters around the nation will see that you are supplied with the items of clothing and household equipment that you still lack."

48) Willie Gibson is a six-foot, 200 pound foundry worker at the Ford Motor Co.—a strong man in a tough, dangerous job. He had accepted the loss of all his possessions with dry-eyed stoicism.

49) But when he stepped forward to express his thanks, it was too much for him. He started to speak but his eyes welled with tears and a sob came instead.

50) Finally, he was able to say:

51) "I never knew people could be so nice. This has been the most wonderful week of my life."

52) His wife, Mildred, had been prepared to find work as a domestic after the disaster, although she was needed at home to care for the four youngsters—Sandra, 11, Cynthia, 9, Bennie, 8, and Sylvia, 5.

53) "What this means most of all to me is that I can continue to be a full-time mother to the children," she said.

54) "Until we got those wonderful gifts, I thought I would have to go to work but I hated leaving the children to shift for themselves all day long.

55) "Please tell everyone who has helped us how grateful we will always be."

56) In addition to the gift to the Gibsons, Sigma Gamma Rho earlier had presented a $2,000 check to Mayor Cavanagh for the Detroit Conference Emergency Relief Fund to assist other victims of the riots.

57) The plight of the Gibson family had been discovered by United Community Services. This group and the Neighborhood Service Organization, both Torch Drive agencies, are assisting riot victims to find new homes and are providing clothing and household furnishings. [33]

In the second question following article [32], you were asked to evaluate the _____ impact of that article on the (average, sensitive)

emotional
average

| | |
|---|---|
| reader. According to article [33], (a few, hundreds of) people responded to article [32] with action to (help, sympathize with) the Gibsons. | hundreds of<br>help |
| Since the Gibson's plight was not otherwise publicized, it is reasonable to infer that these people were (not, deeply) affected emotionally by article [32]. | deeply |
| Considering that (some, many) people can be emotionally affected quite a bit by such an article without taking any action, it is reasonable to infer that most readers (were, were not) affected emotionally by this article. Furthermore, it is reasonable to _____ that they were affected (only a little bit, quite a bit). | many<br><br>were<br><br>assume<br>quite a bit |

Question 1 follows the instructions below.

*Problems 2–20:* Following are 17 statements. On the basis of your knowledge of the world and the two articles, mark each statement in one of five ways:

   T—true without question
PT—probably true
PF—probably false
   F—false without question
   ?—not enough information to justify one of the other four answers

Here are the rules: You may refer to the articles as often as you like. In order to simplify your decisions, accept everything in the articles as true. Assume that quotation marks are used correctly. Assume that the writer did not make any false implications. Assume that everything the Gibsons said, either individually or jointly, is true. Assume that expressions of emotions and feelings are genuine. Notice that these instructions apply to problems 2–17, and not to question 1, which immediately follows.

1. Since the second rule in the instructions above tells you to accept everything in the articles as true, why was it necessary also to instruct you to accept everything the Gibsons said as true?

According to the second rule, the article could tell you that the Gibsons said something and you would have to accept the fact that they said it; but without the other rule, you wouldn't have to assume that the Gibsons told the truth. With both rules, you must not only accept the fact that they said certain words, but you must also accept their words as being true.

Following are the problems to which the instructions above apply:

2. Most readers were emotionally affected quite a bit by article [32].

PT. This answer is supported in the discussion immediately following article [33].

3. Not everything in the articles was true.

F. The instructions above told you to accept the articles as *true* for the purpose of evaluating the truth of the statements made in problems 2–17.

4. Maybe not everything in the articles was true.

F, for the same reason that statement 3 is false.

5. The Gibsons didn't know what caused the riots.

T, per paragraphs 24–26.

6. The entire block of buildings where the Gibsons had lived was leveled by flames.

T, per paragraphs 4–5. If you answered PT or ?, you may be thinking, "Yes, we know that the Gibsons lived on Kercheval, but we don't know that they lived in the block between Townsend and Baldwin, so we don't know for sure that the block where *they* lived was leveled by flames." By mentioning this block of Kercheval immediately after telling us that the Gibsons lived on Kercheval, the writer implies that the Gibsons lived in this block. Although, in fact, this implication may be false, you were told to assume that the writer did not make any false implications.

7. The Gibsons had no intention of going on welfare, despite their losses.

T, per paragraph 21.

8. Most readers of article [32] felt happiness for the Gibsons after reading article [33].

PT. We have already agreed that most readers of article [32] were probably upset by the Gibsons' plight. It is then highly unlikely that they would not be glad that the Gibsons had found another home, complete with household goods, furniture, clothing, cash, and a car.

---

9. The Gibsons' rent for their new home on Hurlbut was $60 a month.

T, per paragraphs 15 and 38.

---

10. Based on rental values at the time of the article, the Hurlbut home was worth only about $60 a month.

PF. First, the Hurlbut home would seem to be more desirable than the Kercheval flat, so the rent for the Hurlbut home should be higher than the rent for the Kercheval flat. Second, the Kercheval flat had seven rooms, so $60 does not seem an excessive rent in 1967. It then follows that the rent for the Hurlbut home should probably have been higher than $60 a month.

---

11. The people who helped the Gibsons with a home, a car, furniture, etc. were all Negroes.

F, per paragraph 36.

---

12. The Gibsons intended to make sure that about $400 they owed on destroyed household furniture and goods was paid.

T. In paragraph 16, Mrs. Gibson says the $400 *must* be paid, not that it *should* be paid or *maybe* it should be paid or that they couldn't afford to pay it.

---

13. The Gibsons had nothing to do with setting the fire which destroyed their Kercheval apartment.

T. Paragraph 3 says they were *innocent* victims.

---

14. The people who helped the Gibsons all asked to remain unidentified.

PF. It is doubtful that the newspaper would publish their names if they had asked to remain unidentified, and some names were published.

---

15. The Gibsons had been getting some help from nonrelatives before their story appeared in article [32].

T, per paragraphs 19–20.

---

16. The newspaper in which article [32] appeared was the first organization to discover the plight of the Gibsons.

F, per paragraph 57.

17. The Gibsons will never forget the kindness of the many people who helped them.

T. Per paragraph 55, they will always be grateful to everyone who helped them, and they can't always be grateful if they forget that these people were kind to them.

In the special report, paragraphs 99–127 and 134–39 tell us about snipers during the riot. Although these paragraphs were written primarily from the viewpoint of the difficulties involved in restoring law and order, daily articles in the newspapers were written from other viewpoints as well—the effect of the snipers on individuals, neighborhoods, law forces, firemen, tenants of buildings in which snipers were thought to be; whether or not race was involved; what it's like to be in the middle of a battle between police and snipers. Two reporters even interviewed snipers.

It can be assumed that one purpose of the articles was to let the public know what was happening, of course; but the inclusion of descriptive details, the use of the present tense to describe past events, the "short story" style of writing, the abandonment of standard journalistic procedure for reporting news indicate that most of these articles were written with more in mind than giving a straight news report.

Following are excerpts from some of these articles. They have been arranged so that you can see an emerging pattern: how the snipers harassed the firemen and what was done about it; how the snipers turned the streets into battlegrounds; how the days and nights of fighting snipers affected the law forces; how this, in turn, affected the law forces' treatment of citizens. As you read these excerpts, look for this emerging pattern, and try to decide what each writer is trying to convey to his readers. Also decide whether or not you think these articles had any emotional effect on the Detroiters reading them, and if so, what effect. Notice that the impact of some of these articles is greater than the impact of others. Notice also that this difference in impact is caused more by the way the information is given, rather than by the information itself.

7/26/67:
1) The latest trap into which fire fighters were lured was set last night with a false report of a fire at Lawton and Blaine, Chief Charles J. Quinlan said.

2) Despite an escort of national guardsmen, members of Engine Co. 10 were pinned under sniper fire from second-floor windows for more than 10 minutes after responding to the false alarm at 9:30 p.m., he said.

3) The apparatus was dispatched after the department received a telephone call from a "homeowner" promising that firemen would be protected when they arrived, Quinlan said. . . .

4) Another instance of a sniper trap came early Tuesday, Quinlan said, when firemen returned to a house fire at Linwood and Vicksburg.

5) Fire fighters had been forced to abandon this fire four times previously because of gunfire from snipers, he said.

6) A fifth attempt to fight the blaze was made after a caller said he could "guarantee" that homeowners would stand guard if the firemen returned, Quinlan said.

7) "They went back, and the men had to crawl under the trucks to escape the gunshots," the chief said. [34]

7/25/67:

8) At Davison and Dexter an entire block of businesses was going up in flames as firemen, acting under orders, stayed with their cruising fire trucks instead of stopping to fight the fire.

9) A Negro employee of Chrysler Engineering, Eugene Lofton, ran to his home at 3280 Waverly and grabbed a .22 rifle. He rallied his neighbors and they ringed the entire block.

10) There were old men and young men, armed with rifles, shotguns and pistols.

11) Lofton said:

12) "I hollered at the firemen, 'Aren't you going to put out the fire?' They said not till the police came to protect them from snipers.

13) "I told them to go ahead and we'd shoot any SOB that tried to stop them."

14) The firemen accepted the offer, but the fire was out of control. Famous Cleaners went up in flames, then the Red Satin Dining Room, then the Salvation Army Store, then Hawkins Apparel.

15) "This whole block is owned by Negroes," Lofton said. "These people are not fighting against the white man, they just want to burn and loot." . . .

16) Police said vigilantes were in evidence in various parts of the city, but it was impossible to estimate their number.

17) "We're guarding the firemen and our homes and property," one man said. He had a pistol strapped to his side and a .16 gauge shotgun in his hands.

18) A fire lieutenant at Livernois and Seven Mile was asked how he liked being guarded by amateur gunmen.

19) "I like having anybody around who's got a gun and is on my side," he said. [35]

1. What is the *main* idea of article [34]?
*a.* Firemen are being lured into sniper traps.
*b.* Firemen are responding to false alarms.
*c.* Firemen are being pinned down by sniper fire.
*d.* Snipers are preventing the firemen from fighting fires.

*a.* Paragraph 1 starts out with the clause, "The latest trap into which fire fighters were lured," and the rest of paragraph 1, along with paragraphs 2 and 3, details this clause. Paragraph 4 starts out with the clause, "Another instance of a sniper trap came early Tuesday," and the rest of paragraph 4, along with paragraphs 5–7, details this clause.

2. Did the writer of article [34] appear to have more in mind than giving a straight news report? If so, what?

No. This is an example of an ordinary news report.

3. Did the writer of article [35] appear to have more in mind than giving a straight news report? If so, what?

Yes. Assuming that the news to be reported was that vigilante groups were being formed and that one such group was formed too late to do any good, the writer tried to give a picture of one vigilante group in action and the firemen's acceptance of them as allies. In doing this, he also succeeded in implying that more such groups are needed and that fire damage would be considerably less if more such groups were formed.

4. Why is the word "homeowner" enclosed in quotation marks in paragraph 3?
*a.* This shows that Chief Quinlan is being quoted.
*b.* This shows that the writer questions the use of the word.
*c.* This implies that the caller was believed not to be a homeowner.
*d.* Quotation marks are improperly used in this case.

*c.* The writer does not indicate that he personally questions the use of the word (not *b*), for the article is a straight news item. Quinlan is being paraphrased, not quoted in paragraph 3. When a speaker is being paraphrased, a single word should not be included in quotation marks unless it is an unusual word or unless it has unusual connotations or implications. "Homeowner" is not an unusual word, but in view of the account of events in paragraphs 1 and 2, it has here unusual implications (*c*, not *a* or *d*).

5. Why is the word "guarantee" enclosed in quotation marks in paragraph 6?
*a*. This shows that Chief Quinlan is being quoted.
*b*. This shows that the writer questions the use of the word.
*c*. Quotation marks are improperly used in this case.
*d*. None of the above.

*c*. Not *a* or *b*, for the same reasons as discussed in answer to question 4 above. In paragraph 3 the lack of quotation marks around "homeowner" would mean that a homeowner called; however, with the quotation marks, paragraph 3 implies that someone who *claimed* to be a homeowner called. However, paragraph 6 already states that the caller *claimed* he could guarantee protection, and the quotation marks around "guarantee" seem to serve no useful purpose.

6. You have already read of the tremendous amount of damage caused by fires during the riot. Coupling this knowledge with the information in articles [34] and [35], what are some of the implications of these two articles?
*a*. The police were inadequately trained for dealing with snipers.
*b*. More fires could have been extinguished if snipers hadn't kept the firemen away.
*c*. Some citizens were afraid to form vigilante groups.
*d*. Some citizens did not join vigilante groups because they thought it would be better if some of the old buildings burned down.
*e*. The answering of false alarms probably allowed real fires to go unchecked.
*f*. The snipers wanted the fire to destroy buildings.
*g*. Some of the snipers were also arsonists.
*h*. The snipers worked in conjunction with the arsonists.
*i*. Some of the snipers were probably building owners who wanted to collect the insurance on the buildings.
*j*. The damage from fires would have been considerably less if the firemen had been unhampered by snipers.
*k*. The snipers were white men who wanted to see the property of Negroes destroyed.
*l*. The snipers were Negroes who wanted to see the property of white men destroyed.
*m*. Negroes were burning and looting Negro-owned buildings.
*n*. White people were not burning and looting Negro-owned buildings.
*o*. White people were not burning and looting white-owned buildings.

*b, e, f, j, m.* Answers *b* and *j* follow naturally from our knowledge of fires. Answer *e* follows from our knowledge (from reading previous articles) of the great number of fires and the comparative shortage of firemen and equipment. Answer *f* is implied by the fact that the snipers kept the firemen from extinguishing the fires. Answer *m* is implied by paragraph 15. However, the implication that Negroes were burning and looting Negro-owned buildings in that particular block implies nothing about the actions of white people (not *n* or *o*). Not *k* or *l*, for nothing is implied in either article about the race of the snipers. There is nothing in either article to justify the inference of statements *a, c, d,* or *i.* Furthermore, since the vigilante groups were able to deal with snipers, it certainly seems reasonable to suppose that the police could also deal with them (not *a*). There is nothing to indicate that the snipers themselves set any fires (not *g*). And since the fires were so widespread, anyone who wanted to snipe at firemen could find a fire without working with an arsonist (not *h*).

---

| | |
|---|---|
| Paragraph 12 implies that the firemen (were expecting, did not expect) the police to arrive and protect them from _____ , but we are not told why the police were not already there. | were expecting<br>snipers |
| However, since critical reading involves drawing logical inferences from our reading, we will see if we can make a reasonable conjecture as to the reason for the absence of the _____ from that scene. | police |
| First of all, we know that sniping at firemen (is, is not) a serious offense, and this tells us that the police (would, would not) be there if they had been notified and if they could be there. | is<br>would |
| Since paragraph 12 (implies, does not imply) that the police had been notified, this allows us to draw the conclusion that the_____ could not be there. | implies<br><br>police |
| The question follows, ("Why weren't the police there?", "Why couldn't the police be there?") | "Why couldn't the police be there?" |
| Two possibilities suggest themselves: Either the police were too busy elsewhere and had no more men to send immediately, or they had been notified of the sniping only a few minutes | |

before and were (ignoring the call, on their way).

on their way

From reading paragraph 8, we know that the fire trucks were cruising, which implies that they (were, were not) on their way to another fire.

were not

Paragraph 12 tells us that the firemen did not intend to stop until the _____ arrived to protect them from the snipers.

police

Between the times in paragraphs 8 and 12, a vigilante group was formed and ringed the block, which must have consumed (only a few, several) minutes.

several

Also, paragraph 14 tells us that the fire was (beyond, brought under) control by the time the firemen stopped, even though paragraph 8 tells us there was more than one fire truck.

beyond

This again implies that (only a few, several) minutes had elapsed between the time in paragraph 8 and the time in paragraph 12.

several

Therefore, we are led to believe that the police were notified of the sniping (only, more than) a few minutes ago.

more than

Since we have already agreed that the police would probably be there unless they were too busy elsewhere or unless they had been notified only a few minutes before, we can now conclude that the _____ were probably (too busy, not busy) elsewhere.

police
too busy

We now have the question, "But what could possibly be so important that the police couldn't leave it to protect the firemen?" Excerpts [36] and [37] which follow (7/27/67 and 7/26/67) give us an idea of what the police were doing:

1) Ba-lam! Ba-lam! Rat-a-tat-tat! Pow!
2) A fusillade of shots thundered in the night air and caught me, running across the street at the corner of Lawton and Carter in the middle of one of Tuesday night's vicious shoot-outs between law enforcement officials and snipers. . . .

3) . . . In this particular neighborhood the closeness of the homes and the higher rising apartment houses caused bullets to ricochet and whine down the streets and sidewalks. Echoes made it sound as though shooting came from several directions.

4) Police cars screeching to the scene left their radios blaring. Multiple sniper fire across a 140-square-block battleground was their message, a direct attack on the fire department's command post at West Warren and Lawton, a shoot-out in the New Center area, one at Virginia Park and 12th, one behind the Algiers Motel.

5) Another massive burst of gun fire sounded along Lawton. Then a single pow and it seemed to come not from the direction of Gladstone but rather from across the street on Carter. Police and state troopers retreated down Lawton knocking out the street lights as they went. . . .

6) Pop-pop-pop! An automatic sounded like tiny firecrackers. Ba-lam! Ba-lam! Police answered with shotguns and another deafening volley was underway. . . .

7) "Motor squad, down here! Motor squad, down here!" The police barked orders. . . . We could see the smoke rising from their guns.

8) "Hold your fire!" sounded a voice over a loudspeaker.

9) Pow!

10) "Snipers are all over. Snipers are all over." It was the police radio.

11) "Get in the house! Get back!" It was the police loudspeaker chasing residents into their homes.

12) In the distance you could hear more firing from the direction of almost totally ravaged Linwood. . . .

13) Pow! Pow! The sniper's fire set off another massive barrage. There was the rat-a-tat-tat of a sub-machine gun, which later I learned was a Thompson .45 being fired by the sniper who was ultimately slain. A city policeman was critically injured, shot by the sniper in the stomach. A state trooper was less seriously wounded.

14) "Everybody hold your fire!" said an officer over the loudspeaker. "All right come on out! Come on out!" The command was obviously directed at the sniper.

15) "There's a sniper on top of the bar at Brisbain," blared a police radio. [36]

16) Backed by tanks and armored personnel carriers, national guardsmen and police last night and early today fought a house-to-house war on 12th Street.

17) The scene was incredible.

18) It was as though the Viet Cong had infiltrated the riot-blackened streets.

19) Snipers in what sounded like at least two dozen locations snapped off rounds as police and riflemen slid past the dingy houses.

20) They were answered by quick volleys from M-1 carbines, blasts from shotguns and bursts from submachine guns.

21) Then there was the clanking whine of a tank or a personnel carrier.

22) A 50-caliber machine gun roared in 30-second bursts, sweeping a roof, building or alley.

23) Silence for a second, broken only by the soft sounds of moving troops.

24) Another sniper round and the battle resumed.

25) Then the darkness vibrated with a sound that made the troops' skin crawl.

26) "Help . . . help me . . . help me," the voice screamed.

27) It sounded like the man was about a half-block away.

28) "It sounds like a white man," a Guard rifleman whispered.

29) A Negro patrolman clutching a shotgun nodded.

30) Then the voice stopped.

31) I crouched under the rear of a Guard jeep at Virginia Park and 12th. . . .

32) The patrol . . . [had been] led by a jeepload of police and guardsmen. We were in the truck behind the jeep with three riflemen and a police officer. A second truck carrying riflemen followed.

33) With all lights out, the patrol crawled along West Grand Boulevard. Then it turned up Linwood.

34) "Watch that apartment building on the left," a police officer said. "We took fire from there last night."

35) The patrol moved slowly past but nothing happened.

36) Then it wheeled down Virginia Park. The first breath brought the smell of two-day-old fires.

37) As we rumbled down Virginia Park past darkened homes, a rifleman gave me a short course in sniper warfare in city streets.

38) It's a technique the young citizen-soldiers have picked up the hard way in the last few days.

39) "Watch for houses with one screen off a window on the second floor," he said matter-of-factly. "And keep your eye peeled for second floors where one window has the shade down and the other is open a crack."

40) "Can you spot them by muzzle blasts when they fire?" I asked.

41) "No, not any more," he said. "They've gotten smart. They open the window a little, move way back in the room and then fire.

42) "They can snipe away for hours and you can't see them. We were even taking fire from burning buildings last night."

43) Suddenly the patrol lurched to a halt. Without a word the riflemen leaped out of the trucks and followed police north on 12th, ducking behind parked cars and trees and along buildings as they ran.

44) After a few moments . . . it became obvious to Wellman [a *News* photographer] and me that we were alone with the trucks and jeep. . . .

45) After about 40 minutes of intermittent gunfire, three riflemen returned to guard the vehicles. . . .

46) The rest of the men returned and we scrambled back aboard the trucks. The engines started.

47) A sniper round cracked over our heads and everyone dived for cover.

48) "The son of a bitch waited for us to come back," a rifleman said.

49) An armored personnel carrier wheeled up and blasted out the lights in the looted store that were silhouetting our vehicles.

50) Riflemen lay prone in the trucks, peering at a half-dozen houses on the north side of Virginia Park, looking for the sniper.

51) They couldn't find him so we rumbled off down Virginia Park.

52) The guardsmen seemed remarkably cool considering their youth and the weird battle they were fighting.

53) "Get the hell out of that window," they shouted when they spotted someone.

54) The head popped out of sight and no shots were fired. [37]

1. Did the writer of article [36] appear to have more in mind than a straight news report? If so, what?

Yes. Aside from reporting a battle at Lawton and Carter, the writer tried to give a running account of the battle in a way calculated to make the reader a witness. He also tried to convey the enormity of the sniper problem (paragraphs 4, 10, 15) and what the police were going through to end it.

2. Did the writer of article [37] appear to have more in mind than a straight news report? If so, what?

Yes. Aside from reporting that a patrol had run into a battle at Virginia Park and 12th St., the writer tried to give the reader an idea of the way the snipers operated (paragraphs 46–48). He also tried to portray the danger accepted routinely by police and guardsmen (paragraphs 33–42) and to give a glimpse of the restrictions on civilians in the area (paragraphs 53–54).

3. Was either of these two articles written by a reporter who had personally witnessed the sniper battle described?

Yes. Paragraphs 2, 7, 31, 37, 40, 44, 46, and 51 make it clear that both articles are eyewitness reports.

4. Were these two articles describing two different battles?

Yes. Article [36] describes a battle at Lawton and Carter (paragraph 2); article [37] describes a battle at Virginia Park and 12th St. (paragraphs 31, 37, 43).

5. Aside from the fact that the Viet Cong were our enemy, what is implied by paragraph 18?

If you answered something like, "The enemy had infiltrated the streets," you have not answered the question, for the question says to ignore the fact that the Viet Cong were our enemy. The Viet Cong were noted for their ability to infiltrate and show up where they weren't expected to be. They were also clever at keeping themselves concealed and they were adept at using hit-and-run tactics. Then paragraph 18 implies that the snipers seemed to have infiltrated and were shooting from everywhere, yet were nowhere to be found.

6. What does the writer imply by the words "matter-of-factly" in paragraph 39? The guardsman made the statement
a. in an off-hand way.
b. unemotionally, as though it were something the reporter should know.
c. irritably, as though the reporter were bothering him.
d. in a condescending way.

b.

7. What is meant by the last sentence in paragraph 42?

Snipers shot at guardsmen from in or on burning buildings.

8. In paragraph 49, the phrase, "blasted out the lights," indicates the use of (explosives, bullets).

bullets

9. Why were the lights blasted out (paragraph 49)?

By saying, "the lights . . . that were silhouetting our vehicles," in this context, the writer implies that the lights were blasted out so that the vehicles would no longer be silhouetted.

| | |
|---|---|
| So far, we have (read, inferred) that the law forces were not always able to be at fires to give firemen protection from snipers. | inferred |
| We can then infer that this was probably (normal routine for, frustrating to) the law forces. And we know from (reading, further inference) that the law forces were engaged in warfare with snipers. | frustrating to<br>reading |
| More often than not, the _____ had a good idea of where the _____ was hiding, but when they tried to find him he (could, could not) be found. | law forces<br>sniper<br><br>could not |

Now consider that each man in the law forces was working at least 12 hours a day trying to hunt down snipers, trying to protect firemen, trying to arrest looters, trying to keep certain areas roped off from outsiders, trying to keep cool when provoked by hostile citizens; consider that he knew he could be shot down at any moment; consider that he was away from his wife and family and was also worried about them if he was from the Detroit area; consider that he was in unfamiliar territory if he was not from the Detroit area; consider that if he was a policeman or a guardsman he had never received training for dealing with such large-scale sniping. Now mix these all together for two or three days and nights, and what do we get? The next excerpt (7/27/67) tells us.

1) Bone-weary policemen and National Guardsmen showed the edges of their frayed nerves early Wednesday as the rioting moved into its fourth day.
2) Sleepless after the long nights of looting and shooting, they showed signs of tension and fatigue as they sought the source of rifle shots in the darkness.
3) For anyone who went into the areas of violence after darkness fell, it was easy to see why the troopers and police had become jumpy.
4) It was the equivalent of night fighting in the jungle—shots coming out of nowhere. Few of the guardsmen or policemen had had experience in this kind of fighting.
5) "I worked from 12 to 12 yesterday and then had to go home and guard my house until dawn," said a bleary-eyed Detroit policeman.
6) "That makes you sleepy and on edge and you are bound to make mistakes.

7) "We've been conditioned so long to under-reacting and holding our fire that it's hard to adjust to this thing. There's a very thin line.
8) "They (the National Guardsmen) haven't been trained in this sort of thing and when you remember that, I think they do a pretty good job.
9) "Certainly they're skittish, but after three days of this, I'm skittish." [38]

1. In the paragraph immediately preceding the last excerpt, a question was asked. What is the answer expected to that question?

We get law forces that are nervous, jumpy, on edge.

2. Did the writer of article [38] appear to have anything more in mind than giving a straight news report? If so, what?

Yes. He tried to tell us why the police and guardsmen were jumpy.

3. In paragraph 7, what did the Detroit policeman mean when he said, "We've been conditioned so long"?
a. "We've been told for so long."
b. "We've been trained and have been doing for so long."
c. "We've had these present conditions [sniping, etc.] for so long."
d. "We haven't had these present conditions since long ago."

b. One who is "conditioned" to do something has been more than *told* to do it (not a); he has *learned* to do it.

4. In paragraph 7, what did the policeman mean by "under-reacting"?
a. Not reacting in an appropriate way to provocation by citizens
b. Not arresting citizens who break the law unless the infraction is a felony
c. Not responding in kind to provocation by citizens
d. Reacting to provocation by citizens with a well-controlled temper and as little force as possible

d. As indicated by the source [6] editorial, Detroit policemen have been trained to keep cool heads when confronted by an explosive situation (answer d). Since keeping cool is an appropriate way to act, answer a is incorrect. It should be obvious from the nature of police work that answer b is incorrect. The fact that one doesn't react in kind to provocation could mean that he over-reacts, so the expression "under-reacting" is not adequately described by "not responding in kind" (not c).

5. In paragraph 8, what does the policeman mean by "this sort of thing"?

Under-reacting and holding fire.

6. What does the policeman imply in paragraph 9?
a. "If even *I'm* skittish after being trained for these situations, it's natural for guardsmen to be skittish."
b. "The guardsmen have not received proper training for situations like this."
c. "Even though the guardsmen have not received training for such situations, they should not be as skittish as they are."

a. Consider the policeman's line of reasoning in paragraphs 7–8: "I've been trained to handle these situations. The guardsmen have not been trained for such situations. Therefore, I can be expected to do a better job than they can." Answer *a* follows naturally from this line of reasoning.

All right, now we have some idea of the conditions under which the law forces have been working for three days and nights, and we know that the guardsmen and police are feeling the strain and so are nervous, on edge, skittish. It is natural for this state of mind to be reflected in their treatment of the civilian population, but to what extent is it reflected? The next excerpt (8/14/67) gives us an idea of how people in the streets were treated.

1) The guardsmen that night were manning roadblocks and stopping cars and every one of them was jittery and jerky, like men who now have realized that this was a real thing.
2) They had been out there some hours by now, and they had fired their guns—not at practice targets on a rifle range, but at real, living, human shapes behind shades in windows on the streets of the city they live in.
3) And then, out of the shadows, stepped three colored persons.
4) An old woman. A younger woman, maybe a girl yet. A man.
5) Slowly they walked toward the guardsmen.
6) Each of them, the old woman, the girl, the man, carried paper bags.
7) "Halt!" said one of the guardsmen, and the three colored people halted.
8) The old woman reached her hand into the big supermarket bag she was carrying, and the guardsmen barked:
9) "Get your hand out of there!"
10) "We have food for you," the old woman said.
11) "I said get your hands up," the guardsmen shouted.

12) Now the smell of fried chicken enveloped the guardsmen, tired and hungry.

13) "It is food for you," said the old colored woman. "We have brought it for you."

14) The guardsmen looked at the Negroes and the Negroes looked at the guardsmen. Then one of the guardsmen said:

15) "Don't touch that stuff. It's poisoned."

16) And at that, the old woman bent over and set her bag on the street in front of her and reached into the bag and took out a piece of fried chicken and, so all the guardsmen could see her, took a bite out of it. And another. And another.

17) "We felt so foolish," one of the guardsmen who was there that night said.

18) "Here they come out of their houses on a night like that to feed us, because they knew how hungry we were, and we stop them and make them put their hands up and we say the food is poisoned and all they want to do is something decent.

19) "It was fried chicken and meat loaf. It was so good. And they have nothing, but they bring what they have to us." [39]

1. What is the purpose of paragraphs 1–2?

The purpose is to give the reader an idea of the mental strain the guardsmen were under.

2. Do the first two paragraphs succeed in accomplishing their purpose? Support your answer.

Yes. Two expressions remind us that these men had been trained only in dummy situations and that this was their first real-life application of this training: in paragraph 1, "like men who now have realized that this was a real thing"; in paragraph 2, "not at practice targets on a rifle range, but at real, living, human shapes . . ."

3. Do you think most readers felt an emotional impact from this article?

Probably. It is difficult to imagine a reader's having either no reaction or a reaction only of, "So what?" or, "That's interesting."

4. Aside from paragraphs 1–2, did the writer use emotive language?

Not particularly, at least not in the same way that emotive language was used in some of the other articles which had emotional impact—for example, articles [23], [32], [36], and [37].

5. What, then, accounts for the emotional impact of this article?

It seems to be a combination of the quality of suspense and the vacillating feelings aroused in the reader (who are the good guys? who are the bad guys?), as well as discovering that three people who had almost nothing unselfishly offered what they had to the guardsmen.

The preceding excerpts gave us an idea of how people in the streets were being treated by police and guardsmen. The next article (7/27/67) tells us how a tenant in an apartment building was treated.

1) Like a dozen other incidents that night, it started with the terse, understated radio call: "Man with a gun, shooting."
2) Patrol cars from Livernois Station's unit four careened through sniper fire to an apartment at 2753 Hazelwood, where shots were coming from a third-floor window, Apt. 32.
3) Under cover of rifle and machinegun fire, Patrolman Roger Poike and other officers dashed into the building and up the three flights of stairs to No. 32.
4) Crouching, Poike burst through the door.
5) A bullet ripped into his abdomen and he crumpled to the floor. His fellow officers blasted the apartment with a solid torrent of gunfire.
6) Outside, National Guardsmen, police and police commandos poured into the area, shooting.
7) A tank roared up and was stationed on Lawton beside the besieged apartment.
8) On police and military radios reports crackled that the contingent was caught in a crossfire being rained down from snipers all over the area. Three blocks south, firemen were pinned down.
9) State Trooper Jerome Lange, crouched beside a patrol in the intersection of Lawton and Hazelwood with Detroit Patrolman Salvatore Pallazzola, suddenly jerked, wheeled and collapsed with a gunshot wound in the right chest.
10) He lay bleeding for 35 minutes before he could be rescued and rushed to Ford Hospital.
11) The word flashed two blocks in seconds as police and soldiers screamed: "Two officers shot! Officers shot!" And then: "Get the bastard."

The apartment shook under withering volleys of police gunfire, which only let up when the commanding officer grabbed a bullhorn, and blared: "Officers in the building. Hold your fire!"

12) Under a cloud of tear gas, officers re-entered bullet-riddled apartment and moved to the bedroom.

13) They spotted the sniper lying on the ground three stories below a rear window.

14) The sniper, Jack Sednor, a 38-year-old Negro, was dead with bullet wounds in the chest and abdomen.

15) The body lay in a pool of blood until morning. Sniper fire made it impossible to move it out. . . .

16) Sednor was slain, but the other snipers in the area are probably still alive.

17) As police and troopers fought Sednor the other sniper fire crackled and rang against the pavement from any one of a hundred windows overlooking the area.

18) "Keep away from your windows or you'll be shot," the man on the bullhorn called.

19) Across Lawton a face peeked out a window. A blast of bullets greeted it.

20) A squad of police swept up the back stairs of the building and into a hallway.

21) Screaming for anyone inside to open up the door, officers unleashed a burst of machine gun fire through the doors and shot off the locks.

22) Crashing through the living room door, they swept into the apartment and ordered a woman out at gunpoint. She had been cowering on a bathroom floor.

23) Forcing her arms behind her, police handcuffed the woman and dragged her downstairs into the back yard.

24) There, ringed by three officers with shotguns, the shackled woman was pushed into a corner.

25) Two of the officers left the scene. The third kept a shotgun leveled at the woman's chest.

26) Then, Photographer Ira Rosenberg, part of a Free Press team reporting in the heart of the riot area, moved toward the group to photograph the capture of the alleged sniper.

27) "I took one look at her," Rosenberg said later, "and knew damn well she was no more a sniper than my mother."

28) As the woman's knees began to sag, Rosenberg stepped to her side and said: "It's all right, nobody's going to shoot you."

29) Lowering the terrified woman to the ground, he continued to comfort her.

30) At this point an officer emerged from the building after a frenzied search of the woman's apartment to report: "There's no gun."

31) It was only then that police looked closely at their "sniper"—a terror-stricken woman of 47, moaning hysterically, a crumpled heap in a purple bathrobe and pink hair curlers. It was learned later that she had been seen while in her bathroom and had no idea she was a suspected sniper.

32) Fumbling with the key, an officer snapped open the cuffs. The woman staggered to her feet, lurched and embraced photographer Rosenberg. "Don't leave me," she pleaded, "don't leave me."

33) Holding her, Rosenberg assured her, "I won't." He led her to the stairway where she stumbled inside and was helped upstairs to what, 45 minutes before, had been a neat apartment.

34) The kitchen door had been riddled by machine gun fire. Locks and night latches on two doors had been blown off by shotgun blasts. The living room door was in splinters, smashed by gun butts.

35) Seven holes were stitched in a staggered line across a brown sofa. Three slugs had ripped through the bathroom wall a foot from where the woman had been lying. The kitchen was riddled with bullet holes. What had been a saucepan was now a contorted scrap of metal. The floor was carpeted with broken glass.

36) Later she talked about her ordeal.

37) "The Lord was with me," she said. "I understand that the police were at their wits' end. But they dragged me around and searched me all over my body.

38) "One of them pointed a big rifle at me and said he ought to shoot me, and he called me a name."

39) What name?

40) "He called me a bitch. He said: 'I ought to shoot you right now, you bitch'."

41) Nowhere in the apartment was there a bureau drawer whose contents had not been scattered on the floor. The bed had been dismantled. Towels and linens had been hurled onto the floor in a hurried search for a weapon.

42) The woman, who asked not to be identified, has been a typist for the Detroit Board of Education for 25 years. [40]

1. Did the writer of article [40] appear to have anything in mind other than a straight news report? If so, what?

Yes. He wanted to tell a story about violence, bravery, terror, and error; he wanted the reader to visualize the police in action against a sniper and to appreciate, if not feel, the terror of an innocent woman as police shot their way into her apartment, threatened and handcuffed her, dragged her into the back yard, and kept a shotgun leveled at her chest.

2. Did the author accomplish what he tried to do in this article? That is, did he succeed in convincing the reader that
*a.* there was violence? Support your answer.
*b.* there was bravery? Support your answer.
*c.* there was terror? Support your answer.
*d.* there was error? Support your answer.

*a,* yes: His abundant use of colorfully descriptive verbal expressions—such as "screaming," "crashing," "shotgun blasts," "dragged her downstairs," "roared up," "caught in a crossfire being rained down by snipers"—assured the reader that there was much violence.
*b,* yes: Patrolman Poike tried to enter an apartment where a sniper was known to be (paragraphs 2–4); law forces "poured into the area," knowing there were snipers there (paragraph 6); despite knowing that Poike had been shot in the stomach when he tried to enter a sniper's apartment, other officers went into an apartment when they thought a sniper was there (paragraphs 18–21).
*c,* yes: We can well imagine the woman's terror after we read paragraphs 22–25, 34–40, and 42.
*d,* yes: Paragraph 27 tells us that an error had been made; paragraphs 31–32 tell us that the police, too, realized their mistake.

3. Why would paragraph 42 add to the reader's impression of the terror the woman must have suffered?

This paragraph gives us the impression that the woman was quiet and respectable, unfamiliar with the violence she had undergone.

4. What led the police to choose this particular apartment to smash into? Support your answer with paragraph numbers.

The police saw someone peeking out of a window of that apartment (paragraph 19), and they thought that it was one of the snipers (paragraph 31). Count your answer as wrong if you did not realize the police knew that the window of paragraph 19 was in that particular apartment.

5. Do you think most readers of article [40] would be understanding of the actions of the police (in regard to the woman), depite their possible feelings of revulsion for these actions?

Yes, if they read carefully enough to determine that the face peeked out of a window of her apartment; however, if they did not connect the window with the woman's apartment, they are likely to think that the police smashed into a random apartment, and then it is doubtful that they would be understanding of the actions of the police. This answer is somewhat determined by the woman's own understanding of their actions—"I understand that the police were at their wits' end" (paragraph 37).

---

6. Are we justified in inferring that the writer wrote his article in a way calculated to arouse sympathy for the woman? Support your answer.

---

Yes. Our first clue is in paragraph 22, to which we react, "Was it necessary to point a gun at a frightened woman?" To paragraphs 23–24 we react, "Why did they have to drag her and push her and surround her with officers holding shotguns?" To paragraph 25 we react, "She's in a corner, she's frightened, and they have her hundcuffed with her hands behind her back. It seems to be going too far to keep a shotgun pointed at her chest."

---

7. Suppose the writer had felt that the woman's encounter with the police served her right for looking out the window after hearing all the shooting and being warned to keep away from the windows (paragraph 18). Could he have written about the same facts so that we, too, would possibly feel some sympathy but would have a feeling of, "It serves her right," which was stronger than the feeling of sympathy? Support your answer with specific examples.

---

Yes. Consider the difference in effect if the following paragraphs were rewritten.
Paragraph 18: "'Keep away from your windows or you'll be shot,' the man on the bullhorn called. His voice was clear, the message was clear, and everyone in the whole block heard it."
Paragraph 22: "Crashing through the living room door, they swept into the apartment and rapidly searched the rooms. They found a woman hiding in the bathroom. Keeping her covered as a precaution against her making a run for it, they ordered her out of the apartment."
Paragraph 23: "Police handcuffed the woman's hands behind her and took her downstairs into the back yard."
Paragraph 24: "There, they took her to a corner where three officers were standing."
Paragraph 25: "Two of the officers left the scene. The third stayed and guarded her."
Paragraph 29: Leave out the word "terrified."
Paragraph 31: Leave out the first sentence.

Paragraph 32: "An officer snapped open the cuffs. The woman got to her feet and asked photographer Rosenberg to stay with her."
Paragraph 33: "Rosenberg said he would, and they both went to her apartment."
Paragraph 35: Change "lying" to "hiding."
Paragraph 36: "Later she talked about her experience."
Paragraph 41: "The dismantled bed, the towels and linens and bureau drawer contents on the floor were mute testimony of the efficient, though hurried, search for a weapon."
Paragraph 42: Add another sentence: "Hopefully, she has learned a lesson which isn't taught in school; if so, she'll stay away from her windows the next time."

Now, remembering the content of paragraphs 1–16, try rereading the article starting with paragraph 17 and inserting the above changes. The effect should be quite different than the original effect.

---

One article was written by a reporter who interviewed two Negro snipers identified only as "Eddie" and "Frank" in the article. Among other things, Eddie is reported to have said that the rioting was organized. The excerpts which follow are included only to illustrate some miscellaneous things you should be aware of when you read, so it should not be inferred that these excerpts comprise a shortened version of the article (7/31/67). The writer had just quoted Eddie in the paragraph before the following:

1) The organization, he said, had a specific purpose in the rioting. It was to burn every Whitey store to the ground. Thus, when the firemen came to put out the fires, they had to fight back. That's when the sniping began in earnest.
2) "Who were you shooting at?"
3) "The firemen. That's what we were trying to do, shoot the firemen and police." . . .
4) Once some people came through Eddie's home neighborhood in one of the Twelfth Street hot spots and the shooters [snipers] had to take time off from firing at the authorities.
5) "We had to go shoot some guys that were going to burn down a building near where I live," Eddie said. He did not say whether they hit any of them. [41]

---

1. According to Eddie, what was the purpose in the rioting?

---

Per paragraph 1, "It was to burn every Whitey store to the ground."

---

209 Applying What You've Learned

2. Who or what was meant by "Whitey store"?

A store owned by a white person.

3. Who is "they" in the third sentence of paragraph 1?

The people in the organization.

4. According to Eddie, why didn't the organization want the firemen to extinguish the fires?

The organization wanted the white-owned stores to burn down.

Considering paragraphs 1–3, then paragraphs 4–5 of the excerpts from article [41] indicate a possible inconsistency in Eddie's thinking. Before reading further, see if you can find this inconsistency and a logical reason for it, and name the fallacy indicated by this reasoning.

| | |
|---|---|
| Paragraphs 1–3 of the excerpts from article [41] (make it clear that, leave some doubt as to whether or not) Eddie was a part of the organization he spoke of. Eddie's tone in paragraphs 1–3 leads us to infer that he (approved of, disapproved of) the goal the organization had set for the riot to accomplish. | make it clear that<br><br><br><br>approved of |
| Since this goal was to (cause general chaos, burn down all white-owned stores), it follows that Eddie would (approve, disapprove) of burning down as many white-owned stores as possible. He would also (approve, disapprove) of trying to save any white-owned store from burning. | burn down all<br>   white-owned stores<br>approve<br><br>disapprove |
| Eddie's use of the word "go" in paragraph 5 (indicates, does not indicate) that he had to leave his current sniping post in order to prevent the burning of a building near his home. | indicates |
| This then indicates that someone told Eddie of the planned burning; which, in turn, indicates that this someone knew where Eddie was; which, in turn, indicates that this someone was (probably, probably not) a member of the organization. | probably |

The fact that this "someone" knew that "some guys were going to burn down" the building (indicates, possibly indicates) that it was the organizers who planned the burning of this building.

possibly indicates

But if it was the organizers who planned this, then it is reasonable to assume that this was a (white, Negro)-owned building.

white

But we have already said that Eddie would (approve, disapprove) of trying to save a white-owned store from burning.

disapprove

Then if this was a white-owned building, Eddie's thinking is being (consistent, inconsistent).

inconsistent

And if this building was white-owned, then the question arises of why Eddie (wanted, didn't want) it burned.

didn't want

Paragraph 5 specifies that the building was near where Eddie (lived, was sniping).

lived

Since the fires during the riots often went (out by themselves, unchecked), destroying the homes of the people living near the burning stores, we can reasonably infer that Eddie (may have been afraid, hoped) that a fire in this building might spread to his own home.

unchecked

may have been afraid

If this is true, then it appears that he (minded, didn't mind) helping fires spread to other people's homes in order to achieve the goal of the riot, but he didn't like the idea of having _____ spread to his own _____ in order to achieve the _____ of the _____.

didn't mind

fire/home
goal/riot

This, in turn, indicates that Eddie may be guilty of the fallacy of _____ (see page 19).

special pleading

Paragraph 173 of the special report mentions the slaying of a Negro youth by a state legislator. (The legislator was white.) Following is an article (7/26/67) about this slaying.

1) A state representative who fatally shot a teen-age looter in the legislator's Pontiac [a city about 15 miles from Detroit] grocery store, said Tuesday that civil authorities should order police and National Guardsmen to shoot to kill on sight in the Detroit area's strife.

2) The 61-year-old representative, Arthur Law, D-Pontiac, has long pushed for tougher law enforcement against violent crimes.

3) "Had the authorities in Detroit, including the governor and even the President, put a stop to the violence earlier, this would not have happened in Pontiac," Law said.

4) "Something drastic has to be done. The only answer is a double-barreled approach. The police and National Guard must shoot to kill and the courts must back them up by giving maximum sentences on all offenses."

5) Law fatally shot 17-year-old Alfred Taylor of Pontiac when Taylor and half a dozen other Negro youths swarmed around Law's Supermarket, 200 Earlemore, about 10 p.m. Monday.

6) Two others were wounded.

7) "They were nothing but hoodlums," Law said. "First they fire-bombed the store and then they hurled a trash can through the window.

8) "It was a point of having your back to the wall with no place to turn. My wife and I worked too hard for that store to let a group of lawless hoodlums destroy it."

9) State Sen. Basil Brown, D-Highland Park, a Negro, sent Law a bitter telegram Tuesday.

10) "What was contained in your place of business and what property interest were you protecting when you decided to execute an unarmed 17-year-old boy?" the telegram read.

11) "Your answer may help me to determine the extent of the vicious hatred that I have seen demonstrated in the last 2½ days in my senatorial district."

12) Law, who bought the store in 1948, said Monday night's incident left him with smoke damage, burning shelves and broken glass windows and door.

13) "It's a crying shame people have to be afraid for their businesses and lives," he said.

14) "It's a disgrace. All those troops do is stand around and watch the looters take whatever they want. If nothing else, it shows an absolute lack of civilization."

15) Law said his store has been the object of several attempted robberies. Almost two years ago, his son Charles fatally shot an armed robber after the intruder had fired three shots.

16) Charles, 27, was in the store with Law during Monday's incident. Both fired on the intruders.

17) The senior Law fired the fatal blast from a 12-gauge shotgun which he has kept in the store for several years.

18) Law's store is in a district which has about 15,000 Negro residents.

19) He said: "The people who live around the store are decent people who are just trying to live. The boy I killed lives more than two miles away, but he puts all of them (the neighbors) in a bad light."

20) Law, former mayor and city commissioner of Pontiac, has served the state legislature for the last nine years. [42]

1. What does Rep. Law imply in paragraph 3?
a. Detroit officials are responsible for what happened in Pontiac.
b. Pontiac people do not start trouble unless someone else gives them the idea.
c. The fever of Detroit's unquelled riot spread to Pontiac.

_____

c. Statements a and b may also be at least indirectly implied in paragraph 3, but they do not consider the context of the situation as statement c does. Count your answer as correct if you chose all three answers, however.

_____

2. What does Rep. Law mean by "a double-barreled approach" in paragraph 4?

_____

Apparently he is not talking here about the use of a shotgun. His meaning seems to be clarified by his next sentence: the law forces "must shoot to kill, and the courts must back them up by giving maximum sentences."

_____

3. Does Rep. Law believe that if someone tries to destroy your property, then you are justified in killing that person? Support your answer.

_____

Apparently, per paragraphs 7–8.

_____

4. Does Sen. Brown believe that if someone tries to destroy your property, then you are justified in killing that person? Support your answer.

_____

Although the words "you decide to execute an unarmed 17-year-old boy" in Sen. Brown's telegram do sound bitter, the first part of the question (paragraph 10) asks what property interests were being protected. It is possible that Sen. Brown heard that Rep. Law shot the boy for nothing more than walking around outside the store and harassing Rep. Law. Consequently, the article does not give us enough information to be able to answer more than, "We can't tell," to question 4.

---

5. Of what race was Taylor? Support your answer.

Negro. Paragraph 5 says, "Taylor and half a dozen other Negro youths." The phrase "other Negro youths" indicates that Taylor, too, was a Negro.

---

6. What is the racial makeup of the neighborhood in which Rep. Law's store was located?

Paragraph 18 leads us to believe that it was either a Negro or a mixed neighborhood.

---

7. Why should the actions of a boy who lived more than two miles from the store put the neighbors of the store "in a bad light" (paragraph 19)?

This is unclear. The article reports that Rep. Law made the statement, but it does not give us any clue as to why he believes it to be true.

---

8. What is the implication of the last sentence in paragraph 19? The boy's actions reflected upon the characters of
*a.* the people in the neighborhood around the store.
*b.* the Negro race in general.
*c.* all white people.
*d.* all people.

---

*b.* Not *c* or *d,* for Rep. Law's statement said "all of *them,*" thereby implying exclusion of himself. Since we know that the boy did not live in the neighborhood of the store, and since Rep. Law says in paragraph 19 that the neighbors are decent people and he implies that the boy was not, he cannot be indicting the neighbors per se as part of the boy's group. Therefore, we reject answer *a,* despite the reporter's parenthetical insertion in paragraph 19. And yet the reporter *did* indicate that Rep. Law was indicting the neighbors, so the question remains, "On what basis?" The most obvious answer is, "On the basis of race," which, in turn, implies an indictment of the Negro race in general (answer *b*).

---

Following is a letter (7/31/67) to the editor of the newspaper in which article [42] appeared.

1) I resent the remarks made by Rep. Law: "The boy I killed lives more than two miles away, but he puts all of them in a bad light."

2) God forbid that one 17-year-old Negro youth should represent all of the Negroes or all of a neighborhood. How can the people of his district let a man with this pathetic narrow-mindedness represent them?

3) I am a Negro and I do not feel that the three white youths arrested for sniping on 14th and Davison represent all of the whites.

[Name withheld] [43]

1. What does the letter writer imply in paragraph 3?

a. Rep. Law would not feel that the actions of one white youth reflects on all white people.

b. Rep. Law let racial prejudice interefere with his common sense.

c. The actions of three white youths arrested for sniping really do reflect on all white people.

d. Negroes have more common sense than white people.

---

a, b. Paragraph 2 makes it clear that the writer believes Rep. Law's generalization to be without foundation. By saying in paragraph 3 that the writer is a Negro and doesn't believe that the actions of one white person reflect upon all white people, the writer is implying that the reason for Rep. Law's generalization is racial prejudice (answer a). The combination of making a generalization without foundation and making it because of racial prejudice supports answer b. Not c, for the writer makes it clear in paragraph 2 that she does not agree with such generalizations. Not d, for she is talking about the reactions of one Negro person (herself) and one white person (Rep. Law), not about Negro people and white people in general.

---

2. Assuming for the sake of argument that Rep. Law really did believe that the actions of one Negro boy would reflect on all Negroes but did not believe that the actions of one white boy would reflect on all white people, Rep. Law was guilty of a fallacy in thinking. What is the name of this fallacy?

---

Special pleading (page 19). If you said "proof by selected instances," you may be thinking, "He is willing to say that all Negroes are bad just because one Negro was bad, and this is a proof by selected instances [page 49]." If so, you are not answering the question asked; instead, you are answering the question, "Of what fallacy in thinking is Rep. Law guilty if he thought that the actions of one Negro boy reflected upon all Negroes?"

---

The following paragraphs summarize some of the more popular theories of the cause of Detroit's riot.

1) Throughout the riot and afterwards, the question was asked, Why did it happen in Detroit? Negroes here, unlike Negroes in many other places across the country, form part of the so-called power structure. They hold important jobs in business and industry and within the labor movement. They help run this city's progressive, racially enlightened government. [44]

2) One columnist observed that the fact that Negroes in Detroit were not confined to specific ghettos—as Negroes in some other large cities hit by riots had been—served to show only that the fires could burn brightly all over Detroit instead of in only one spot.

3) Observers agreed that this was not a race riot in the usual sense of the word: "There were Negro and white looters and snipers fought by Negro and white policemen and soldiers." [45] Articles told time and again of the lack of antipathy between races—Negro citizens feeding white soldiers and offering shelter from snipers to white reporters, Negroes and whites jailed together and sharing cigarettes, a pair of Negro looters holding a door open for a white man so that he could more easily get his loot out of the store, the telephoning of a white store owner by the store's Negro neighbors after these neighbors had saved the store from being burned, the offering of citizens in all-white suburbs to share their homes with Negro riot victims.

4) The theory has been advanced that this was a revolt by Negroes against the white power structure rather than against the white man, but this theory does not explain the burning and looting of Negro-owned stores, nor does it explain the nonburning and nonlooting of some white-owned stores in the midst of the ravaged areas.

5) Some who support the "revolt against the white power structure" theory say that the Negro-owned stores were not deliberately burned but caught fire as a result of the spreading of fires set to white-owned stores, but this does not account for the burning of at least one block of all Negro-owned stores (article [35]).

6) Some say it was a war of the "have-nots" against the "haves," but this doesn't explain the deliberate burning of apartments without allowing the occupants time to remove their personal possessions (reported in a part of article [26] which was deleted from this book). Nor does it explain the looters' permitting people to drive up in new Cadillacs and join in the looting, as was reported in other articles.

7) Some say it was a protest against store owners who gouged their customers and treated them like dirt, but this does not explain the burning and looting of stores owned by men who treated their customers with courtesy, fairness, and respect; nor does it explain the looting and burning of at least one white-owned store which Negro neighbors tried in vain to save.

8) Some say it was part of an overall protest against injustice to Negroes, but it seems unlikely that the thousands of Negroes made homeless in Detroit's riot felt that the rioters had treated them with more justice than they had been getting.

9) Some say it was all the work of groups of local hoodlums, but this does not explain the looting done by family men who were steadily employed in Detroit's industries (reported in various articles).

10) An occasional voice is heard saying that it was a protest against police brutality, but this does not explain the spread of the riot despite the admirable restraint shown by the Detroit police being harassed by the early crowds; nor does it explain the looting and burning of stores; nor does it explain the sniping at firemen.

11) Some say it was the work of black nationalists, but this does not explain the burning and looting of Negro-owned stores, nor does it explain the leaving of thousands of Negroes homeless.

12) Some say that it was the result of a long pent-up frustration, that the Negroes accepted as Negro leaders in the community had been out of touch with the man in the street. But this does not explain the comments of the many Negroes living in the riot areas who were interviewed during the riot and who time and again said something like, "This is senseless," or "I don't understand this," or just, "Why? Why?"

13) As of this writing no satisfactory explanation for Detroit's riot has been found.

1. What was the purpose of the preceding 13 paragraphs? The purpose was
a. to explain the cause of the riot.
b. to explain some of the causes of the riot.
c. to discuss some of the alleged causes of the riot.
d. to prove that the riot had no definite cause.

---

c. As evidenced by paragraph 13, neither a nor b is an acceptable answer. The above paragraphs did name some of the alleged causes of the riot and reject each of these as being an explanation (answer c). The fact that many alleged causes were discussed and rejected does not prove that the riot had no definite cause (not d).

---

*Questions 2–12:* Paragraphs 1–12 either name or imply alleged causes of the riot. What is (are) the alleged cause(s) named or implied in
2. Paragraph 1?

---

Negroes wanted to protest against not being a part of the power structure, against not being able to advance in position in business, industry, and the labor movement, and against not having anything to say about the city government.

_____

3. Paragraph 2?

..............................

Negroes wanted to protest against being forced to live in ghettos or in specific areas of Detroit, or they wanted to protest against not being allowed to live where they chose to live in Detroit.

_____

4. Paragraph 3?

..............................

Negroes wanted to show their hatred of white people (or vice versa).

_____

5. Paragraphs 4–5?

..............................

Negroes wanted to protest their treatment by the white power structure.

_____

6. Paragraph 6?

..............................

The "have-nots" wanted to protest against the "haves."

_____

7. Paragraph 7?

..............................

Negroes wanted to protest their treatment by merchants who treated them unfairly, regardless of the races of the merchants.

_____

8. Paragraph 8?

..............................

Negroes wanted to protest the many injustices done them.

_____

9. Paragraph 9?

..............................

Groups of local hoodlums wanted to cause trouble.

_____

10. Paragraph 10?

..............................

Negroes wanted to protest police brutality.

_____

11. Paragraph 11?

..............................

Black nationalists wanted to stir up (or express) discontent with the treatment of Negroes in Detroit.

12. Paragraph 12?

Negroes wanted to express long pent-up frustrations which they had been unable to express before.

13. As indicated by paragraph 13, I do not believe that any of the alleged causes explains Detroit's riot. Judging from the contents of paragraphs 1–12, why don't I believe that these causes suffice as explanations?
a. Because each alleged cause is a generalization, and I don't believe that any generalization is wholly true.
b. Because my living in a Detroit suburb tends to make me feel protective toward Detroit, and I don't want to put Detroit in a bad light in this book.
c. Because for each cause named there were conditions present during the riot which conflicted with the cause.
d. Because I don't believe a riot like Detroit's is ever justified.
e. Because I don't believe that these alleged causes are enough to explain the size and intensity of the riot.

c. You were asked to judge my reason from paragraphs 1–12, and nothing in these paragraphs says or implies anything about answers a, b, or d. Statement e begs the question (page 23): it says, in effect, "I don't believe because I don't believe." Therefore, it does not answer the question of why I don't believe, and it is not an acceptable answer. However, each of the paragraphs 1–12 did give evidence of conditions during the riot which conflicted with the alleged cause (answer c).

The sources referred to by bracketed numerals in this chapter are:
1. Lowell, Jon: "Street of Nightmares," p. 1-A, *The Detroit News*, July 24, 1967.
2. "Blind-Pig Raid Was Spark," p. 1-A, *Detroit Free Press*, July 24, 1967.
3. Wolff, Joseph E.: "Coincidence Played Role in Raid That Led to Riot," p. 1-A, *The Detroit News*, August 3, 1967.
4. Aumente, Jerome: "Detroit Errors May Change Riot Tactics," p. 20-D, *The Detroit News*, August 4, 1967.
5. Meyer, Philip: "Putting the Riot's Pieces Back Together," p. 3-B, *Detroit Free Press*, July 30, 1967.
6. "Did Restraint Fail?" (editorial), p. 14-A, *The Detroit News*, July 27, 1967.
7. "Cavanagh's Role Criticized" (letter to the editor), p. 6-A, *Detroit Free Press*, July 31, 1967.

8. "Lauds Restraint . . ." (letter to the editor), p. 4-A, *The Detroit News,* August 5, 1967.

9. Stanton, Barbara: "An Orgy of Pillage Erupts Behind Fires and Violence," p. 1-A, *Detroit Free Press,* July 25, 1967.

10. Goltz, Gene: "The Tension of Years Echoes in Shouts of Glee Amid the Litter and Rubble that Was 12th Street," p. 6-A, *Detroit Free Press,* July 25, 1967.

11. "She's Horrified . . ." (letter to the editor), p. 8-B, *The Detroit News,* August 1, 1967.

12. "Questions Motives . . ." (letter to the editor), p. 8-B, *The Detroit News,* August 1, 1967.

13. "Raps Pussyfooting . . ." (letter to the editor), p. 8-B, *The Detroit News,* August 1, 1967.

14. (letter to the editor), p. 6-A, *Detroit Free Press,* August 2, 1967.

15. (letter to the editor), p. 6-A, *Detroit Free Press,* July 31, 1967.

16. "Cavanagh Put Detroit Before Politics" (letter to the editor), p. 6-A, *Detroit Free Press,* August 2, 1967.

17. "Bad Politics . . ." (letter to the editor), p. 8-B, *The Detroit News,* August 1, 1967.

18. "While Detroit Burned—Who Was Fiddling?" (editorial), p. 4-A, *The Detroit News,* August 12, 1967.

19. Meyer, Philip: "387 Buildings Burned in Riot, City Says," p. 3-A, *Detroit Free Press,* August 2, 1967.

20. Greene, Doc: " 'Couldn't Erupt Here'—a Smug Wrong Answer," p. 8-A, *The Detroit News,* July 24, 1967.

21. Breslin, Jimmy: "Civil Rights Movement Becomes a Rebellion," p. 10-A, *The Detroit News,* July 24, 1967.

22. "Weary Fire Fighters Finally Given First Break," p. 5-B, *Detroit Free Press,* July 28, 1967.

23. Weston, Mary Ann: "A Hero Goes to His Grave as Wife—and City—Mourn," p. 1-A, *Detroit Free Press,* July 30, 1967.

24. "Neighborhoods Burn as Residents Watch," p. 3-A, *Detroit Free Press,* July 24, 1967.

25. Ryan, Richard A.: "Inferno Madness Unchecked—So Are a Mother's Tears," p. 10-A, *The Detroit News,* July 25, 1967.

26. Kerwin, James L.: "Fire and Snipers Force Family Out," p. 6-A, *The Detroit News,* July 29, 1967.

27. Heard, LaRue: "In a Ravaged Neighborhood—a Festive Air," p. 1-B, *Detroit Free Press,* July 25, 1967.

28. Walker, George: "The Horror of Violence and Its Trembling Victims," p. 7-A, *Detroit Free Press,* July 25, 1967.

29. Holmes, Susan: "Detroit's New Refugees—The Flames Left Little," p. 1-B, *Detroit Free Press,* July 25, 1967.

30. Stanton, Barbara: "Twelfth St.: A City Within a City of Both Honest Men and Criminals," p. 1-B, *Detroit Free Press*, July 28, 1967.
31. Simon, Max E.: "Widow Suffers 2nd Riot Blow," p. 1-A, *The Detroit News*, August 12, 1967.
32. Gebert, Armand: "Hope Rises in Riot Ashes," p. 3-A, *The Detroit News*, August 7, 1967.
33. Batchelor, E. A., Jr.: "Good Outshines Flames of Riot," p. 9-B, *The Detroit News*, August 13, 1967.
34. Nehman, John F.: "Tricks Lure Firemen Into Sniper Traps," p. 8-B *The Detroit News*, July 26, 1967.
35. Goltz, Gene: "Vigilante Groups Formed," p. 2-A, *Detroit Free Press*, July 25, 1967.
36. Hamilton, John A.: "That Was No Racial Incident on Lawton," p. 4-A, *Detroit Free Press*, July 27, 1967.
37. Lowell, Jon: "Guerilla War Erupts on Riot-Scarred 12th," p. 1-A, *The Detroit News*, July 26, 1967.
38. Walker, George: "Fatigue Adds to Tension on Troops, Police," p. 8-A, *Detroit Free Press*, July 27, 1967.
39. Stark, Al: "The REAL Detroit—Poisoned Moment," p. 2-A, *The Detroit News*, August 14, 1967.
40. King, Wayne: "Sniper Hunt Claims The Guilty and Innocent," p. 5-A, *Detroit Free Press*, July 27, 1967.
41. Goltz, Gene: "Snipers' Tools: Hate, Guns and Whisky," p. 3-A, *Detroit Free Press*, July 31, 1967.
42. Wax, Judy: "Legislator Defends Shooting of Looter," p. 3-A, *Detroit Free Press*, July 26, 1967.
43. (letter to the editor), p. 6-A, *Detroit Free Press*, July 31, 1967.
44. "Collision of Subtle Forces Contributed to City's Riot" (editorial), p. 6-A, *Detroit Free Press*, July 28, 1967.
45. "Sift Ashes for Reasons Behind Ghetto Outbreak" (editorial), p. 4-A, *Detroit Free Press*, July 27, 1967.

**BIBLIOGRAPHY**

1. Keyser, Cassius Jackson: *Thinking about Thinking,* The National Council of Teachers of Mathematics, Washington, D.C., 1953.
2. Thouless, Robert H.: *Straight and Crooked Thinking,* Simon and Schuster, Inc., New York, 1932.
3. *The Holy Bible,* ed. by Rev. C. I. Scofield, Oxford University Press, Fair Lawn, N.J., 1945.
4. Hawthorne, Nathaniel: *The Scarlet Letter,* Henry Altemus, Philadelphia, 1899.
5. *The Detroit News,* Detroit, 1967.
6. Barron, John: "Tyranny in the Internal Revenue Service," *Reader's Digest,* vol. 91, no. 544, p. 48, August, 1967.
7. *Detroit Free Press,* Detroit, 1967.

0360